Bad Catholic

A Memoir

Joe Thomas

Also by Joe Thomas

Fasten Your Seat Belts And Eat Your Fucking Nuts

Flight Attendant Joe

I'm Just Here For The Layovers

First Class Cocktails with Flight Attendant Joe

For Mémé.

Thank you for your love.

Contents

PART 1

THE FIRST ATTACK

I know now the attack was planned. Most are. But to my six-year-old self, it came like a lightning strike on a clear night. I was safe in my bed, wrapped in the warmth of my blanket, drifting toward sleep. My eyes traced the *Sesame Street* wallpaper decorating my bedroom walls—Ernie, Bert, and the rest of the gang keeping me company.

My mother, Irene, had tucked me in for the night, as she always did before going out. Melvin, my new dad, and I were alone in the house. I was almost asleep when he called me from the living room.

"Joe, come in here." He summoned me. I heard my name, soft at first. I wasn't sure if I was dreaming. I stayed still until he called again, more forcefully, "Joe. Get in here."

I crawled out of bed in my Spider-Man pajamas and padded toward the living room. It wasn't far, just around the corner. In the doorway, I stopped and watched him. Melvin lay on the sofa, still as a statue, the television casting light across his face.

"Yes, Melvin," I replied, waiting. The room felt heavy.

"What did I tell you about calling me Melvin?"

"Sorry, Daddy."

"Come here and sit next to me." He shifted against the back of the sofa and patted the space between his waist and the end of the cushion.

I shuffled over, my padded feet quiet on the rug. I slipped into the spot and leaned back against his body, my eyes on the television. It felt safe and friendly, the kind of loving father-son moment my mother always wanted.

The living room was dark, lit only by the soft glow of the television. Melvin wrapped his arm around me and pulled me closer.

I felt an intense warmth radiating from him, and I couldn't have asked for a happier moment—to be held by this man who loved me like his own. My biological father, whom I'd never met, didn't want anything to do with me. After feeling rejected, I found Melvin's arms around me warm.

"I want to talk to you about something important," he said, pushing my long bangs behind my ears and touching my cheek. "The important thing is that this is a daddy-and-son conversation, which means it's just between you and me." He poked my chest and tickled me. I giggled and smiled.

"Like a secret, Daddy?" I asked, gazing into his dark brown eyes.

"Yes. It's a secret between you and Daddy."

The thrill of having a secret with my father felt enormous. It seemed like the kind of thing other boys shared with their dads, and now I was finally going to have it, too. I'd never had this kind of relationship with a man. The men in my life were usually temporary—my mother's boyfriends who came and went as quickly as I learned their names.

"You know I love you more than anything in the world. I would never do anything to hurt you," he confided, stroking my cheek.

"I know that, Daddy. Why?" I asked, worried he was sick or about to deliver bad news. Maybe he would leave. That was my greatest fear, that I'd wake up one morning to find him gone.

"Of course, everything's okay. I love you more than anything in the world." He paused. "I love you more than I love Mommy," he murmured, his voice soft as he rubbed my cheek.

"More than Mommy?" I asked. How could he love me more than my mother? I couldn't understand.

"Yes. I love you more. And I love you more than Mommy does. That's what you need to understand." He pinched my leg. "Daddies and sons have a special relationship. You want me to be your Daddy, right?"

"I love you, Daddy. You leaving?" I started to whimper. I knew he was about to drop the bomb. What could I do to stop him? I stared into his eyes as he lay on his side, his gaze unsettling.

"I want to talk to you about becoming a man. Do you want to know what it's like?" He sat up on his elbow and glared at me.

What did I know about being a man? I was wearing Spider-Man pajamas. I worried about having loving parents, not about what it meant to be a man. I didn't understand where he was going with this, but I nodded anyway. I didn't want to disappoint him.

The attack was imminent, though I couldn't sense it. If I were older, I might have felt the tension mounting, but I was an innocent six-year-old who knew nothing about predators, so I stayed put, waiting for the exciting secret we were about to share.

My mother had drilled into my head that I should never keep secrets from her. But I figured it was different if my daddy were the one sharing it. A child's mind is easy to bend, and Melvin had me eating out of his hand.

He continued rubbing my hair and face, his hand slowly moving down to my neck and then to my chest. He touched me gently in a way that felt comforting. I trusted him.

Trust is an open door, letting the predator step inside.

The caressing continued across my chest. "Does this feel good?"

I agreed.

"Good. I'd never hurt you." He kept massaging me.

I leaned back against him, desperate to absorb his love. I wanted to cling to him and never let go. I wanted a father to share secrets with, play ball with, and catch me when I tripped and fell.

"I want to talk to you about something important," he said softly.

I shook my head, distracted by the television.

"Look at me when I'm talking to you, Joe!" His voice rose. "Don't worry about the TV."

Melvin gripped my chin and turned my head until our eyes locked. I couldn't look away, trapped in the cobra's gaze. His affection was the sweetest candy, and I craved it.

"You know, sometimes daddies show their sons love like this," he continued, petting my soft skin. "This is how we show each other love. Daddy wants to show you how to be a man, but you have to promise not to tell anyone, okay?"

I agreed, but everything started to feel wrong. Butterflies battered around in my stomach, desperate to escape.

He guided me off the sofa. "Take your pajamas and under-wear off for Daddy."

The room shrank. My breath came fast, nerves crackling with electricity. My heart pounded. I forgot about the butterflies.

"I'm scared. No, Daddy. I don't wanna," I said, frozen. Secrets weren't supposed to mean taking off my clothes.

"Do as I say, Joe. Or I'll tell Mommy you were a bad boy tonight. Do you want to make Mommy mad? If she gets mad, she might make me leave."

He knew exactly how to play on vulnerable children like me.

I slowly pulled down my pajamas and underwear, and they dropped to my ankles.

I stood there, silhouetted by the television, shivering in the cool air. Melvin looked at me like I was his prize, his eyes scanning my body. Then his hand disappeared into his underwear.

"Daddy. I'm scared."

"There's no reason to be scared." He took a sip of his drink, his other hand still inside his briefs. I didn't move. His threats started to register; fear built in my chest, waiting for my heart to burst.

"Why are you standing there like a wimp? Turn around."

My trembling wasn't from the breeze. I was naked from the waist down; I saw his arousal. Melvin stared at my body, then pulled me back onto the sofa, pressing me against his crotch. I tried to move, but he yanked me back. His moans made me wince. I tried to break free.

"Sit the fuck down. I'm trying to teach you something." He growled, pulling me closer. The chase had ended; he was finished playing with his food.

He rubbed my behind. "Yes," he groaned to himself. "That's good." He turned me around to face him. "You're a good son. Do you love me?"

I nodded, stunned. I wanted to run, but my body wouldn't move. How long would this last? Where was my mother?

"Daddy... no." My voice cracked. "Please call Mommy. I want Mommy!"

I tried to stand up, but he'd pull me back down, his hand pressing me forcefully against him.

His temper flared. "Don't fucking make me mad, Joe."

"I want Mommy," I said. My eyes blurred with tears.

"You want your Mommy?" he mocked. "You're no son of mine, crying for your fucking Mommy." He gripped my neck. "If you want your Mommy, you don't want a Daddy. Mommy doesn't love you like I do."

He ran his cold fingers along my leg, up my stomach, then placed my six-year-old penis between his fingers and squeezed it gently. This unfamiliar touch was painful. I jerked forward, but he held me tightly, keeping me beside him.

"Let's see if we can wake him up," he said.

Tears streamed down my face, uncontrollable. What could I do? I'd already told him I was scared and wanted my mother. My needs didn't matter. I knew it was wrong, but I didn't know why. It was frightening and uncomfortable, making me feel sick. If this was what it meant to have a dad, maybe I didn't want one.

Melvin smiled at me as if he were doing something good. He was violating me, and he looked happy and proud. He smirked, removed his hand from my private parts, and put his finger in his mouth, tasting my scent.

While he kept sucking his finger, I stared at the shadows on the wall. The window was open, and I could hear the traffic on the road. I glanced at the TV—*Star Trek*. He coughed, snapping me awake. Then Ernie and Bert from my bedroom wallpaper materialized through the haze. They didn't speak, but their message was clear.

Run

And I did.

I tore out of the living room, my short legs carrying me away from danger. I stumbled, fumbling to pull up my pants, too scared to look back.

I didn't stop to wonder whether he was following me. I barreled down the hallway into my bedroom, certain his hands would close around my neck and drag me back. I flew down the back stairs into my grandparents' living room, where Mémé and Pépé sat watching television.

GASLIGHTING

I slipped into Mémé and Pépé's living room and closed the door behind me. Tears streamed down my face, and Mémé rushed to me as I entered. She locked the door and guided me to the sofa.

I was a wreck—shaking, crying, unable to articulate what had just happened. Sitting beside Mémé, I replayed it all in my young mind. I couldn't comprehend it. Only minutes earlier, I had been on the sofa with the man I trusted most, someone I never thought could frighten me. Then it spiraled into a nightmare. Melvin went from professing his love to pressuring me to take off my pajamas and underwear. Was this what fatherly love was supposed to feel like?

It felt wrong.

I barely understood simple things like birthdays and Santa Claus. Now, the man who was supposed to love and protect me had done something I struggled to name. I didn't even know what to call it. He touched me in a wicked, unloving way that terrified me. Mémé pulled me close, her arms a shield. Pépé never turned from the television. Maybe he noticed I was there; I can't remember. My focus was on my grandmother, and I nestled against her.

Mémé held me tightly, rubbing my back. "Jesus, Mary, and Joseph, you're shaking like a leaf." She waved at Pépé. "Victor. Something happened upstairs." She wiped away my tears. "Did Melvin hit you? Is he drinking? Joseph?"

Pépé looked over. "He's safe down here until Irene gets home. Stay out of it, Lo. That asshole is a drunk."

No love lost between my grandfather and Melvin.

I kept crying.

"Stop crying and tell Mémé what happened."

She wanted answers, but the questions made no sense. It was as if she spoke another language, clear to her, but not to me. I wanted to explain, to let it out. My brain fogged over. The words wouldn't come. Only tears.

I couldn't speak; I only nodded in response to her rapid-fire questions. She had no idea what my nods meant. I wanted her to ask the one question that mattered: Did Daddy touch you inappropriately?—but it never came. Mémé knew he drank and had a temper, but the idea that he'd try to violate me was unthinkable. As she spoke, I stared at the living room wallpaper, white with shiny gold shapes stamped across it. Fear of what he had done and what might come next consumed me. He would leave, just as he said. My mother and I would be alone, and it would be all my fault.

Melvin was upstairs, likely concocting his defense. I wondered whether he was thinking of me, already packing to leave before my mother came home.

The silly innocence of my childhood mind.

I didn't want him to leave. I wanted him not to touch me like that again. To rewind ten minutes, back to before he called me from my bed. Melvin had shattered my little heart, yet left me carrying the guilt of his leaving. Irene had ingrained in me the idea that I needed a father, and I didn't want to be the one to prove her wrong.

Children carry guilt for their parents' emotions and behavior. In abusive homes, children become peacemakers, comforting, smoothing things over, even defending the very people hurting them.

Melvin was clearly wrong, yet I found myself doubting. Did he intend to scare me? That question surfaced as I fought the memory—his touch, his curses, the fear he instilled. I had no answers then; the questions remained only half-formed.

I wrapped myself in my grandmother's housecoat and closed my eyes. Time passed until my mother's white Dodge Monaco pulled into the backyard. Mémé left the back door open so she could hear Irene pull in and intercept her before Irene went upstairs to our apartment.

Irene woke me by gently placing her hand on my face. Pépé had gone to bed. I sat up, pushing the housecoat aside, and, like a cornered cat, stared at her. Her touch usually comforted me, but after what happened with Melvin, nothing felt safe.

"What happened, Joseph?" she asked, sitting beside me and pulling me onto her lap. I smelled the mix of alcohol and cigarettes on her. Usually, I was asleep when she came home, free of the bar's stench clinging to her skin, clothes, and hair.

Irene looked from me to Mémé, who stood by the living room archway, watching. To an outsider, it might even be unclear which of them was my mother.

"Tell me what happened, Joseph. Is Daddy drinking?" Irene pressed.

Mémé interrupted. "Irene, look at him. He's frightened."

"Joseph, I need you to talk. If you don't answer, you'll be in trouble."

Nothing.

"Do you hear me?"

"That's right. Scare him until he talks," Mémé snapped.

"Ma, let me talk to my son. Stay out of it!" Irene hissed, and I shrank back.

Their interactions were always the same whenever Irene had been drinking.

I should have felt safe, but safety didn't exist. Monsters did. I felt disoriented, like a child crossing a busy street alone. I had to be brave and find the words to tell them what happened.

Too much responsibility for any six-year-old.

The words tumbled out of my mouth, though I had no control over them. It was as if another boy had stepped inside me—had taken over my soul, my voice. He swallowed my fear and turned it into strength. I watched from the sidelines as this New Joe took charge, speaking words my mind barely comprehended.

"Mommy, I was scared," my robotic self whispered, eyes fixed on the floor. I glanced at Mémé, my only source of safety. Her loving gaze gave me the final strength to do the unthinkable, to break my mother's heart.

"What happened, baby? You can tell me," Irene asked, her body swaying like a tree in a windstorm as she struggled to keep me on her lap. I stared into her tipsy eyes, unsure of her allegiance. Would she believe me or blame me for ruining her happiness?

"Mommy… Daddy… he talked to me," I stammered, then fell silent. The words were on the tip of my tongue, but my stomach churned.

"Daddy… he… he…" I couldn't say it. I didn't want to betray him. If I stayed quiet, kept our secret, I'd protect him. The grooming had already taken hold of my mind. I'd save our family; I'd mend Irene's broken heart. The fear of being a bad boy haunted me. "I'm sorry, Mommy. I don't want to be bad."

Irene pressed harder, insisting I stop my shit and speak. Mémé walked closer and touched my head, and I knew it was time.

"He rubbed me," I squeaked, trying to pull away and sit by myself. I felt dirty, the filthy little boy who spills father-son secrets, the bad son who tells.

She stared. A tear slipped down her cheek and landed on my arm.

The sound was barely there, but her next words were immediate: "Daddy touched you where?" she asked, wiping at her face. Her beautiful face was distorted by fear and sadness, mascara streaking her cheeks.

I remember the shame. Darkness pressed in, a heavy halo pressing me down—into the sofa, into the earth, into nothing.

"Here," I answered, pointing to Spider-Man on my pajamas, between my legs.

The moment my hand touched my pajama bottoms, Irene's body began to tremble. Her inner tectonic plates shifted in response to her emotions. She calmly wiped my face, kissed my forehead, and slid me back onto the sofa.

"It's going to be okay, baby. Stay here with Mémé."

I cried again. The words were out. I was unsure of what it meant for Melvin, or for my mother and me.

Irene stood up. "Lie down. Rest. I'll go talk to Daddy." She covered me with an afghan and walked toward the kitchen, moving like a zombie.

Mémé stopped Irene in the dining room before they went into the kitchen. From the sofa, I kept my eyes barely open and listened. They were in plain view; the living room and dining room were open to each other.

Irene lit a cigarette and stared at my grandmother.

"Do you want me to call the police?" Mémé asked quietly.

She didn't respond.

"Irene? Answer me."

My mother drew on her cigarette and stared at Mémé. Her voice began low and heavy with hurt, then climbed. "I have to talk to Melvin. Find out what happened. If he touched my son, I'll kill him. You'll have to call the cops, 'cause I'll fucking kill him!"

She stubbed out the cigarette in the amber ashtray on the dining room table. "I'll be right back. Stay with Joseph. Don't let him come upstairs."

Mémé hesitated. "Do you want me to wake up Victor so he can come upstairs with you?" Without responding, Irene disappeared into the kitchen.

I sat up as Mémé entered the living room. She gave me that *it's going to be okay* smile and settled beside me. With my head resting in her lap, we sat in silence, the kitchen light casting us in sepia tones.

Time passed, and I drifted off. Safe. I woke to Irene's voice from the kitchen: "Ma. Come in here."

Mémé shifted me gently, pulled the blanket over me, and tiptoed out to meet her. She thought I was asleep, but I was awake. And nosy. Once she was in the kitchen, I pushed the blanket off, stood, and snuck into the dining room. I crouched between the beautiful antique oak bar and the wall, listening.

"I told you, he misunderstood Melvin," Irene explained. "Yes, Melvin's been drinking, but we talked, and he told me he was only trying to have a man-to-man conversation. Joe is just a confused six-year-old."

"Irene, are you listening to yourself?" Mémé snapped. "I'm sorry, but as your mother, I have to say this: you've had too much to drink tonight. You're completely wrong. Joseph isn't misunderstanding. Did you see how hard it was for him to say that? If Melvin touched him, then I don't know what you—"

"Ma! Stay the hell out of it. Joseph is my son. It has nothing to do with you. I don't care how drunk you think I am. Do you understand?"

"I know Irene, but I think—"

Interrupting my grandmother again, Irene said, "Listen, you just take care of Victor and stay out of our business."

Irene confused me. She lashed out at Mémé with the heat of a house fire—for what? For believing me? For daring to question Melvin's motives? None of it made sense. I didn't want Melvin to leave, but I also wanted my mother to believe me, to know I wasn't lying. What I wanted was impossible.

I could hear them moving around in the kitchen, their voices rising and falling, but nothing improved. Irene had fully accepted Melvin's tale now, deciding I had "misunderstood" him.

A chill ran down my tiny frame. My brain whispered, *"Don't go upstairs."* It was that instinct we are all born with, the one that flares when danger is near.

Like a horror movie, where the terrified teenager knows better than to enter the dark, abandoned house in the woods, yet steps inside anyway. I did not want to step inside the scary house. I loved my new dad, but this new fear of him felt disorienting. In an instant, the comfort of our apartment turned into danger. I couldn't piece it all together at my age, but one truth was crystal clear: facing Melvin was a bad idea.

But what if Irene was right and I was wrong? Maybe I would be blamed for jeopardizing her relationship with the man she swore would bring us a new life, the one who was supposed to save us from ourselves. He was the happiness she had fantasized about since I was born, yet that so-called happiness felt more like a punishment.

"Irene, I don't agree with you, and I think you're making a big mistake," Mémé pleaded.

My mother didn't hold back. "Well, whatever mistakes I make, and don't forget this, Ma, he is my son, not yours. I'm taking him upstairs."

I sensed them leaving the kitchen and ran for the sofa. I didn't make it.

"Joseph, what are you doing? I told you not to move," Mémé's voice was sharp as she and Irene crossed from the dining room into the living room.

I froze, turning to face them without a word. They knew I had been eavesdropping, but neither said a word. Mémé gently guided me back to the sofa.

Irene staggered in behind her, looking drunker than before she'd gone upstairs, and plopped onto the sofa. She grabbed Mémé's pack of Winstons, tapped one loose, and lit it. The scratch and flare of the match cut through the silence. Irene motioned for me to come closer. She inhaled deeply, then exhaled slowly. The cigarette smoke curled between us, filling my youthful lungs with poison.

Irene smoked in silence. Mémé stood as still as stone. I sensed my mother's glare, as if I were the one who should speak first. I couldn't meet her eyes. Instead, I stared at the coffee table. The silence weighed on me, leaving me uneasy.

When Irene finally spoke, her voice was raspy. "Look at me. I think you're confused. Daddy wouldn't do anything to hurt you. He was just trying to explain what it's like to be a big boy. There's nothing Daddy wouldn't do for us. He loves us very much."

She paused, then, almost as if to convince herself, repeated, "He loves us."

I listened, the words pressing down on me as the silence had a few moments earlier. I wanted to tell her he'd said he loved me more than her, but I kept it to myself.

"Mommy," I whispered, but nothing else followed.

This is what gaslighting feels like the first time: like you're the one apologizing for getting injured.

My words carried no weight. My mother didn't believe me. That was the second betrayal of the night—from someone who was supposed to protect me. The two of us would be back upstairs, facing him. I'd explained as best I could, tears and all, but she didn't seem to care. The worry that had filled her eyes earlier was gone, replaced by confidence in her boyfriend. To her, I was a confused kid. Maybe even a brat. But there were countless ways I could have been a brat; telling a story like this was not among them. Before Melvin, Irene had taught me that adults touching me inappropriately was wrong. And now, everything she told me conflicted with the reality before us.

Mémé tried to speak, but Irene's stare left her momentarily speechless.

"Let's go upstairs," Irene said, smiling. "Daddy loves you. He's not mad. Okay? Mommy and Daddy aren't mad."

"I want to stay with Mémé." I clung to the sofa with all the strength a six-year-old could muster. I couldn't face Melvin. He would hate me. Worse, he wouldn't want to be my dad anymore.

"Come on, we're going." She pulled at me, but I stiffened. If she wanted me to go upstairs, she'd have to drag me.

And she did.

"Joseph Thomas, get off this fucking sofa and go upstairs. Let's go!" She took one last long drag, crushed the cigarette in the overflowing ashtray, and seized my arm. She yanked me up. I stumbled.

We passed Mémé without a word; she followed us into the kitchen. I waited for her to stop us—why wasn't she stopping us? When we reached the kitchen, I pulled free from my mother's grip and ran to my grandmother, wrapping my small arms around her legs.

"I love you, Mémé," I said, looking up at her.

"I love you, too," she said, her voice soft but steady. "Irene?"

My mother stood in the kitchen doorway, staring out into the hall. Perhaps she didn't hear my grandmother call to her.

Mémé focused on me. "Listen to Mommy. You'll be okay. I'll see you tomorrow." She knelt and hugged me, and I believed her. My six-year-old innocence couldn't imagine she'd ever send me into danger, but the adult me knew she had no choice.

She released her embrace and addressed my mother: "Take care of your son, Irene."

Irene hesitated, then smiled. She looked at me, then at her mother. "Come with Mommy," she said, taking my hand. The smile never left her face. Looking back, I know she wanted to remind Mémé that I belonged to her and Melvin, not to Mémé and Pépé.

"Goodnight, Mémé," I said, glancing up at her. Then I crossed the threshold of safety into the unknown. I stepped carefully, but Irene pulled me close, so close we nearly shared each step up the spiral staircase.

Irene opened the front door to our apartment. The air reeked of nicotine, and I coughed as it filled my lungs. Of course, Melvin had been chain-smoking.

I broke free from Irene's grasp. "I have to pee," I blurted, turning down the long hallway toward the bathroom.

"Joseph. Get in here," she snapped.

I stiffened, then edged toward the kitchen doorway. "But Mommy, I have to go," I said, grabbing myself, trying to hold it in.

She let me use the bathroom, but soon I was back in the hot seat.

"Daddy needs to talk to you." Her voice was flat, serious. Ernie and Bert came back to me—*it's them against you, kid.* The smoke-filled air seemed to vanish from the room, and I fought to stay calm.

I stepped into the kitchen, seeking my mother's reassurance. She lit a cigarette, brushing me off with a wave of her elbow toward Melvin. Head down, I crept to his side. He lifted his cocktail glass, took a long swig, and set it down with a quiet thud.

Melvin was an expert at manipulation—a master. The stage was set, and he cleared his throat, ready to deliver a monologue he'd been rehearsing since I ran downstairs to my grandmother. Maybe longer.

He placed his hand on my shoulder. It felt heavy. "Joe, you know I would never hurt you."

The alcohol on his breath stung my nose. The intoxication seeped into me. I stood motionless.

"You know that, right? You misunderstood me." He kept his hand on me. "I just want you to be a big boy—a man. Do you understand?"

I stood there, numb, as if filled with Novocaine. I could only nod. I didn't know what to say; I didn't dare move. The room felt staged, rehearsed, like everyone had been waiting for this exact moment.

Everyone but me.

We were three players caught in Melvin's performance. He wrote the script, built the stage, and cast himself as the hero. He removed his hand from my shoulder and continued, "It's okay to be wrong. Daddy can be wrong sometimes. So can Mommy. But we forgive and forget."

Beat.

"You were wrong, Joe."

He stood as he finished talking, then moved to the counter and refilled his glass with clear liquid from a glass gallon jug—vodka, his favorite.

I watched him, speechless, my stomach aching. The night's tears and confusion felt like my fault. Still, something was off; the toys didn't fit in the toy box. Nothing made sense.

And still, I loved him. I wanted him to be my dad, not to love me more than Irene, but at least more than his vodka. He stared at me with a vacant expression I'll never forget. It was filled with confusion and accusation: How could you do this to me?

"I love you, Joe. You're my son," he said, closing the act with a sip of his drink. His smile at Irene was a curtain bow. Job accomplished. She rose and went to the refrigerator for another beer.

I wanted to hide under my covers while my *Sesame Street* friends watched over me. If Mémé couldn't protect me, it would be up to Ernie and Bert.

"I have to go again."

Melvin pulled me close. "Go pee. Then I'll tuck you in." He held my arm. "Do you love me?"

"I love you, Daddy," I said with a smile. I went to my mother. She hugged and kissed me. For a moment, I felt safe. I felt loved. Now, when I replay that night, it feels more like an episode of The Twilight Zone: images spinning, impossible, and misshapen. Surreal. Again, the script was his; the confusion was mine.

I'll never know what was said when Irene went upstairs to confront him about my accusation, but I know this: whatever it was, it cost me everything. I became a fawn trapped in a coyote's den. I was told I was wrong and confused, but I wasn't. Because everyone knows an inappropriate touch is a bad touch.

Everyone.

BASTARD

Take a breath. That was a lot to process.

Child abuse doesn't begin with one defining moment—as if you could point to a single day and say, *There*—that's when it started. It doesn't work that way. It grows in the ordinary, in countless small explosions and outbursts that wear a child down until chaos feels normal.

Years before Melvin entered our lives and unmasked himself on the sofa, I had already been desensitized to violence and aggression by the adults around me—especially my mother, Irene, who never cared where or on whom she unleashed her fury. After drinking, she often erupted at anyone who crossed her. In her haze, even the smallest slight became a threat. There's a cliché about words being weapons; for Irene, they were flaming arrows aimed straight at the heart of her enemy. On this particular afternoon, her enemy was our Aunt Juliette.

I tugged Irene's shirt as she lunged at Juliette. Mémé pulled me back, trying to shield my ears from Irene's profanity.

"If you ever call my son a bastard again, I'll knock your fucking teeth out," Irene hissed, her venom poisoning the kitchen. "Do you understand me, Juliette?"

"Get your hands off me, you crazy bitch," Juliette snapped, struggling to break free from Irene's grip and salvage what dignity she could. She turned to Mémé. "Lorette! Do something about your daughter!"

But Mémé didn't know what "do something" meant.

Juliette was my grandmother's sister, my great-aunt, a devout Christian by her own definition. A hardcore Catholic. She lived and breathed Jesus Christ, trying to baptize everyone into her faith.

Maybe I can give Mémé more grace for her beliefs in Jesus Christ because, unlike Juliette, she never called me a bastard. Like many zealots, Mémé's life revolved around Jesus, but she carried herself differently. She showed compassion. Even though she believed a man in the sky judged her actions, she didn't act holier-than-thou. She treated people with kindness.

I wish there were more Christians like my grandmother.

As I grew older, I realized Juliette saw Jesus everywhere—in the steam rising from her coffee, in the swirl of cigarette smoke, in the rain clouds overhead. Every moment of her life was a sermon: from *"Jesus is Lord"* to *"Your Son's a Bastard."* Juliette's faith ran amok—distorted, dangerous, unyielding. She awaited the Rapture with the same giddiness I felt watching Fred Rogers put on his cardigan on PBS.

On the day I was branded Irene's bastard, the kitchen was full of older women, mostly my aunts, fresh from Sunday service and brimming with sanctimonious fervor, gathered for the weekly lunch. Mémé loved hosting after church; I was too young to realize those lunches were as dull as the sermons. A kitchen full of ladies discussing Jesus, casseroles, and their children would send most kids running, but not me. I soaked it all in.

It didn't matter that the youngest woman there was decades older than me or that most of their conversations went over my head; I never wanted to leave. From the start, I was drawn to gossip. My aunts shooed me toward cartoons, but that rarely worked, especially when Mt. Irene erupted.

Raised voices were my call to action: Get in here and bear witness to the family turmoil. I'd climb into the first available lap, settle in, and soak up the foul language, my first lesson in profanity, taught by Irene, the Professor of Crass. If swearing were an academic discipline, I'd hold a PhD—summa cum laude.

Bastard. A child born out of wedlock. One of the greatest sins, I'd been told—the kind that destroyed the image of a wholesome Catholic family. I was very young when this confrontation erupted—three, maybe four—so my memory is blurred. I do recall a flash: Irene pinning Juliette against the refrigerator, lifting her a few centimeters off the ground. The rest I pieced together later from Irene's retellings, stories reaching back to a time before memory.

Irene's rage continued: "At least I didn't have to take fertility pills to have a kid, Juliette. And look at him. He's a cripple."

Juliette's son wore a brace; one leg was shorter than the other. When Irene was mad at Juliette, she took it out on our cousin.

Mémé pleaded with Irene to let go. By then, I was crying, squirming in the lap of an older woman who held me tight. Irene kept her hands at Juliette's throat until someone finally pried her fingers loose.

Did I mention that Juliette was my godmother?

A choice my mother made and regretted. Out of all the blue-haired ladies in our lives, I never understood why she chose Juliette. I asked her once, "Why Juliette?" She had no real explanation, just another bad decision. However questionable Irene was as a mother, I often wonder what my childhood would have looked like under Juliette's eye. And under Jesus's.

But seriously, was it my fault that Irene fooled around with a guy who vanished? It wasn't her fault either; it was his, the one who abandoned us. No blame was placed on the man who put her in this situation; it all fell on the innocent. A faithful Christian like Juliette might have praised Irene for choosing not to end the pregnancy and for deciding to raise a child alone in the 1970s. I wouldn't wish that on anyone. Instead, Juliette did the opposite. To her, a sin was a sin. In Juliette's eyes, we were damned if we did, damned if we didn't.

We were just damned—period.

Young Joe didn't understand. Today, I'm grateful that Irene defended me. But I also see the paradox: Juliette was wrong to devalue my existence, yet she was right; I am a bastard, born out of wedlock, with no father to claim me.

Maybe we should expect more from our holy-water-bathing, Jesus-praying family members. Calling a child a bastard within earshot is the opposite of the love Jesus preached. I expect more from the faithful. Foolish me. But I digress.

Before Melvin, I clung to the belief that I had a father—distant, out of reach, a figment of my young imagination, yet still out there somewhere. I believed he'd find me. As I got older, I asked about him, and Irene would snap: *He didn't want you.* I didn't realize my curiosity was picking at her wound of abandonment.

Maybe my "bio dad," as I'd call him later, disliked Irene and assumed I was a smaller version of her. I grasped at straws, trying to piece the puzzle together, but too many pieces were missing. Still, I convinced myself that if he met me, I could prove I wasn't like Irene. I never got the chance. She was right: he didn't want me.

Case closed.

Even after Melvin took over our lives, I pressed Irene for my prequel story. My biological father, Frank, was the missing chapter. Melvin became our present and our future, but what about my past? Why didn't Frank want me? Where had he gone?

For as long as I could form questions, I asked them. Then, one night, around the age of twelve, Irene's truth slipped out. In the years that followed, she returned to the story whenever we were alone, and the alcohol loosened her tongue. She never mentioned Frank in front of Melvin, as if erasing any trace of life before him. What I know about Frank, I stitched together from decades of her fragments and half-confessions.

This is her story.

"Frank was the greatest thing that ever happened to me," she began. "After my first divorce, I thought that was it, no more love for me. Nobody wants a divorced woman. But Frank wanted me, Joe. He did.

"I'd given up on love until that morning in 1971. He walked into the grocery store where I worked back then. The second he walked in, I knew. I did. So handsome. A full head of salt-and-pepper hair. Strong. Masculine.

"Sometimes, I see him in you.

"We started dating right away. Frank got me. We were both divorced, ya know. He understood. We swapped stories. He said his ex-wife cheated. My ex-husband beat me. I never learned. Never.

"Things were going well, even though your Mémé warned me. I didn't listen. I dove headfirst. He took me dancing. Dinners. I enjoyed sex. I don't enjoy sex anymore. *Irene often overshared.* He was forty-two. I was twenty-six. Frank treated me like a lady. Nobody had ever done that before. It felt… new.

"But then the shit hit the fan. After six months, I missed my period. I worried. I told your Mémé. She stared at me, silent. Frank was driving a taxi. He usually picked me up from work most nights. But that day, I told him not to. I said I had plans with friends. I was afraid to tell him the truth, Joe. I took the bus to Hartford Hospital and pissed in a cup. I knew before they told me. Pregnant.

Irene's voice cracked as she spoke. She didn't want to relive this memory, but she had liquid courage, and my ears were desperate for the missing piece of my history.

"I cried to the nurse. 'Do you need to call someone?' she asked. Yes, I needed to call someone. Who? I couldn't call my mother. I didn't want to hear her say, 'I told you so.' I couldn't call him, either. Things were going so well. I didn't want a baby to ruin it.

Ouch. But continue—

"The bus passed three times while I sat at the stop. I had to tell him. He had a right to know.

"I finally got on the bus and went home. The moment I saw my mother, I cried. The tears wouldn't stop. She held me. I told her I was pregnant. My life was ruined. *Ouch, again.* She comforted me, assuring me that everything would be all right. I wondered if I could ever be the kind of mother she was to me.

"I calmed down. Had a few cigarettes. You know, to calm my nerves. Don't look at me like that. It was a different time. Then I called him. Asked him to come get me. The excitement in his voice made me think I could tell him anything. He loved me. Our baby would bring us together.

"He picked me up in a taxi. I told him I was pregnant. He didn't react at first. He pulled over to the side of the road and turned to me.

"He was different.

"Frank wanted to know who I had been sleeping with. He didn't believe it was his baby. 'It's not mine,' he started yelling.

He was so angry with me. I kept telling him, 'It's your baby. I've only been with you.' He didn't believe me. He turned the car around and headed back to the house. I begged him to listen to me. This was his baby. But I remember his exact words: 'I have three kids. I don't need any more.'

"He dropped me off in front of the house. Before I could close the car door, he sped off. Asshole.

"The next day, he called. He wanted to see me. I was thrilled. He seemed calmer, which I thought meant everything would be all right.

"First thing out of his fucking mouth: 'I want you to have an abortion.'

"I had never considered an abortion. Your grandmother would kill me. I told him it was out of the question.

"He spoke calmly, but he was hurting. He said he would forgive me for cheating, but he could never raise another man's child. He truly believed I had fucked around on him. I kept yelling, 'It's yours. It's yours. It's your fucking baby," but I was talking to the dashboard. He didn't want to hear it. He insisted I have an abortion. It was his way or the highway. We didn't go to dinner that night. No dancing. No drinks. Instead, I sat in his car, smoking a cigarette and crying.

"I could've had an abortion. I thought about it a few times. Everything would go back to normal. He told me to think it over. He'd pay for it. Italian Catholic. Such bullshit. If I decided to keep you, I'd be on my own.

"He pulled away from the house, from our lives, for a while.

"I kept working at the grocery store, getting fatter each day. Everyone told me I was having a girl, but I knew deep down you were a boy. Frank came to the market to check on me. He offered me money, but I told him to shove his money up his ass. I didn't want his fucking money. I didn't want anything from him.

"You were a perfect baby boy. I picked your name before you were born. Joseph Thomas. Joseph, after my father. Thomas, after my grandfather. Mémé watched you during the day. I loved having you. I always counted your toes in the morning. I couldn't believe you were mine. I didn't need him. We didn't need him. We would be fine.

"And we've been all right, ya know.

"After I returned to work, he'd show up almost daily. He'd come into the store, pestering me while I rang up customers. He asked to see a picture of you. I refused. He didn't want you before you were born; he wasn't going to see you now. You were mine. Not his. 'Take care of the kids you have, Frank,' I told him. He tried to give me money again. I threw it at him. The manager started walking me out to my car. By then, Pépé had bought me a used one.

"I hated him for leaving me all alone. But then I'd come home, hold you, and I knew. I'd made the right choice. All the hate for him turned into love for you.

"The day I threw his money at him was the last time I ever saw him. He stopped coming to my job. Cut me off. No calls.

"Around that time, Mémé started noticing a cab parked outside the house every afternoon. Was he going to kidnap you? Take my baby? I told your grandmother not to let you stand near the window.

"He never saw you. He just gave up."

This story was retold throughout my childhood; the missing chapter of my DNA was solved. On the surface, I know myself. Underneath? I'm not so sure. I spent decades walking through life with half a stranger inside me, never knowing which parts belonged to a father I'd never meet, like a board game with missing pieces.

I was frustrated with Irene for keeping me from Frank. Would my life have changed if he'd met me, held me, and placed me on his chest, our hearts beating as father and son? I'll never know. Then I remember he wanted Irene to abort me, and all those questions and dreams became a nightmare.

For years, I questioned the authenticity of Irene's story, though her account never changed. It sounded fantastical yet true. The sadness and loss in her voice were real. Maybe I just didn't want to believe her. If she were lying, then Frank hadn't abandoned me. Us. It would've been easier to imagine he'd died in some terrible accident. Easier for a child to process than the truth: *He didn't want you.*

Irene always insisted she was protecting me from Frank, saying that if I'd met him, he'd have disappointed me and broken my heart the way he'd crushed hers. Likely. But she never gave me the chance to find out.

EATING DIRT

The concept of family has always puzzled me. Unlike most people, I find the idea of unwavering loyalty to blood relatives doesn't resonate. Many proudly declare, "I'd die for my family," and my honest response is, "Why?" I'd die for my freedom. I'd die for my husband. I might even die for my cats. On some days, maybe even for a slice of cake. But an entire family? I just don't get it.

For decades, even the word family made me queasy—like I needed to turn and run the other way. I couldn't shake the belief that a family's real purpose was to hurt you, to rip you apart and scatter the traumatized pieces across the backyard.

A boyfriend once told me I sabotaged relationships. His parents treated me like family; his mother adored me. But when we'd get in the car after visiting them, I'd say something stupid: "Your parents hate me," even after they'd welcomed me with open arms.

Maybe the ex was right. Maybe I did sabotage love early in my life. Better to cut yourself off from imagined pain than wait for it to strike.

***

My grandparents' house had three levels, and my entire family lived under that shingled roof. Mémé and Pépé claimed the second floor; Irene and I were above them on the third. On the first floor, my mother's brother, Vinny, lived with his wife, Sonya, and their three kids. We were stacked together, floor upon floor, like a layered cake, sweetened and heavy with rum.

That house buzzed with life, every floor alive with kids and adults yelling. A rhythm of slamming doors and voices carried through the walls and stairwells of a house built in 1919. Mémé adored it: chaos woven with devotion. Me? I'd have been flipping through the Yellow Pages, searching for nearby boarding schools. From what I've heard, it drove the adults crazy. Maybe that's what family really is—loud, dramatic, relentless.

Threads stitched just tight enough to hold the family together under one roof.

During those summers of my preadolescence, my grandparents disappeared for weeks at a time, hitting the open highway. Pépé, a truck driver, spent the summers moving families' belongings—furniture, boxes, entire lives— to places like Texas, Florida, and small cities across the Southeast. Mémé rode shotgun in the cab, keeping him company mile after mile.

I loved it when she tagged along with him because she always came back with gifts. One summer, she returned from Texas with a pair of cowboy boots and a shirt that read: *My Grandmother Went to Texas, and All I Got Was This T-shirt.* I wore it until I looked like a sausage about to burst from its casing. I refused to take it off.

With my grandparents away and my mother working her cashier job at the grocery store, the only available babysitter was my Aunt Sonya—a woman who swore like a sailor lost at sea. Sonya treated childcare like community service. Honestly, I wouldn't have trusted her to care for my cats.

The routine was always the same: when Mémé was away, Irene dressed for work and sent me downstairs to Vinny and Sonya's apartment on the first floor. Sonya would throw together something that looked like breakfast for my cousins, Timmy and Tommy, and me, then promptly shove us outside. Not such a terrible command, especially in the 1970s, when kids spent more time outdoors than indoors.

Rainy days threw me into a tailspin. I hated being cooped up inside, but when I was outside, I longed to be back inside. Maybe what I really wanted was the choice. Independence and freedom appealed to me, but with Sonya holding all the power, I had none. A restless bird can never be happy in a cage, and that's exactly how we felt when she pushed us out the door, angry, flightless birds who turned on each other.

When I was born, Pépé built a fence that turned the backyard into a corral. A kids' corral. Three sides were enclosed by an eight-foot wooden wall anchored to the detached garage. A heavy wooden door, locked from the outside, kept the adults out and the riffraff in.

We were the riffraff.

Inside the pen, the yard had a few patches of grass and mounds of dirt—just enough terrain to mimic a small, pathetic wilderness. This pen became our detention center until Irene came home or until one of us might have accidentally died.

On good days, my cousins amused themselves by tormenting whatever unlucky bug crawled across the yard. On bad days, their attention turned to me. In that backyard, it was always two against one, and I was the lone soldier in a losing battle. The clink of the breakfast bowls as Sonya cleared them signaled the end of the morning's safety and the start of fear.

"You're going to be sorry today, Joe," Tommy muttered as we tied our shoelaces.

"I'm going to tell on you," I said, my voice trembling, knowing my threats meant nothing. My cousins weren't afraid of punishment; I couldn't understand that then. They simply didn't care what happened. Nihilism at such a young age. When I warned them about consequences, they mocked me. Punishment wasn't a deterrent for Tommy and Timmy; it was a challenge. Getting in trouble became a twisted badge of honor they wore on their foreheads: *We're proud screwups.* It puzzled me as a kid. As an adult, I know it was a cry for help.

"Tell on us. You'll be even sorrier. Right, Timmy?" his brother warned, slapping me on the forehead.

"Right," Timmy echoed. "No babies in the prison."

The march to the corral felt like a chain-gang procession, and it always began with tears—mine. I begged. I screamed. On a few occasions, I even threw myself onto the porch in protest, desperate to stay inside. None of it mattered. Sonya would grab me by the arm and toss me into the backyard. A five-year-old doesn't weigh much. My cousins walked in willingly; they had nothing to fear. The idea of me standing up to them was laughable.

Once inside the pen, Sonya slammed the gate shut. "I'll check on you at lunch," she'd call over the fence. The latch snapped. We were locked in. No—I was locked in with lunatics.

The slap of the screen door hit us like a physical blow. I sprinted to the far end of the yard while Timmy and Tommy huddled by the gate, whispering. Birds sang. Squirrels chirped. Alarms went off in my head. My mind raced. I figured if I looked busy, maybe they'd forget about me. If they saw me playing with my Luke Skywalker figure—in the middle of a vital fight scene, ready to battle Darth Vader—these maniacs might postpone whatever torment they had planned. As if to say: *Joe, we'll beat your ass later. You look busy.*

Right. Like bullies *ever* reschedule.

Foolish child. I could've staged a full-blown Star Wars orgy with my toys, and Timmy and Tommy would still have flung every toy over the fence. Within minutes, my possible-future-convict cousins slinked across the dirt mounds toward the little haven I'd carved out behind a bush. Of course they came. They always did.

Sometimes the torment began when the gate clicked shut; on other days, they made me wait, letting the anticipation consume me from the inside out. Once, the suspense got so bad I shit myself. Or maybe it was Sonya's idea of breakfast. Hard to tell.

When I did, we all screamed for Sonya. My cousins knew they'd gone too far; they loved it. With no fear of their parents, their summer pastime became trying to scare the shit out of me—literally. Thankfully, it never happened again.

That day, though, I sat in my own shit while we yelled for hours. I'm sure the neighbors heard. Sonya didn't show up until lunch, three hours later.

"Hey, Joe. Come here. We've got something for you," Tommy said, heavy with malice.

"Leave me alone. Stay over there," I whimpered, clutching my R2D2 as if a piece of plastic could save me from my cousins.

There was a narrow gap between the back of the garage and the fence where I could squeeze myself whenever I thought my life was in danger. At that age, surrounded by bullies, everything felt like a matter of life or death. I screamed for Sonya—anyone—to save me, but she was too preoccupied to notice my high-pitched, echoing cries. How did no one ever call the cops? Nobody came. These days, a kid stubs his toe, and it's on Instagram within minutes.

My safety was an illusion. Tommy charged, dragging me from my hiding spot. Timmy blocked. I had nowhere to go. I covered my face, curling into a ball to shield myself from Tommy's onslaught. They left no bruises, no welts, no scratches. Their smirks were enough to instill fear, to keep me guessing. I lay on the rocky ground, jagged pebbles piercing my tender skin. I peeked through my fingers. The sun was hiding behind them.

Timmy had something clenched in his hand. He glanced at his brother. "You know, Tom, I don't think Joe had enough to eat this morning."

"Yeah. I think you're right. You hungry, Joe?"

Tommy slammed me onto my back, drove his knees into my chest, and pinned my wrists to the dirt. Pain shot through my back as a rock dug into my spine. If I thought I'd screamed for Sonya before, these new cries from deep within didn't even sound like me.

"Stop! Aunt Sonya! Help!" I gasped. "Get off me! Mom!"

Tommy pinned me down harder as Timmy knelt beside my head, a handful of earth in his hand. He pried my mouth open with his clean hand, careful not to put his fingers inside. I'd have bitten them off. With a swift motion, he smashed a fistful of dirt into my mouth. I gagged. I kicked and thrashed, to no avail. Timmy pressed his hand over my mouth.

Were these fools trying to kill me?

If only I could get away and make it behind the garage. I twisted into what I would later learn were my first yoga poses, trying to break free. The silt in my mouth tasted woodsy and dry.

I don't remember how I broke free; maybe I kicked Tommy in the balls—I hope I did. He yelled and toppled over. Timmy froze, paralyzed by the sudden shift in power. I flipped over and spat out the sludge. I scrambled to my feet, saliva streaming down my chin, and bolted straight for the space behind the garage.

Safe for the moment, I gathered my thoughts. My only option was to sit cross-legged behind the garage and wait for Sonya to serve lunch. Time crawled, and I regretted not grabbing my *Star Wars* figurines; they were left behind, alone and defenseless. Tommy and Timmy had wandered off, distracted by whatever had entertained them after they tired of feeding me a dirt appetizer.

The sound of the gate unlocking signaled that an adult had arrived. I leaped from my hiding place, making myself known, and my heavy breathing slowed. My cousins were feral, but I knew they wouldn't dare attack me in their mother's presence. When Sonya finally appeared inside the corral, she carried a platter with three plates and three glasses. If I hadn't been trapped inside this prison with her unpredictable sons, I might have looked forward to the picnic. If such a thing as a prison picnic existed.

"What's all this noise?" she snapped. "I'm trying to watch my stories. You boys are upsetting Bonnie."

Bonnie was my cousin by circumstance, Sonya's daughter from a previous relationship. Older than all three of us boys, she lived with severe developmental challenges. Back then, many in our family used the word "retarded." It was the language I grew up hearing; I never thought to question it.

Locked in the backyard, I often envied Bonnie. She stayed inside with Sonya while I was left outside, trapped in my family's version of *Lord of the Flies*. I imagined Bonnie lounging on the sofa—a chocolate bonbon in one hand, a TV remote in the other—while I fought to survive another day locked away with her brothers.

As I grew older and the wooden fence finally came down, I spent more time inside with Sonya and Bonnie. That's when I realized that choking down a dirt snack before lunch hadn't been the worst fate after all.

Bonnie often had accidents around the house, the kind that came with her body maturing while her mind remained childlike—a cruel hand life had dealt. I remember walking from the kitchen to the bathroom and noticing red dots on the linoleum in the hallway. For a moment, I thought someone had been painting. To avoid blame, I pointed them out to Sonya.

She erupted: "Goddamn it, Bonnie, you whore! Wipe your bloody snatch and put on some underwear."

Careless, vulgar, cutting—that's how she spoke to children. Sonya was no poet.

I don't know what triggered Sonya's spiral into verbal abuse, but let's not sugarcoat it: this woman needed medication. Lithium for breakfast, Prozac for lunch, and a Valium nightcap.

Family lore insists that in the early days of her marriage to Vinny, Sonya was "normal." She spoke calmly and respectfully. A clean freak, she insisted that visitors remove their shoes before setting foot on her freshly waxed floors. Every day, she dusted, made the beds, and folded the clothes, placing them neatly in dresser drawers. In her 1960s wedding photograph with Vinny, she embodies the all-American wife and mother—smiling as she cuts the cake beside her new husband, her future shimmering with promise and hope.

But something had shifted between that wedding photograph and now. Sonya had darkened. Her vocabulary, once suited for Tupperware parties and elementary school bake sales, now belonged on late-night Cinemax—never meant for ears under sixteen.

Sonya's delivery of lunch marked a ceasefire in the backyard. The afternoon shifted from *Timmy and Tommy versus Joe* to *Timmy, Tommy, and Joe versus Sonya*. Mornings were reserved for the relentless assault on the United States of Joe; afternoons escalated into open war against the Union of Sonya Socialist Republic.

Sonya despised the backyard. She'd heard that one of us had shit inside the fence, and from then on refused to venture more than a few steps in—avoiding landmines at all costs. Her slippered feet carried her just far enough to set our lunches on the uneven ground, then she retreated to the safety of her sofa and *All My Children*.

The three of us scrambled toward the paper plates and cups of orange Hi-C. Our behavior was more *National Geographic* than OshKosh B'Gosh catalog. Three flimsy plates sat on the gravel, each holding a meal fit for inmates: a ketchup sandwich and a handful of potato chips.

Along with being a terrible babysitter, Sonya was equally awful at preparing lunch. She deserved a trophy for *Least Effort Put into Nourishing Children* at the 1978 Bad Parenting Awards—if such a ceremony had ever existed.

We sat in the grass, leaning against the garage, trying not to let the dirt steal our food. If a chip fell, we brushed it off and ate it. A speck of dirt on a Lay's potato chip was nothing compared with the mouthful of soil I'd almost swallowed earlier.

Though basic, the sandwich and chips filled our stomachs: two slices of Wonder Bread glued together with a thick smear of ketchup. By the time I picked it up, the bread had gone limp, surrendering to its own soggy weight. No lettuce, no meat, no cheese—just bread and ketchup, week after week, all summer long. The official lunch ration of Sonya's Socialist Republic.

After lunch, my cousins and I collapsed into the shadiest corner of the yard, waiting for Irene to liberate us. The lack of protein, really, the lack of anything nourishing, left us plotting revenge on Sonya in whatever ways we could invent. My cousins were always one lap ahead of me in the revenge pool. Tommy's eyes glazed over with excitement, and, to fulfill Sonya's prophecy, he would announce, "I'm gonna poop." And he did, right there in the far-left corner of the prison yard. We declared it a rebellion against Sonya's rule—a backyard revolution. In reality, it was nothing more than what kids will do when they've lost control of their own narrative.

Years ago, I told this story to my husband, Matt. He didn't hesitate: "You know that's child abuse, right?"

Back then, I didn't have a word for it, but now I do. Sonya, her foul mouth, the fenced-in yard, those mushy fucking sandwiches—I know exactly what it was.

Child abuse.

Shattered Garage Window

Alcoholism runs through my family's veins like red blood cells, tracing back to my mother's biological father, Josephat. Irene once told me she'd considered naming me after him. While I'm rarely grateful for anything she did, I'll admit this much: I'm thankful I didn't grow up in the '80s as a chubby kid saddled with a name that ended in *fat*.

I fought off the demon of alcohol, but my mother and her brother, Vinny, never escaped the disease that destroys families and dreams. Irene often told horrific childhood stories about Josephat. One stands out: when she was still small enough for a crib, Josaphat came home drunk one night, furious that his firstborn was a daughter instead of a son. He turned belligerent with Mémé, found Irene wherever she was playing, lifted her into the air, and hurled her across the room. She bounced off the wall and landed back in her crib.

In her twenties, Irene reconciled with her father through letters—he even sent her checks while she was pregnant with me—but her earliest memories of Josephat were steeped in fear and violence.

Eventually, after too many years of beatings at his hands, Mémé divorced him. A few years later, she married Victor, my Pépé—the only grandfather I ever knew.

After Mémé married Pépé and moved the family from Maine to Connecticut for better job opportunities, Irene and

Vinny still spent their preteen summers back in Maine with their father. Irene told me more than once how Josephat would give Vinny alcohol, then lean in to warn her: *Don't tell your mother, or you won't be allowed to visit me.*

Desperate for her father's approval, Irene kept the secret. She never told Mémé. So every summer, she and her brother were driven to Maine, where Josaphat continued funneling alcohol down his son's throat.

***

Vinny was destined to become a functioning alcoholic—and he didn't disappoint. Though, honestly, "functioning" might be too generous. In my earliest memories, when Vinny and Sonya lived on the first floor of my grandparents' house, toxic outbursts were the daily soundtrack, seeping through the walls into our third-floor apartment. Our house on Prospect Avenue was rarely quiet. There was always something unsettling going on—a place of twisted safety among chaotic adults.

Some nights, it was Pépé arguing with Vinny because one of his sons had punched a hole in the plaster. On other nights, it was Mémé clashing with Irene over how I was being raised. Most often, it was Sonya calling the cops after Vinny staggered home drunk. Whatever the trigger, the adults' dysfunction poured down on every child in that house.

Usually, when Mémé's adult children misbehaved, she swept it under the rug, keeping it out of Pépé's sight. Irene and Vinny were *her* children, and she guarded them with fierce instinct, even when she disagreed with their choices. Pépé felt no such obligation. He had married my grandmother, not her tormented children. He believed in holding adults accountable. Pépé did not suffer fools.

Even with the drunk adults controlling most of the narrative, Irene and Vinny knew there were lines they couldn't cross—especially under Pépé's roof. But alcohol blurs lines, and once blurred, they're easy to cross.

Vinny had been unfaithful to Sonya more than once, as I'd learn years later. My young mind couldn't process the damage infidelity does to a family, but I understand it now. Strangely, everyone—except Sonya and Pépé—enabled his behavior. He'd vanish for days or weeks, then stroll back in as if nothing happened.

Mémé tolerated the fighting and turmoil, feeling sympathy for his family while still guarding Vinny, her golden child. Perhaps she identified with having an unfaithful husband. Maybe it cut deeper—that Vinny mirrored Josephat, whose drinking and abuse had once driven her to divorce.

I realize now that Mémé escaped her abusive husband but still lived inside the bubble of his influence on her children: the drinking, the adultery, the violence—the seismic shift of uncertainty whenever Vinny pulled into the driveway. It must have exhausted her to see her ex-husband living on in her son. I feel her sadness. It lives inside me too.

I wouldn't understand everything until I was much older, but when I was five, I was there the night Vinny came home after a multi-day bender. I remember fragments—the air still heavy with heat as the sun began to set, voices rising through open windows. The sharper details came later, filled in by Irene when I was old enough to understand the trauma that unfolded that night.

An argument between Vinny and Sonya had been brewing for weeks, and when he finally staggered into their kitchen, the air burned with tension. The shouting spilled into the backyard while Irene and I stayed in our third-floor kitchen. She busied herself with dinner; I hovered at the screenless window, craning over the porch roof, desperate to catch the action below. Their words blurred—muffled by distance and my age—but their voices carried: harsh, angry, climbing higher and higher until their rage felt so close it could have been standing behind me. The house seemed to brace for an explosion.

"Get away from the window, Joe," Irene said, moving to close it. Just before she shut it, something outside caught her eye. She crushed her half-smoked cigarette into the ashtray, a curly puff of smoke still wafting from the tip, as she bolted down the back stairs.

"Stay here. Don't come downstairs," she warned.

But, as usual, I ignored her—trailing closely behind, desperate to be part of whatever was unfolding. That half-dead cigarette smoldered in the ashtray, burning down on its own. By luck alone, Irene avoided setting the house on fire.

When we reached the bottom landing, Irene didn't seem to care that I was behind her. She was my mother; she knew I'd follow out of curiosity. The screen door slammed as I stepped onto the back porch. Irene darted toward Vinny. My grandparents stood near the front of the garage. Sonya was screaming at anyone who would listen. Panic engulfed the family.

Timmy and Tommy lingered behind my mother's parked car. I walked toward them. Tommy was in tears, and Timmy was wide-eyed and stunned. Bonnie was nowhere in sight.

"What the fuck are you doing?" Irene shouted, rushing toward Vinny. He stood by the side garage window—the same window my cousins and I sat beneath while eating our ketchup sandwiches during our afternoon imprisonments. It took me a moment to understand. Then I saw it: his head and neck smeared in sticky, maroon-colored liquid.

"Sonya! Get some fucking towels. He did this because of you!" Irene screamed.

Then, like Tommy, my tears came.

Mémé waved me over, and I ran to her as Sonya sprinted inside for towels to clean the blood from Vinny's head. Pépé was livid and did not attempt to hide it. From what I could see, he wasn't the least bit concerned that Vinny's face looked like skirt steak.

"I want him out of this house, Lo. That's it. I'm done with this bullshit," he growled, his face flushed purple with fury. I had never seen him this angry; I never would again.

Pépé helped raise Mémé's kids since they were six and eight, but now Vinny was destroying property and putting everyone in danger. Driving his head through the garage window was the final straw. Part of Pépé's outrage, I imagine, came from the shame—especially with a neighbor standing on their porch, watching the whole mess unfold.

Irene guided Vinny toward the porch just as Sonya burst out of the house. Ignoring our grandmother's warning to stay away from the garage window, Tommy, Timmy, and I bolted into the backyard, a place I usually avoided unless forced.

We saw it together. The terror hit all three of us at once.

As kids, we weren't allowed to watch horror movies, but what we saw that evening was far worse than anything on the big screen. Linda Blair's head spinning around in *The Exorcist* — that was child's play.

The lower pane of the garage window now held a clean, head-shaped hole—Vinny's head. Blood streaked the jagged glass, bright and wet, like paint slashed across shark teeth. On either side of the break, handprints smeared with dirt and blood clung to the frame, a ghostly reminder of his struggle to pull himself free. Even now, I get chills remembering it.

The shouting snapped my attention. It was Pépé: "Get the fuck out of my house. All of you. You have a week."

I wondered if Pépé meant Irene and me, too. He didn't. His emotional gun was aimed squarely at Vinny and Sonya. Vinny still hadn't spoken. Losing that much blood will silence a man. His eyes fluttered open and shut. Barely conscious, he managed to drag his legs as Irene eased him onto the steps and began wiping clotted blood from his hair, her hands trembling as she tended to her baby brother.

Sonya rushed over to gather her boys. I can only imagine the shock. She was a long way from the perfect life she'd envisioned on her wedding day.

"Get in the house," she yelled. The boys didn't react. "Now. Go check on Bonnie." Still, they stared at the jagged hole in the window. She finally snapped. "I said, get in the fucking house!"

Irene spoke up for Vinny, turning to Pépé. "Victor, you can't kick them out. He's hurt." Then she faced Mémé. "Ma, you can't do this to your son."

Caught in the headlights of her dysfunctional family, Mémé replied softly, "Irene, I stand with Victor. They have to move."

My cousins were leaving. None of it felt real. Since the day I popped out of Irene, we'd all lived under the same roof. What would this mean for me? Would I finally be free from having dirt shoved down my throat? If so, good riddance. Don't let the wooden fence gate hit you on the way out.

Pépé brushed past Irene and Vinny on the stairs. "They're out."

Vinny struggled to his feet and finally spoke. "Fuck you. We'll be out."

Mémé wept as she passed her children on the steps and fell in step with Pépé—a devastating decision for her, but a necessary one. Vinny's unpredictability became too dangerous for everyone under our roof. The screen door slammed behind her, snapping us out of our daze and back into the nightmare.

Then came the sirens—soft at first, swelling louder until red and blue lights washed across the driveway. A cruiser pulled up in front. Moments later, an ambulance arrived, and a wave of uniformed men carrying medical gear marched up the driveway like a military unit.

Irene pulled me behind her car. She didn't send me upstairs, but Mémé stepped onto her second-floor porch and pleaded, "Irene, send Joseph up to me."

"Go with Mémé," Irene said, already moving toward a police officer.

I headed for the stairs as the medics approached Vinny. Sonya tried to stand beside him, but he shoved her away. Maybe he already thought it was her fault—after all, she'd started yelling when he came home.

I slipped past them and disappeared into the house.

Mémé's kitchen door stood open, but when I stepped onto the landing, instead of turning right into her apartment, I turned left onto the porch she'd just beckoned me from— to get a bird's-eye view. From there, I watched the paramedics lead Vinny to the back of the ambulance. He refused the stretcher. They helped him climb inside and shut the double doors with a thud. The siren wailed first. The lights flashed. Then, they were gone.

The cop questioned Sonya, who babbled through incoherent thoughts, before turning to Irene, who responded with quiet nods and shakes of her head. After the halfhearted interrogation, the cruiser drove away—no sirens, no lights. Silence.

Irene waved up at me. "I'll be back soon. Stay with Mémé." She climbed into her car and backed down the driveway. Heading, I assume, to the hospital.

Sonya was standing on the gravel beneath me. We exchanged a glance before Timmy showed up on their porch and shouted, 'Mom, Bonnie pooped her pants." Sonya quickly retreated into the house, her life feeling as shattered as the glass in the garage window.

I stared down into the backyard. A strange calm lingered over the scene. The neighbor had gone inside. Turning, I took the few steps back into the house. Pépé had retreated to his brown, overstuffed recliner in the living room to watch television or nap. Mémé, knowing I hadn't eaten dinner, moved around the kitchen. A pot of water steamed on the stove.

Things seemed, dare I say it, normal.

But they were far from it. This exhale was the calm every family feels after surviving a tornado. The quiet that follows the noise. Those brief moments when the drunk has left the house, when the mother apologizes for her crass words, and when the father regrets throwing his daughter across the room. That calm deceived me. It warped my mind, making me crave it—confusing it for hope.

Uncle Vinny and his family left shortly after that night.

I'd learn later that when Vinny came home, Sonya unleashed every accusation you'd expect from a wife confronting her unfit husband. Their shouting escalated until it wasn't just their fight anymore. It felt as if the entire family had cracked, sharing the same psychotic break.

Then the shouting stopped, and Vinny tried to kill himself by slamming his head into the garage window, in the presence of his children, his wife, his mother, his sister, his nephew, and his stepfather.

Eventually, we become numb.

IRENE'S DILEMMA

Growing up in a half-American, half-French household, Irene longed for a sense of belonging and a connection to her heritage, but not in the way you might expect. For Irene, "learning" to be French meant drinking alcohol with other French people—not cooking, learning the language, or even visiting any French-speaking countries.

In the mid-to-late 1970s, one of her regular haunts was The French Club, a members-only gathering place for French expatriates in Hartford. Membership required French ancestry, and though Irene spoke little of the language, her maiden name was enough to grant her entry. It even drew cheers. The truth was, the party started when Irene walked in.

At least now I know where I get that from.

She craved community, a place where no one would bat an eye at a single mother with her child in tow. The French Club provided exactly that. From about age four, whenever Mémé refused to babysit me, Irene would toss me in the back of the car and bring me along. If anything, my cuteness might've earned her a few free drinks. I like to think it did. Listen, if she was going to drag me into a bar at a young age, there better be complimentary cocktails. In those days, Irene's go-to order was a Seagram's 7&7 with ginger ale—her signature drink. At home, though, she was a Budweiser girl. At the bar, she leveled up.

One of Irene's biggest party influences during that era was our Aunt Jean, Mémé's youngest sister, *le mouton noir.* Jean wasn't just a firecracker; she was the whole explosion—the total opposite of their sister Juliette. Where Juliette prayed to Jesus, Jean prayed to Frenchmen. Rich, poor, short, tall, ugly, handsome—it didn't matter. If these men spoke French and had a pulse, they were targets for her womanhood.

I'm not judging Jean. She was my favorite aunt, and I loved her sparkle. If I'd been old enough to drink and party in 1977, I would've been right there with her, hooting and hollering. Jean was a fun-loving, up-for-anything gal. That's how I imagine people would describe her. Picture Blanche Devereaux from *The Golden Girls*, but swap out the Southern charm and hospitality for Northern bluntness and unapologetic selfishness.

For reasons I never knew, Jean eventually divorced her husband and needed a place to go. I don't know whether her promiscuity began after her marriage ended or helped end it, but either way, she needed a roof over her head. Mémé encouraged Irene to let her "stay for a little while, just until she gets back on her feet," and that was that.

After Jean moved in, I was displaced for a while. We shared my bedroom. You have to be pretty down in the dumps to share a room with a four-year-old, but the arrangement was meant to make Jean as comfortable as possible. Me—an afterthought. On nights when she stayed overnight with her suitors, at their house or a motel, I had access to my room and my bed. But when she found herself manless, she stayed at our apartment and took over my bedroom.

Most nights when she was home, I'd sleep downstairs with my grandparents. Occasionally, when Jean's plans changed— maybe the man's wife came home earlier than expected—I'd be woken in the middle of the night and carried into Irene's bed. I never minded sleeping with my mother; she was still my sense of safety. My blanket. Even if that blanket was stained, crusty, and faintly smelled of sadness.

One of Jean's bad habits was bringing men back to our apartment when the motels were full—late-night visitors. Today, we'd call them *tricks*. Again, no judgment. I'm a gay Gen Xer. I spent my twenties in the nineties. We didn't even worry about motels. A car in a dark alley was all we needed. Get in. Get out. Stop at Krystal's on the way home for a few Chili Cheese Pups and fries. Perfectly fine behavior for a single woman, or man, in their twenties or thirties, but less ideal when there's a kid around.

That kid was me.

On any random morning, while kneeling on a chair at the kitchen table, crunching my sugary cereal, I'd see a strange man stumble through the house. Sometimes muttering in French, usually wearing nothing but white briefs and a white T-shirt. Maybe that's why, to this day, my favorite outfit on a man is just a pair of tighty-whities and a smile.

"On se revoit bientôt?" I'd hear him say from the hallway. Jean and her extremely hairy suitor stood just beyond the wall. Out of sight. Definitely not out of mind. As I drank the sugary milk from the cereal bowl, I heard louder slurping from the hall. Then came the light sound of smacking wet hands, like water balloons colliding and splashing to the floor. Were they washing each other?

Soon they'd appear. The Frenchman nodded toward me as I set my bowl down—a silent acknowledgment. *One day, kid, you'll have your own woman to tongue-lash.* Jean would usher the mysterious stranger out the front door, assuring him she'd see him again the next time she was at The French

Club. I'd hear his boots clomp down the stairwell, the air thick with Brut. Then he was gone for good. I rarely saw the same man twice.

That seemed to be her plan. The more men, the better. Bravo, Jean. Those men were getting a taste of what it felt like to be tossed aside for the next hot thing. Her power lay in her prowess, her command of her mind, body, and desire. I think this impressed Irene. My mother wanted to emulate that, but she didn't have what Jean had—confidence. The ability to be comfortable in her own skin.

I'm sure Jean had men she cried over when they rejected her, but she moved on quickly. A tear. A tissue. A splash of perfume. And she was back in the game. Jean desired men only until she climaxed; her discarded lovers rolled under the sofa like forgotten cat toys.

Irene was nothing like that when it came to men. She didn't just want one. She needed one like another drink.

Later, I'd ask Irene, "Mommy, who's that with Aunt Jean?"

She'd gently rub my hair. "That's one of your uncles."

On nights when Irene and Jean went out hunting men for sport, they'd try to sneak up the back stairs to avoid my grandmother. It was always a failed attempt. Mémé was wiser than anyone gave her credit for, and she was looking after me, which meant keeping tabs on her daughter as she galavanted around Hartford into the late night.

It didn't take long for Mémé to realize Irene and Jean were bad news together. Still, there wasn't much she could do. After all, it was her idea for Jean to move in. Maybe she thought Jean, being older, would be a positive influence. That backfired. Jean only added fuel to the fire.

Now Mémé had to worry about both of them. Two full-grown women stumbling up the winding staircase, whispering and giggling, thinking they were quiet. They woke everyone in the house, including me.

Irene spent countless hours perched on a barstool at The French Club, pursuing one goal: to find a man. A single mother living in the attic apartment above her parents, she wasn't searching for a companion. She was searching for a savior.

Mémé hoped Irene would find her savior in Jesus Christ. But Irene was looking for salvation in the house of drunks, not the house of God. Besides, when had Jesus ever helped her? He hadn't stopped her father from throwing her across the room as a baby. Jesus was a no-call, no-show when she needed him most. In her eyes, Catholicism was for Mémé. It sure as hell wasn't going to send a man to sweep her off her feet in those 1977 taupe open-toed wedge heels. Jesus hadn't helped her, so she turned to a man who seemed like salvation and drank like sin.

This man was a gentleman named Larry Lovex, whom she had met one night at the club. If Irene was looking for a sign from above, she didn't have to look far; his name said it all: *Lovex*. She believed love had found her.

From what I learned later, their relationship was a tsunami of drinking, dancing, and forgetting she had a child at home. In her mind, spending less time with me was a sacrifice for the greater good. Becoming Mrs. Irene Lovex became her new religion.

Irene seemed confused about the relationship's prospects, specifically about the difference between two competing feelings: love and lust.

Love doesn't clock out at the end of the day. It's magic—rainbows after a storm, the scent of petrichor in the air. It's spinning vinyl late into the night, laughing for no reason with your person. It doesn't vanish once you find the right person. Love can be overwhelming, exhausting, and rewarding all at once.

Lust, on the other hand, is heat—bodies in motion, electric energy strong enough to keep your apartment lights on for days. It's novelty, not longevity. A dopamine rush. An addiction to a person. Like any high, it fades.

I don't think Irene understood the difference. With all her might, she climbed the ladder to a high diving platform, her breath heavy with each step, inching closer to her version of Heaven. When she reached the top, she didn't look down for sharks. She extended her arms above her head. Her heart fixed on Larry. She gathered momentum and a dose of delusional bravery. Then she dove straight into lust.

When she surfaced, she was surrounded by chum.

"I love him, Ma. We're getting married," Irene declared, standing before her bedroom mirror, fastening a gold chain around her neck. Mémé sat on the bed; I sat beside her. The smell of Winston 100s and perfume clung to the walls. Dressed in her favorite outfit, a black-and-white oversized blouse, tan pants, and, of course, the wedge heels, Irene was focused on getting to The French Club, *tout de suite*.

"That Larry drinks too much, Irene. And you have a son to take care of right here," Mémé reminded her, but my existence fell on deaf ears. Ignoring her mother, Irene gave herself one last primp in the mirror, grabbed her purse, scooped me off the bed, and, careful not to wrinkle her blouse, carried me through the apartment toward the stairs.

Mémé followed, head down. No words left to say.

At the bottom of the landing, Irene kissed my cheek. She told me to be "good for Mémé." Then she dropped me off in the kitchen like a package waiting to be delivered. UPS-style.

Irene desperately wanted to marry Larry and was willing to give up the party life she'd shared with Jean. Ready to trade nightlife for married life, she became obsessed. There were no other men, only Larry. While Jean juggled suitors like a cabaret act, Irene clung to one man as if he were the last life raft on a sinking ship. It was predictable, really. Irene tried to imitate Jean's carefree confidence, but they were opposites—an Inuit trying to live among an Amazonian tribe.

In 1977, devastation lurked in the shadows. My mother learned she was pregnant with her second child, Larry's. It was a monumental shift in how she imagined her future. Finally, she could say goodbye to the bar life. Goodbye to The French Club. Surely Larry would be as thrilled as she was, ready to trade his nights of drinking for fatherhood and to care for her and her two children. Her delusion blurred with reality, but to her, the dream felt real. Maybe she'd finally be a stay-at-home mother—raise her new baby and me while being loved by Larry.

The thing was, Larry didn't want a child. He wanted to stay the handsome stud, with women fawning over him day and night. Larry lived to walk into bars and drink until he stumbled out. He wasn't there to change diapers or be a stepfather to someone else's kid.

Irene was planning a wedding. Larry was planning his escape.

When Irene confessed she was pregnant with his child, he asked her to have an abortion. *Jesus Christ. Again. This woman couldn't catch a break.*

For him, it was the logical choice. He wasn't fit or ready to be a father.

A strangely happy memory of Larry slips in: I remember him lifting me onto the refrigerator and walking away, leaving me six feet off the ground, longer than any young child should ever be left alone. Some might file that under *childhood neglect*, but it was the seventies, and honestly, leaving your kid perched on a refrigerator was one of the safer options. It was fun. I giggled, legs dangling, waiting for him to return.

What I didn't know then was that the refrigerator was my babysitter. It kept me occupied while they closed Irene's bedroom door at the other end of the apartment. They were unknowingly producing another child. But lightning struck twice, cruel and familiar. When Irene told Larry she had no intention of having an abortion, he vanished.

My heart breaks for my mother at this moment. As I write, I feel the sting.

As a child, I didn't understand Irene's suffering, but it was always on display. After Larry disappeared from our lives, tears stained her face every night. Still pregnant, she drank heavily and chain-smoked, slumped at the kitchen table, head down, listening to Patsy Cline's "I Fall to Pieces" until the 8-track tape ribbon snapped. Jean would put her to bed.

Irene hadn't followed Frank's request to abort me, but she couldn't bring herself to have another child without a father figure. It gutted her. The action shredded whatever hope she had left and darkened whatever light she tried to hold.

For the time being, my mother stopped seeing the world as a place where anything could last, especially her happiness. After discussing it with Mémé, Irene decided. She went to the hospital and terminated the pregnancy. The fetus was female, my unborn sister.

Although Jean enjoyed Irene as a bar buddy, she disappeared when things got hard. Jean wasn't someone Irene could always rely on for support. What Irene needed was someone to hold her up, to teach her how to walk again, to show her how not to feel lost, and to remind her she still had an important responsibility. Her son.

That someone became her new friend, Linda, whom she'd met at the annual French Club picnic. Linda had no idea Irene was pregnant or that she'd chosen abortion. When whispers spread through the club about Irene's absence, Linda reached out. Mémé directed her to Hartford Hospital. Irene stayed in the hospital for a few nights after the procedure, and Linda was the only friend who visited. Out of one of the saddest moments in my mother's life, a true friendship began to blossom. Linda became Irene's biggest ally. Her best friend, really. A sisterhood born from tragedy.

Sitting by her hospital bed, Linda listened. Irene confided in her, telling her how the relationship with Larry had fallen apart and explaining the weight of the call she'd had to make.

I stayed with Mémé until Irene was discharged, constantly pestering her with, "Where's Mommy?"

"She'll be home soon," she'd reply softly, then redirect me. "Let's put on *Sesame Street* and see what Ernie and Bert are up to."

The day Pépé brought Irene home, I ran to her as she stepped into Mémé's kitchen. She knelt and hugged me as if one of us were leaving, never to return. Whether she held me that tightly for herself or for me, I'll never know. I like to believe that hug was for both of us.

Maybe she'd realized I was all she had. I was her savior. Even though the men she loved always abandoned her, I was constant. I couldn't leave. I was underage. But even then, I knew: I'd never leave her behind. I'd be there, waiting for her every night when she came home.

That first night back from the hospital, I remember her crying into the phone, talking to Linda. Her voice cracked as I sat on her lap, one hand pressed to my back, the other holding a cigarette, ash dangling from the tip like a burning thread. The green receiver rested between her ear and shoulder.

Through the nicotine haze, she whispered, "Linda, I just couldn't do it again."

THROUGH THE KEYHOLE

I loved spending the night in my grandparents' apartment. Honestly, the line blurred about where I actually lived. I spent more time with Mémé than with Irene. You could say I had two domiciles under one roof.

Lucky me.

I always felt safer downstairs with my grandmother. With all those strange French "uncles" wandering around in their underwear, I never turned down a sleepover with Mémé, especially when Pépé traveled for work.

When Pépé left for a weeklong job, I was the man of the house, or so I thought. At five, I was already convinced I was the protector of Mémé, of Irene, of anyone who might need saving. The truth, of course, was that they were protecting me. But that sense of duty to guard the women in my life took root early.

One night, a few weeks after her pregnancy ended, the ghost of Larry had finally evaporated from our lives. Or so it seemed. Jean cajoled Irene into sending me downstairs with Mémé for the night. They wanted to "have some fun." That night felt no different from any other.

"Come on, Irene. Get dressed. Linda's gonna be there. It's been a tough few weeks for you," Jean pressed as the two women sat at our kitchen table. I sat across from them, listening to every word.

Hearing this and not wanting my mother to leave, I began to whine. They ignored me. So I took matters into my own hands: I slid off my chair and climbed into Irene's lap before she could stop me. If I could have, I would've surgically attached myself to her hip to make sure she couldn't leave without me. I loved being with Mémé, but my heart belonged to Irene.

That attachment, the fear of being left, was a behavior that, sadly, followed me through life. Back then, though, it was simple: if I could convince her to stay home, I believed she would. She never did.

Irene and I rarely spent quality time together. So whenever we were in the same room, I tried to sell her on the idea that hanging out with me was far more exciting than drinking at a bar with Jean and Linda.

My argument always fell flat.

One of my most meaningful memories of Irene comes from this period. It's the story I tell when people share fond memories of their loving, attentive parents.

Mémé kept pressuring Irene to spend more time with me. It became a daily plea—my grandmother doing everything she could to convince her daughter to show up for her son. Sad. But then, one random Friday morning, after Irene buttoned her cashier's smock and slipped into her jeans, she helped me get dressed for pre-K at Our Lady of Sorrows Catholic Church.

"When I get home from work tonight, I have a surprise for you," she said, wetting the brush and combing my hair to the side. "We're going to stay at the Sheraton in downtown Hartford tonight."

I had no idea what a Sheraton was, but I was thrilled because we were going together. Finally, all my whining had paid off. No French Club. No Jean. No Linda. No Larry. Just her and me.

The day crawled by, my small brain running in circles. Each minute felt like an hour, each hour a lifetime. When Mémé picked me up after school, she made me my favorite lunch, Skippy peanut butter and Fluff, and we curled up on the sofa to watch *General Hospital*. By then, I was well-versed in soap-opera drama; sometimes I even felt like a series regular. When Irene's car finally pulled into the driveway, I nearly burst out of my Barbie T-shirt.

Yes, I had a Barbie T-shirt. Didn't every little boy?

"Calm down, Joseph," Mémé laughed, half-scolding, as I leaped off the sofa and made a beeline for Irene.

My mother climbed the back stairs, dragging her feet after nine hours of ringing up groceries. When she reached Mémé's landing, her face said it all. She was spent.

Her exhaustion didn't concern me. I noticed the faint smudges on her fingertips from handling money all day. Those cashier stains always fascinated me. I greeted her with pure joy.

"Mommy, are we leaving soon?"

She smiled. "Grab your things and come upstairs."

I kissed Mémé goodbye, snagged a chocolate-chip cookie, and followed close behind my mother.

Upstairs, I closed the door behind me. It felt like my birthday.

She set her purse on the kitchen table, kicked off her flats, and let out a long, weary sigh. Then came the news:

"Honey, Mommy's very tired. I think we need to stay home tonight."

The cookie slipped from my hand and hit the floor, but I picked it right back up. Tears were already welling in my eyes. I was upset, but a cookie is a cookie.

"Why?" I asked. My bottom lip trembled as tears spilled over. The salty tears mixed with the sweetness of the cookie I tried to swallow. I'd been waiting for this all day. Damn it. All I wanted was to spend time alone with her. She'd sold this night as an adventure. We'd never had a mother-son event. Nothing that resembled a vacation.

But I realize now it was never Irene's idea. She didn't want to spend the night with me in a Hartford hotel. Her legs were ready to give out beneath her. This was Mémé's idea. Her way of forcing Irene to be a mother.

The dam broke.

My howl startled her. The sound filled our apartment, poured through the closed door, down the stairwell, and straight into Mémé's ears.

Seconds later, she'd made her way upstairs. She stood in the hallway of our apartment.

"What's going on up here?"

"Mommy said we can't go." I ran to my grandmother and leaned against her, still clutching the crumbling cookie. If anyone could change Irene's mind, it was her mother.

"Irene, he's been excited about this all day. Don't disappoint him."

Whether it was her mother's pep talk or her son's wailing like the world was ending, Irene gave in. Soon, the two of us were in her car, headed to the Sheraton.

I'm not often impressed by hotel rooms; working in the airline industry will do that. But as a small child, that room, with its queen bed and mustard-yellow 1970s furniture, felt like the Ritz. Better than anything the J.W. Marriott has ever offered me as an adult.

We had two competing agendas: I wanted to spend time with Irene; she wanted to soak in the bathtub. There were no tubs in our entire house, just closet-sized showers, and Irene's idea of luxury was soaking in hot water and soapsuds.

I remember sitting cross-legged in the middle of the bed, peeling candy buttons from their paper strip while *The Love Boat* played on the TV. I had a crush on Cruise Director Julie McCoy. I thought she'd be a great mom.

"Mommy, are you almost done?" I asked, curled up on the bed like a tiny celebrity.

From behind the closed door, she called out, "Yes. Just watch TV. I'll be out soon."

That night has stayed with me for decades. Still does. Years later, as a flight attendant, I had a layover in Hartford, and the Sheraton—now under a different name—was our crew hotel. The facade looked different, but the walls still held that memory. It was strange, almost comforting, to walk those halls again.

But moments like that with Irene were rare.

Jean's prodding worked. Irene was bar-bound. Just one last thing to do: get my grandmother to babysit me. My mother called downstairs and asked Mémé if she'd watch me "just for a few hours," which, in Irene's language, usually meant "until I come crawling up the stairs in the middle of the night."

Mémé never missed a chance to make Irene squirm about leaving me. She offered a handful of excuses before inevitably giving in, because, truthfully, spending time with me was one of Mémé's favorite pastimes.

At least someone enjoyed my company.

As a child and even into my twenties, I wondered why Irene favored bars and strangers over me. But as an adult, I understand. She was unraveling in the late '70s, making poor decisions because they required the least effort. Escaping was easier than facing herself—or me. And when Irene slipped away into a can of Budweiser, Mémé filled the space she left.

Though I didn't want her to leave, I was mesmerized as she got ready for a night out. Irene was glamorous. Movie-star glamorous. She dressed up. To my young eyes, she was Jaclyn Smith. I watched her with pure admiration, perched on the edge of the bed, recording every move.

One of her fanciest outfits was a pair of blue jeans and a black-and-white blouse that hid her soft belly. Not too much makeup, just enough to let the men know she wasn't a slut. She was Catholic, after all; they didn't need to know she'd been excommunicated after her first divorce. Everyone at the bar knew she'd just ended things with Larry. She didn't want to seem desperate. Only available.

The final touch was a splash of Jean Naté perfume. She dabbed it on her neck. The chef's kiss. To this day, when I smell that perfume, it opens the door to memories of my mother.

I peppered her with questions.

"When are you coming home?"

"I don't know. You'll be sleeping when I get home," Irene answered, brushing her long, curly hair.

"Can I go?"

"No."

"Why not?"

"Goddamn it, I said no. You're going downstairs with Mémé."

And that was the end of it.

The next thing I remember was a troubling commotion. Loud voices. Not angry, but fearful. Words like *police* and *ambulance* cut through the noise. Jean's voice carried through Mémé's kitchen, panicked and high-pitched:

"Irene locked herself in the apartment. With pills."

Pills?

The word meant nothing to me then, but the terror in Jean's voice told me everything. They hadn't noticed I'd slipped out of Mémé's bed and was padding my small feet into the hallway between the kitchen and dining room. Silent as a mouse, I listened. I didn't understand what I was hearing, but I heard something else, too: Ernie's voice, soft in my head. *Go find your mother.*

With Mémé and Jean locked in conversation well beyond my age range, I slipped past the two ladies huddled at the kitchen table. The kitchen door to the hallway stood open. I walked out unnoticed—being small had its advantages.

Once in the hallway, I bolted up the stairs to our apartment door.

It was locked.

Strange.

I pressed my eye to the keyhole. The horror that filled the air became real. Panic surged through me as I saw Irene sprawled on the kitchen floor.

My mother can't be dead. I need her.

From my skewed viewpoint, I could see her legs and one arm; the other stretched above her head. The cabinet door hid her face. A few chairs lay overturned around the table. On top sat two cans of Budweiser and an empty pill bottle, tipped on its side, mocking the moment.

My scream tore through the hallway, a horrified shriek that sliced through the adult conversation downstairs.

Banging on the door, I wailed, "Mommy! Open the door. Please!"

My gaze returned to the keyhole.

No movement.

Please don't be dead. Please wake up. GET UP!

Even if Irene was conscious, she might not have heard me. Freddy Fender's "Wasted Days and Wasted Nights" echoed through the apartment, its lyrics and bass thudding against the walls. Country music exists to make devastating moments even more devastating.

This was one of those moments.

Jean appeared on the step behind me. Mémé followed. The adults had come to pull me away from the unfolding horror, but by then I already knew what "pills" meant. It meant my mother might be dead.

In an instant, Jean scooped me up and handed me to Mémé. I kicked. I screamed until I had no voice left. All I wanted was to make sure my mother was safe.

As a child, I blamed myself for every disaster. Frank abandoning us. Larry abandoning us. The pregnancy that ended. I assumed the math was simple. I was too expensive for her to afford another child.

Did she take those pills because I pestered her too much to stay home? What would happen to me if she didn't wake up? Maybe if I'd been a better son—less demanding, less needy—my unborn sister would be here. Someone to keep me company. Someone to help me make sense of these adults.

Would they forgive me? Irene and the unborn?

A small child can't grasp the reasons behind an adult's choices. They feel the dysfunction anyway. It seeps into the walls like charcoal dust.

My family swam in dysfunction. For sport.

"Take him downstairs, Lorette," Jean ordered my grandmother. "Irene! Wake up! Unlock the fucking door!" she screamed, trying to shout over the loud stereo. But Irene had overdosed on pills. The only way she would wake up now was with a stomach pump.

I sat on Mémé's sofa, dazed, with her next to me, until I heard the wail of sirens and saw the flash of lights announcing to the neighborhood that something was wrong at our house.

Again.

I tried to run to the hallway, but my grandmother held me back.

"Joseph, sit here. Don't move. Do you understand?"

I nodded. Mémé stood and hurried toward the kitchen to meet the medics. I followed her instructions as long as a child with the attention span of an orange tabby could.

Not long.

I slid off the sofa and crept into the kitchen.

Boots on the stairs. Male voices. Jean shouting directions up toward our apartment.

The police arrived first, breaking down our door with little effort. The splintering of the frame, the sharp crack of wood, sounded like the house's bones snapping.

Then came the paramedics.

After what felt like hours but was only a few minutes, I stood pressed against the kitchen sink as one of them came into view. Then came the struggle: the stretcher wedged in the narrow stairwell, the thud as it hit the wall, the careful repositioning, and the clipped voices calling directions as they guided it down.

Mémé noticed me and tried to block my view. It didn't work.

The second paramedic arrived, and for the first time, I had a full view of the stretcher.

Irene was strapped in with three thick belts, a blanket tucked beneath her, and her black-and-white blouse from that night still visible. An oxygen mask covered her face. Her right hand was wrapped in gauze, with a length of tubing dangling from it. A clear IV bag swayed from a metal hook, the liquid inside glistening under the hall lights.

Terrifying for anyone to witness. Worse for the child of the woman on the stretcher.

Then came a policeman. Then Jean. He had questions. I often wonder how many times the police questioned a member of my family.

The stretcher made one last turn down the second flight of stairs.

"Mommy?"

They were gone. It all happened so fast that I didn't even have time to cry.

I ran to the dining room window overlooking the driveway. Standing on my toes, I finally caught a glimpse of them. The ambulance doors swung open. The paramedics lifted her inside and slammed the doors shut.

Last time, it was Uncle Vinny; this time, it was my mother.

Can a five-year-old have a heart attack? It felt like it.

The thought that Irene might never come home overtook me, and I rushed back into the kitchen, trying to push past the cop, Mémé, and Jean. The officer stepped in front of me, blocking the doorway. Mémé reached out to grab me.

"I want my mommy!" I shouted, pulling away from my grandmother's outstretched hands.

Recoil. From Mémé. Of all people. That was a first.

She latched onto my arm and positioned me in front of her. Both hands gripped my shoulders. I stood still. Jean answered the cop's questions.

When the policeman finally left, the adults' calm unnerved me. I didn't know where they'd taken my mother. No one said a word. Jean went back upstairs to our apartment. She acted as if nothing extraordinary had happened. Mémé ushered me back to bed.

In my family, denial was part of the foundation. Sweeping catastrophe under the rug wasn't avoidance; it was tradition.

But here is the thing about the trauma we hide. We hide it from others. We hide it from ourselves. We think we can outrun it, trick it into oblivion. Unfortunately, it doesn't work that way. Trauma doesn't disappear. We must look at it deeply. Process it. Learn from it.

It waits.

If we ignore it long enough, we spend our lives tripping over it.

The next morning, I asked Mémé when my mother would be coming home.

Her answer was brief: "I don't know."

Nobody knew what was happening to Irene, but the picture began to take shape once Jean stopped downstairs to chat with Mémé before leaving for work.

"They've admitted Irene to Hartford Hospital," she said. "She'll be there for a few days."

At least she was alive. For now, that was enough.

As Mémé helped me get ready for a day with the nuns at Our Lady of Sorrows, the phone rang. It was my mother. Mémé picked up the rotary phone in the kitchen, and I sprinted into the living room to grab the other receiver.

"Mommy, where are you?"

"Joseph. Hang up the phone right now," Mémé demanded.

I did not.

Irene spoke in a low, scratchy voice. She listed what she needed. Bathroom supplies. Clothes. The book she was reading. Cigarettes.

And one reminder: if Larry called, Mémé was not to tell him what had happened.

Larry never called.

I'd later learn that Irene had been admitted to the psychiatric ward.

When their conversation paused, I jumped in. I wanted to keep Irene on the line. "I miss you, Mommy."

"I love you, baby. Mommy will be home in a few days. Listen to your Mémé. There's no need to worry," her voice cracked. "Now let me talk to Mémé alone."

I placed the receiver back in its cradle.

When I walked into the kitchen, my grandmother was finishing her call.

"I'll have Jean drop off your things, okay? I love you, too. Be safe." She hung up, then turned to me with a smile that didn't match her eyes.

"Alright. Let's get you ready for school."

I mustered the nerve to ask, "Why is Mommy in the hospital?"

She ignored me. I didn't ask again.

Then she helped me put on my shoes. I still hadn't mastered tying the laces.

The truth was simple. Mémé was struggling, too.

Her son had once put his head through a garage window, and now her daughter had tried to end her life. Mémé was left as my de facto guardian. I'm sure she wanted a grandson, not another son. Irene was selfish. She put that pressure on her mother. Mémé had already raised her children.

My grandmother wasn't emotionally equipped to explain that Irene had tried to die because another man had jumped ship. But I wanted answers. I wanted to be a grown-up. I spent so much time around adults that I thought I was one of them.

But I was a child, and I was treated as one.

Adults interact with children in such fascinating, fucked-up ways.

That old saying: kids should be seen and not heard. Hilarious.

Small humans sit quietly in the room, absorbing the chaos, with no way to understand what's actually happening. Their voices muted by age. Forced to witness behaviors that the same adults would punish them for. If you're going to let a child watch his mother being lifted onto a stretcher, at least talk to him. Tell him the truth. Give him the words.

It won't do any more damage than watching her lie unconscious on the floor.

No one ever wants to address the trauma in the room. There's an invisible line: they let children witness the habits but refuse to name them.

As if children are too stupid to understand that adults are completely fucked up.

Kids know. Trust me.

Within the week, Irene was back home as if nothing had happened. Her trauma was shoved a little deeper under the war-torn carpet.

But something had happened.

By dinnertime, Jean's bags were packed and sitting on the landing outside Mémé's kitchen. She'd been banished from our apartment. Lucky for me, that meant no more half-naked men wandering around like extras in a French noir movie.

I was relieved when Jean moved out. I had my bedroom all to myself and, I assumed, my mother. But as I write this now, recalling what I remember and what Irene later filled in, the truth screams in my ear.

You see, in Irene's world, it was acceptable for Jean to coax her into abandoning me nightly to hit bars around Hartford, free from responsibility. But the moment Jean betrayed her by involving the police and having her locked away in the loony bin, their bond broke cleanly. The party was over.

C'est la vie.

Bad Catholic

"Why do I have to go? Mommy doesn't go to church?" I asked Mémé as I buttoned up my Sunday-only shirt—a crisp, light-blue one I wore with dark brown dress pants and a light brown wool coat. The coat itched so badly that it felt as if the skin on my arms were being sanded off. I begged her to let me take it off—*please, no, please, no*—until I surrendered. I didn't believe Jesus cared what I wore. Wasn't it enough that I showed up? Apparently not. Mémé was convinced that a polished child meant a pleased Savior.

Jesus had way more influence than I did.

If my job were to impress Jesus and the status-seekers in the first few rows, then I'd better slap a big ol' *Praise Jesus* smile across my face and pretend I loved wearing that heavy jacket. The truth was, I didn't care about pleasing the parishioners, especially the women, but Mémé always muscled us into a pew near the pulpit when I would've gladly hidden in the last row. While many came to Mass to be closer to Jesus, I preferred to stay closer to the exit.

Church was an education, and I learned a big lesson at an early age—most of the women at our church cosplayed Jesus' message. I could sense the distaste these ladies in the pews had for anyone they deemed beneath them. It wasn't about race or gender—it was about popularity, reputation, belonging. An unofficial Eleventh Commandment ruled our church: *Only the known shall be welcomed.*

If these ladies knew you, they would be tooth-rotting sweet. If they didn't, or they quietly decided you were sinful, their friendliness soured into venom. Out in the community, they smiled like saints, the holiest women in Hartford. The moment they crossed the narthex into the nave, the rot began to show. Jesus lifted the downtrodden and unknown; these women pushed them to another pew.

Try sitting in their row without recognition, and they would spread out—like commuters guarding their turf on a packed subway, using Stop & Shop bags and coats to occupy space. Their elbows became barricades, their purses claimed more real estate than people, and the rehearsed smiles carried a demonic warning: *This seat is taken.* The message was clear—*you don't belong here.*

It was high school for geriatric mean girls.

The men were cool, but I never trusted the ladies. They were unkind. Mass wasn't about welcoming strangers into God's house; it was about judging who they believed deserved to be there. These Christians-in-name-only sauntered into church with their noses so high in the air they probably smelled Jesus. I used to wonder what He smelled like—musty from the cave, most likely. The women in the front pews always wore that curled upper lip, their scowling faces bunching into God-fearing Shar Peis.

Catholicism never struck me as a religion obsessed with kindness—just obedience.

Mémé bent down to finish combing my hair. "Your mother is an adult. And you're not. You have to do as we say," she said, placing the comb on the kitchen table. "And church is good for you."

She took a step back to inspect me—a full body scan, Catholic grandmother edition. Every time I tried to walk away, there was something wrong with my outfit. I'd be halfway to the door before she'd yank me back: *Wait, you have a cowlick.* I'd try again—*Wait, there's a loose thread.*

Then came the scissors.

She fidgeted with my outfit, poking and prying at me as if I were preparing to meet Jesus Christ himself, not disappear into a sea of blue-haired adults kneeling, standing, and sitting in unison. With all that constant up-and-down abuse on aging knees, I'm convinced the Catholic Church was designed to keep orthopedic surgeons in business.

With all that said, I never liked attending Mass, and not just because of the unfriendly hypocrites. I feared the building —the bells, the echo, the ceiling that felt like it touched Heaven. The smell of burning candles erasing sin. The pomp and circumstance. The choreography. It all seemed so… performative.

I thought we were here to praise Jesus, not put on a production of *Joseph and the Amazing Technicolor Dreamcoat*, which, for the record, I would have happily been cast in.

I did, however, enjoy the *Peace be with you* portion of the service. Offering kind words and well-wishes to your neighbors was the part of Catholicism that actually made sense to me, at least according to what was printed in the missal. Truthfully, I liked interacting with strangers, even the ladies who shied away from making eye contact with me. They must have known I was Irene's son. It became my own tiny rebellion: *Oh, you bitches don't want to acknowledge the bastard child? Great. Now you have to hold my hand.*

I'd keep right on shaking hands until the priest started speaking again. Pépé would nudge me back, and I'd return to the hardwood bench.

Sitting in the backseat of their car on our way to church, I'd squeeze my hands together as tightly as I could, praying for any excuse—any miracle—that would make Pépé turn around and take us home. My cousins Timmy and Tommy didn't have to attend Mass. *Did they pray about it?* As unlikely as it was that those heathens prayed at all, I convinced myself they might, which meant I had to pray even harder. I always gave it a try.

I know it seems strange to pray to Jesus *not* to have to see Him, but I was desperate:

> *Hi, Jesus, it's me.*
> *Please crash the car.*
> *Don't kill anyone.*
> *There—hit that tree.*
> *You missed it.*
> *Oh, there's another.*

But we always made it safely into the vacant lot across the street from the church. I felt defeated every time; there was no escaping Sunday Mass, even when I prayed for it.

Most of my fear of religion came from Mémé's beliefs, the delusional "truths" that cemented her in her faith. That holy water could protect you from demonic forces. That every human on earth was descended from Adam and Eve. *(Which, technically, does that make Mémé my grandmother or my sister?)* And my personal favorite: Mary was still a virgin after getting pregnant.

As much as I loved my grandmother, she was a total Jesus freak. Not hateful like Aunt Juliette, but deeply attached in a way that felt uncomfortable. She talked to Him. Oh yes, she did, like He was her live-in roommate. I know plenty of Christians pray to Jesus, but as a kid, I seriously thought something might be wrong with her when she'd stare up at the bumpy popcorn ceiling, clutch her shiny, sterling-silver rosary, and start asking Him for answers.

Mémé ran every decision, every worry, every inconvenience through Jesus before she even considered talking to another human being.

My grandparents' apartment looked more like a church vestibule than a place where people actually lived. A cluttered mess with religious artifacts that were either deeply meaningful or utterly meaningless, depending on your view. Catholicism filled every inch of that space—from a small silver cross nailed above each door to numerous rosaries hanging from hooks. There was always a rosary within reach, of course, to ward off spontaneous demonic possession.

We had it all: crucifixes, ceramic saints, statues of Madonna—not *that* Madonna—the only thing missing was the blood of Christ, though she made up for it with a few bottles of Merlot. And then there were endless images of Him scattered on the walls and shelves in every room.

Jesus on water.

Jesus at dinner.

Jesus at Glamour Shots.

Jesus Jesus Jesus.

There was no escaping Him, not even in the bathroom, which stored decades' worth of palm fronds from Palm Sunday, layered one on top of another like botanical sediment. If anyone suggested throwing out the older ones—say, from 1958—Mémé shut that shit down immediately. So the palms stayed, growing drier and crispier with each passing year.

All these relics turned every open space into a judgment zone. The message was clear: Jesus is watching, so don't fuck up. That warning burrowed into my brain.

Roll your eyes at your mother? Jesus is watching.

Want to sneak a peek at the blurred Cinemax channel when no adults are around? Remember, Jesus is watching.

Sneakingly flipping off your grandfather behind his back because he won't let you change the channel, even while he's asleep? You guessed it, Jesus is watching.

There was no privacy in that house, not even inside your own head.

Mémé didn't just teach me to fear Jesus; she made Him feel like a 24-hour surveillance system.

For example, anytime she caught me gazing at myself in the mirror, she'd start preaching. "Don't stare at yourself in the mirror so much. You'll see the Devil."

I was five when she planted that fear in my head, so I genuinely believed I might accidentally summon Satan by catching my own reflection. I avoided walking past her full-length bedroom mirror as if it were a portal to Hell. The thought of seeing the Devil only fueled my growing fear of going to church. If I were too afraid to make eye contact with myself, imagine the terror of crossing the threshold into God's house.

What would He think?

Did He know I looked into Mémé's mirror? Or that while she was busy in the kitchen, I slipped into her nightgown, wrapped a towel around my hair, and admired myself—Liza Minnelli style? Every night, I promised God I wouldn't stare at myself again, but I always broke that promise.

I had fabulous hair back then, and the mirror loved me. Surprisingly, I never saw Satan.

But what I did get was this: one morning, while I was combing my hair, Mémé looked at me, kissed me on the cheek, and said, "You'd have made such a pretty girl."

Come again, Lorette?

Even at that age, there was no denying that the homosexuality gene had pulled up in a U-Haul, tossed its keys on the kitchen counter, and moved right in. Homosexuality—the sin of sins. The sermons from the pulpit and the judgment from the pews made it clear: difference was a liability. Being gay wasn't just unacceptable; it was treated as worse than a crime, worse than murder, and (according to Leviticus) about on par with eating shrimp.

And apparently, that made me a bad Catholic.

When I look at photos of myself from early childhood—long hair, blue overalls, hand on my hip, head cocked to the side—I can't help but smile at my own gayness. I've always wondered if Mémé saw it, too. We spent so much time together. What if she knew before I did?

She wasn't blind, so how did she overlook it?

I doubt she could have let herself see it. Being as devout as she was, the idea alone would have been unthinkable. If she had realized it, it might have killed her. And we don't need to sugarcoat this with extra fairy dust: I acted very girlish at five years old.

The proof?

When I became a teenager, Pépé, a man who spoke only when he had something worth saying, loved retelling a specific memory whenever family visited.

"When Joe was younger, maybe five, if Cher were on TV, he'd jump up on the coffee table, and boy, he could follow her every move."

See? Gay.

I think my family suspected, but they treated the topic like an unwanted pregnancy—better to ignore the pink giraffe spinning in my grandmother's clothes than to accept it. In Catholic households, the whispers of truth are always drowned out by the screams of denial.

My childhood queerness was like an ignored highway billboard—there for anyone to see, yet never noticed or acknowledged. It was the missing piece in every attempt to explain why I wasn't like my cousins, Timmy and Tommy. While they rocked out to Kiss, Iron Maiden, and Black Sabbath, Sonya gave me Donna Summer's *Bad Girls* for Christmas. I hadn't asked for it. Hell, I'm not sure I even knew who Donna Summer was then, but she would later become a staple in my music rotation.

So naturally, the next logical step was to enroll me in Catholic school—what better place for a terrified little gay boy than a building designed to instill guilt? Mémé convinced Irene to enroll me at Our Lady of Sorrows Catholic School for both catechism classes and kindergarten. A double dose of indoctrination. No chance of escape.

It was 1977, the summer before kindergarten. Mémé dragged me down to the church's musty basement to the main office to register me for both. Irene's signature was stamped across the paperwork like a sentence I hadn't agreed to serve. The idea of school didn't sit well with me. To be away from my grandmother all day? Half a day, maybe—because then I could still catch *All My Children*—but all day? Absolutely not.

"Mémé, can we leave? I don't like this basement."

She patted my hand. "You'll love school and meeting new friends. Don't you want to meet friends?"

I stared at her. "You're my friend."

That's not what she meant.

Catechism classes followed Sunday Mass. As the recession-al began, my grandparents and I bowed and blew our obligatory kisses toward the altar. Then Pépé made a beeline for the car, while Mémé funneled me down to the church basement for catechism. Brutal. I endured countless wasted hours on a wooden pew, being told who was and wasn't going to Heaven, learning hypocrisy as the curriculum and guilt as a second language.

Now I had to do it for another hour without a *Peace be with you* break.

As we descended the steps into what felt like a dungeon, she sensed my panic—my sweaty palms, the way I tried to pull back as we inched toward the classroom glowing at the end of the corridor. I hadn't thrown myself down onto the cold linoleum floor in protest, but I thought about it.

"You'll be fine. Don't cry. I'll be back in an hour," Mémé whispered as we stepped inside.

I cried anyway, reaching for her as the catechist—Sister Nun, as I later named her—grabbed me by the shoulders and pried me away. The audacity. In that moment, I did *not* believe I would be fine.

According to my grandmother, I had nothing to fear. I was being left in a Catholic school basement with a roomful of peers, not at a departure gate at Bradley Airport alone. Honestly, a Catholic school basement does sound scarier on paper.

My issue was that I always needed to be within arm's length of either Irene or Mémé—preferably Mémé. That was safety. I didn't mind being alone with Pépé; he was trusted, but I still needed one of those two women in my line of sight. I hated being the only person I knew in a room; it made me feel as if I'd been dropped off without my emotional support human. I had spent almost every waking moment with my grandmother, so it literally felt like I was missing a limb when she wasn't beside me.

While my classmates zoomed past with their little Catholicism workbooks and smiles for Jesus, I just wanted to go home and watch my grandfather nap in his recliner while Jack Nicklaus sank a birdie on CBS.

It was a terrible experience—realizing that Sunday wasn't completely mine after Mass ended. The worst part was that catechism involved indoctrination workbooks, so there was homework added to church activities.

Mass. Catechism class. Homework. Bed.

A loop that made Sundays feel as if Satan had seen me in the mirror.

"Hurry up with your homework so you don't miss Laverne & Shirley," Mémé called from the kitchen, as if dangling a carrot in front of me would make learning about Jesus' crucifixion go any faster.

I sat at the table with my catechism workbook open in front of me and glanced up at the framed portrait of Jesus on the wall—looking like a white guy who had just finished senior pictures.

When Mémé walked into the dining room, I said, "A girl in class told me that Jesus is not white. Is that true?" Then I casually went back to coloring.

It was an honest question, one that still confuses me today. Looking back, it was probably the first loose thread that pulled me free from my grandmother's belief system.

"What?" Mémé said from across the room, sliding a freshly painted ceramic saint into the curio cabinet.

I asked, "Is Jesus white or Black?" as I kept coloring Him, carrying that enormous cross through the blazing heat of Jerusalem.

"Jesus is Jesus. That's all there is to it." She finally looked at me. "Why would you ask such a silly question?"

She moved to the dining room table and stared down at me, then her gaze drifted to the small, opaque bottle of "emergency" holy water she kept in the center of the table, beside her fancy dishes. Some families keep a first-aid kit for emergencies—Lorette kept holy water in case she needed to perform an exorcism on her grandson.

And it wasn't just that bottle. She had bottles of different sizes stationed in every room of the house. A small one in the bathroom. A medium one in her bedroom. A jug-sized one in the living room—as if spiritual protection required square footage calculations.

I thought it was creepy.

I tasted it once—it tasted like rose water.

Witchcraft, if you ask me.

Like most Catholic kids who eventually escaped the faith, I grew up believing that holy water could burn the skin of Satan's followers. I was terrified to be anywhere near it. After Aunt Juliette preached that I was a bastard child, I figured that if that magical water ever touched me, I'd burst into flames on contact.

As a devout Catholic woman, Mémé smoothly shifted the conversation to a safer topic.

"Now, let me see what you're coloring," she asked, leaning over my workbook.

Her mood lightened. "Oh, Jesus carrying the cross."

She smiled, then crushed her cigarette butt into the golden amber ashtray parked beside my crayons. "Use a lot of yellow and orange to make the sun look bright. It was hot that day."

Leave it to my grandmother to comment on the temperature on the day Jesus Christ was crucified. And of course I believed her—she spoke with the confidence of someone who had personally checked the forecast in Jerusalem that day.

The first three days of kindergarten went well. Our school wasn't in the church basement like catechism class, but in an adjacent building a block away. Honestly, I don't remember my first step into the school building in my crisp-ironed white shirt, black pants, black shoes, and a belt. No tie. I wore what every other boy in the school wore. Some kids had backpacks to express themselves; I did not. Not yet, anyway. Mémé believed the uniform would help me make friends. Because we matched, I'd belong.

But that's not the purpose of a uniform. The point is sameness—to make every kid look identical, interchangeable, and invisible. The message was loud and clear: don't be different. Strip away our identity, our imagination, and our self. A uniform wasn't going to help me make friends. It was going to help me disappear.

And honestly? Disappearing sounded fine. The moment I walked into that classroom, the smell of cleaning fluids hit me like a wall. My classmates were wound up like indoor cats practicing parkour, and all I wanted was to be home on the couch with Mémé. I didn't need the pressure to make friends. I needed a blanket and a handful of Goldfish crackers.

The catechism homework I had battled all summer gave me a preview of what to expect: a lot of Bible stories. Because Mémé forced me to do all my work on Sunday nights, I was technically "prepared" for kindergarten. Besides the gore of Jesus' crucifixion, I also learned about His birth, His mother, Mary, and His stepdad, who, coincidentally, shared my name. (That part thrilled me.) Then came the bloody retelling of Cain murdering his brother Abel—an odd selection for a room of five-year-olds, but fine, sure. And the head-scratcher of all time: Noah stuffing every animal on Earth onto a wooden boat in preparation for a world-ending rainstorm.

No fear was triggered there. None. At. All.

For the first few days, I thought everything was going smoothly—until I was officially labeled the troublemaker who "won't stop talking." Sister Nun had known me from catechism over the summer, so she knew I had loose lips—but she had been more relaxed then. Apparently, she took kindergarten far more seriously, and my constant babble after being told to "be quiet during quiet time" pushed her to act. When she finally did, she lit Irene's fuse, setting off a Catholic-family explosion—Irene-style.

As Irene retold it later, she stormed up to the school after class let out, with Mémé and me close behind, to find out why I had come home crying that afternoon. To be fair, I often cried when I was away from Mémé, but I usually calmed down the second I saw her at student pickup. On this day, I didn't stop crying, not even after we got home.

Five of us were packed into the Principal's office: Irene, Mémé, and I on a stiff sofa against a pale yellow wall, facing the Principal and Sister Nun behind his heavy desk. The room had a faint scent of cloves and aftershave, which was much preferable to the over-bleached classrooms down the hall.

"Okay, tell me again what happened," Irene said, her voice tight. "Why did you need to slap his hands with a ruler?"

Sister Nun looked at the Principal; he nodded. She smiled and folded her hands. "He was talking out of turn. And here at—"

"I don't give a fuck if he was standing on his head, reciting the Lord's Prayer."

Mémé practically broke out in hives. "Irene. Language."

"Not now, Ma," Irene snapped, not breaking eye contact with Sister Nun. I assumed Sister Nun was on the verge of shitting herself. "Explain why I shouldn't take my son out of this school right now?"

Silence. Only blank stares.

"No good answers? Great, we're done. Come on, we're leaving."

"Irene, wait a minute. Let's not be too rash. He needs this school," Mémé pleaded, terrified that her daughter's filthy, sinful mouth might get us all excommunicated by lunchtime tomorrow. If a priest or a nun deemed you a problem, the message went straight to Jesus—no postage required.

In Mémé's mind, pulling me out of Catholic school was as catastrophic as God's punishment of Egypt with ten plagues. In her eyes, it was worse. Irene's choice was a plague upon our family, one meant to destroy any chance that I would grow up to be a God-fearing Catholic. For Christ's sake, my soul was in danger. As devout as Mémé was, I can only imagine the disaster movie playing in her head—the backlash from Heaven, a smiting of Hartford, our family spiritually evicted. And what would the blue hairs in the first few pews say about it?

The Pope might be outraged; the Vatican could revoke our membership.

Jesus might never come back.

The end times were here for sure.

Irene stood, grabbed her purse, and reached for my hand.

"No, he doesn't need this school." She shot daggers at her new adversaries across the desk.

"And the only person allowed to hit my son is me."

Brat!

Next stop: Parkville Community School.

On paper, the transition from one school to another went off without a hitch, with little involvement from me. The previous Thursday, Irene withdrew me from Our Lady of Sorrows Catholic School. On Friday, I was enrolled at Parkville, the public school across the street from our church. Monday was Labor Day, and classes began on Tuesday.

That first morning, Irene dressed me in civilian clothes, no longer weighed down by the guilt of a Catholic school uniform. Lucky for me, as Mémé explained while I drank a glass of milk at her kitchen table, public school started a week later than Catholic school, so I hadn't missed a thing. I'd still have to attend catechism classes—my First Communion was non-negotiable in Mémé's world. Irene may have yanked me out from under the steady gaze of Jesus, but my grandmother was damn sure I wouldn't walk into life without His protection from the bumps in the road little boys like me tripped over.

So, on that crisp September day in 1977, the three of us climbed into Irene's car and drove me to my second first day of kindergarten.

All kindergarten classes met outside on a large playground behind the school, surrounded by jungle gyms, swings with dark-blue seats, and a shiny stainless-steel slide that left a painful burn on our tender, younger skin. You didn't even have to climb the ladder and slide down to end up in the nurse's office—just bumping into the slide was a one-way ticket to third-degree burns. None of us had to endure the slide. There were plenty of other schoolyard shenanigans to choose from, but the second someone said, "I dare you to go down the slide," you were already climbing the ladder. You just hoped it wasn't summer or even close to a sunny day. Being dared meant doing it. No negotiations. No backing out. So we climbed, knowing what was coming, and screamed the whole way down, skin peeling from muscle, hitting the bottom crying and laughing in equal measure.

I hated that slide.

Each grade was divided into separate zones behind the two-story building. The older kids didn't have to line up—they clustered in loose packs, already scanning the kindergarten herd, deciding who might be worth harassing in the hallways later. From where I stood, I could see Our Lady of Sorrows in the distance. I wondered what my old classmates were doing. Were any of them getting their hands whacked by Sister Nun right now?

The three of us approached the kindergarten flock—dozens of tiny humans, each already a fully formed personality, camped beside their parents or mid-play before the bell. The confident ones gathered friends and staked claims in the elementary school food chain. Others hovered solo near the brick wall, waiting for instructions. A few were crying, already wondering when the school nightmare would end. Some kids froze at every sudden sound. Others clicked into place instantly, as if they'd spent their entire lives preparing to claim a desk.

Didn't anyone watch *ABC* soap operas and help their grandmother dry dishes? *That* was education. Soap operas and a mother like Irene had already taught me everything I needed to know about life. School would teach me only one thing: how to count the seconds until it was time to go home.

At least that's something.

I didn't know where I fit in among these kids. I wanted to be cool, to hang with kids my age, but they all seemed dangerous and unknown. Snot ran freely, hair uncombed and unchecked. Frowns and smiles were the extent of their emotional range. One little girl peed herself before the bell.

It all felt wrong.

Within five minutes of arriving, surrounded by an ocean of kindergartners, I scanned the playground and realized this shit wasn't for me. I clutched Mémé's hand like I was dangling off a cliff. Some parents had already peeled away, leaving their kids exposed and trembling, easy prey for the wolves.

And bullies weren't just older kids. Oh no. These little kindergarten fuckers, who arrived shortly after me, were already hunting for someone to pummel the second a teacher looked away. I'd eventually learn that the kindergarten pecking order had a simple formula: kids with older siblings in the school walked in pre-armored. Backup let them terrorize anyone who didn't meet their standards of cool. Kindergarten bullies weren't budding—they were already fully bloomed, circling the kids who were still crying for their parents.

I used to think children were normal before school got hold of them. In the adult world, there were rules and order, but elementary school felt like waking up on a different planet—a planet run by children. Sure, teachers and principals believed they were in charge, but nobody could defend themselves against hundreds of unhinged rugrats all vying for top dog.

Some of these pint-sized demons were cut from the same cloth as my cousins, Tommy and Timmy—products of fractured homes, split in ways no glue could ever repair. I recognized a few kids from the neighborhood. We'd never played together, but I'd seen their bikes in driveways and their shadows shifting behind window curtains. They could have been friends.

But the math changed quickly. The moment the playground assigned ranks, anyone could be reassigned from neighbor kid to threat—no trial, no warning, no reason required.

There was a pretty good chance that at least a few of these five-year-old assholes had shit themselves in the last few months, but on the playground, none of that mattered. What mattered was fitting in and making sure someone below you felt it.

That's why I immediately disliked this school. I knew I'd never fit in.

A kindergarten teacher wove through the crowd, fielding questions from parents who had missed the open house. We were not open-house people. Irene had no questions. She was ready to hand me off so she could go to work. In her mind, I was about to become Hartford Public School's problem until lunchtime, and the thrill of that milestone gave her an unmistakable spring in her step.

One of the teachers—short black hair, high enthusiasm—stepped forward to address the crowd. I'd soon learn that this woman was my new daytime babysitter. Parents and children quieted in unison, giving this cheerful stranger our full attention.

"Good morning, parents and students. My name is Mrs. Rodriguez, and this is my classroom assistant, Mrs. Gonzales. If you're in our class, please line up in front of door 1B."

She turned toward the other teacher.

"And if you're in Mrs. White's class, line up in front of door 1A."

Mrs. White waved, and the migration began—little legs sprinting across the courtyard like a choreographed march.

"Alright, Joe. You have to line up now. Give Mémé and me a goodbye kiss," Irene said, steering me toward door 1B.

Mémé walked on my other side. We joined the line, a slow trickle of small bodies disappearing into the building. Mrs. Rodriguez greeted each child at the threshold, ushering them into what I assumed would be even worse than Catholic school.

What happened next surprised everyone, including me.

"I don't wanna stay here." I looked up at my mother. "I don't like it here. I'd like to go home with Mémé."

I planted my feet; I became part of the pavement. The gap between me and the student in front of me widened.

The last time I'd been handed off to a teacher, my knuckles had been smacked for talking too much, and I had no intention of talking less. If that was the punishment at the last school, what fresh hell awaited me here once the parents were gone?

I didn't want to find out.

Irene knelt to face me. "You can't go home. This is your new school. You have to stay here."

Tears welled up, hot behind my eyes. The second these playground wolves saw me cry, it would be over. I could head right back across the street and offer my hands to Sister Nun and her wooden ruler.

Honestly? The ruler didn't sound so bad anymore.

From what I remembered, Catholic school bullies kept their heads down because their knuckles would get rapped for stepping out of line. Trying to look tough after a hand beating was impossible. Watching a classmate have their hands reddened by a ruler made us all feel equal—a sense of camaraderie. Nobody cared who your older brother was in Catholic school. When Sister Nun brought out her ruler, we all felt it.

As an adult, I know my interpretation of the scenario wasn't accurate. But as a terrified kindergartener on the brink of public school, I convinced myself it wasn't so bad. Having my knuckles reddened by a nun was simply part of the Catholic Starter Pack. Jesus hung from a wooden cross by His hands. Surely, I could survive a ruler for whispering about the girl with the lisp.

Did public school teachers hit students with rulers, too? At least the bullies?

I could only pray.

When Irene confirmed I wasn't going home, something inside me snapped.

"No. No." I pulled away from both of them. "Please, don't make me stay. I hate it here."

Irene looked at my grandmother, then back at me. "Joseph, stop it. You're acting like a brat."

I had nowhere to run. I tried bargaining. "I'll come back tomorrow. Just let me go home now."

When compromise failed.

"NO! I hate it here." The freak-out escalated. I forgot all about the bullies until I didn't. A few were already watching —especially one.

Marilyn Santiago.

The Marilyn Santiago.

The same Marilyn who was assigned to my homeroom all the way through fifth grade. The same Marilyn who, on the second day of kindergarten, knocked every block off the shelf and blamed me. The same Marilyn who, in second grade in Miss Leland's class, barred me from playing with her friends at recess. The same fucking Marilyn who, by fifth grade, would look me straight in the face and tell me I was too gay to have friends.

I disliked her.

Mrs. Rodriguez noticed I'd stalled the procession into the classroom. Kids behind me slipped past. I had no intention of going in. None. They'd have to lift me and carry me inside, and I'd fight them all until my tiny lungs drew their last breath.

I still wonder why I was so terrified. I hadn't felt this uneasy walking into Our Lady of Sorrows, even though that school carried the threat of eternal damnation. Parkville scared me even more.

Quite frankly, it was how feral the kids were compared with those at Our Lady of Sorrows. At the Catholic school, there was order and control, a sense of calm and ease. Sure, those kids could get rowdy, but they were easier to contain. Maybe it was the threat of the ruler. We all wore the same outfit; we were all equal. I liked being like everyone else. It felt safer than being different.

But at Parkville, this new group of rowdy peers seemed untamed—as if they'd never had their hands beaten raw by an angry nun.

"Who do we have here?" Mrs. Rodriguez asked, smiling. I shrank back, interpreting her cheerfulness as a threat. She didn't have a ruler, so I guessed that was a good sign.

Irene said, "This is Joseph Thomas." She looked embarrassed, understandably so. "He's nervous, but he'll be fine."

Mrs. Rodriguez chuckled. "Of course, he'll be all right." She crouched slightly and offered her hand. "Would you like to take my hand? We can walk inside together."

I pulled back. I'd been told not to take a stranger's hand. What was next? Candy in the back of a van? I'd rather stay right here, under my grandmother's watchful eye.

I stepped behind Mémé, using her as a shield. "No. I want to go home."

I kept waiting for Irene or Mémé to understand I meant business. My behavior wasn't a tantrum. It was fear—real, full-bodied fear—of being left with strangers. Mrs. Rodriguez looked kind, sure. Maybe even the kindest woman I'd met who wasn't my grandmother. Compassion lived in her eyes. But whatever kindness I imagined wouldn't stop a pack of older kids and their little brothers from circling me the moment a teacher blinked.

The crying and hyperventilating took me over. Without even crossing the threshold, public school had already ruined me. I'd hate school for the rest of my life. My sobs were loud— the kind that drew attention like a fire alarm. I knew every kid still outside was watching, calculating, and filing me away in the mental folder labeled: weakness to revisit later.

Even then, between gasps for air, spittle dribbling from my lips, I had to stay committed to the performance. I truly believed that at any moment Irene would pull a secret emergency cord and we'd all escape.

Instead, Irene threw her hands in the air and turned to Mémé.

"I can't with him anymore. I have to go to work."

Realizing my meltdown had officially crossed into Academy Award audition-tape territory, Mrs. Rodriguez stepped in.

"Alright," she said, calm but firm. "Why don't you ladies head out? I'll walk Joseph inside. Is that okay?"

She reached for me.

I offered nothing back.

"Oh yes," Irene exhaled, already turning. "That sounds perfect. Let's go, Ma."

Relief practically poured off her. Someone else was taking the wheel.

Having another person manage your out-of-control child is the part of parenting outsiders rarely see—the surrender. The moment the rope is about to snap, and the agonized parent silently prays, another qualified adult steps in before they lose control and beat their child senseless on a school playground. I'd recognize it later in life, every time a parent on a flight looked at me with that same wild, wordless please-help-me stare when their kid went full asshole in aisle twenty.

Mrs. Rodriguez was clearly built for this.

Or so Irene thought.

My tear-soaked cheeks and quivering lip were too much for my grandmother. She was uncomfortable. She knew I had to go to school, but watching me unravel made her feel like a bad grandmother. I wondered if she blamed Irene for taking me out of Catholic school—I hadn't acted like this on my first day at Our Lady of Sorrows. Not only was Mémé about to lose her soap-opera buddy, but seeing me plead as if I were being led to my execution twisted her up inside. I saw it in her eyes. And yes, I used it to my advantage.

"Mémé. Please don't go."

She placed a hand on my head. "Why don't I just stay with him for an hour?"

Our eyes met. I wiped away the tears on my cheek. I grinned.

I wrapped myself around her leg. "Please. Stay with me. I'll be good."

All the students had gone inside. The four of us stood alone in the circular playground, cementing my reputation as a troublemaker. Sister Nun was absolutely right about me being a troublemaker. Here I was, hijacking everyone's time, and I didn't even care. The longer we stood out here, the less time I'd have to spend inside with all these strangers.

Mrs. White closed door 1A. The heavy door slammed shut. We all turned. My time was running out.

Classroom door 1B stood open. The sound of my classmates settling into their seats spilled out. I heard laughter, nothing to fear. Actually, the whole romper-room chaos sounded… exciting. Fun, even.

I wanted to be excited. To be a big boy. To show my mom, my grandmother, and Mrs. Rodriguez that I was brave. But I was the opposite of brave. I was a coward.

If this continued much longer, the school day would be over.

Predictably, Irene was done with my bullshit. She would've left a long time ago if it weren't for my grandmother. Irene knew her son. She knew I was manipulating them because I didn't want to leave Mémé. I think it bothered Irene—her son caring more about his grandmother leaving than about his mother. But I would've done anything to get at least one of them on my side. And if there was a chance of that, I knew it was Mémé. So I did what any grandma's crybaby would do—batted my eyes, wiped my tears, and promised the galaxy if only she'd stay with me a little longer.

"Ma, I gotta go to work. If you're staying with him, I don't care."

Mémé took my hand, and I gave it to her without hesitation.

"Yes, I'll stay for a while if that's okay with you." She looked toward Mrs. Rodriguez.

Mrs. Rodriguez studied the three of us, a hint of apprehension crossing her face. I'm sure she went through this shit all the time. "Yes, that's fine. Let's just get into the classroom, shall we? Mrs. Gonzalez will find you a place to sit—"

She didn't know my grandmother's name.

"Lorette," Mémé said.

"Okay, Lorette. You can stay for a while."

The tears dried instantly upon hearing that Mémé would attend kindergarten with me. There was no doubt in my mind that my grandmother would be here all school year. I was the luckiest kid in this entire concrete child's prison.

I didn't want to manipulate everyone into restructuring the entire first day of school, but I couldn't help myself. I wanted Mémé with me, and that was all that mattered. Irene could go to work. Mrs. Rodriguez could do whatever she needed. As long as my grandmother had eyes on me, I could survive.

I made it happen.

Finally, after I managed to delay the start of my education by a few minutes, Mrs. Rodriguez led us away from Irene toward the door marked 1B—and at last, inside.

Mrs. Rodriguez kicked the doorstop aside. The door slammed shut. Heads turned. The big crybaby had entered the classroom.

Mémé walked me to my chair. "I'm only staying for a few minutes. Do you understand?"

"Yes, Mémé. I understand."

Mrs. Rodriguez greeted the room again in her bright, maternal voice while Mrs. Gonzales found a seat for my grandmother along the wall.

I reluctantly sat in my assigned wooden chair beside a few other kids. One boy, Mark, had hair as long as mine—bangs for days. He smiled at me. A girl in a green dress, who looked like Nelly Olson from Little House on the Prairie, smirked. She looked like a bigger troublemaker than I was.

Across the room, Marilyn locked eyes with me in a way that told me I'd need to watch my back until college.

But I lied to Mémé. I did not understand. If I had to stay, my grandmother did too.

And she did. One day became two. Then a week. Then it was Christmas. Then it was the end of the school year. She stayed with me the whole year.

The joy of being called "Mrs. Lorette" by the other students gave her a sense of purpose. She never said it out loud, but I think my grandmother loved being an unpaid substitute teacher. She bought stickers for the students, passed out supplies, monitored nap time, and played educational games. In every sense, she became an additional teacher in the classroom.

Yes, I manipulated her with my tearful cries—but I think, deep down, she enjoyed being there not just for me but for herself. Being in a teacher's role gave her a spark she didn't know she needed—a glimpse of what her life could look like outside her housewife role. And I know she loved it.

His Name Was Melvin

When people ask me about my mother, I tell them this: imagine a woman standing at a crossroads. One path is peaceful—sunlight through trees, a warm breeze, maybe even a pink unicorn frolicking through emerald grass. The other is a Category Five hurricane with 200-mile-per-hour winds spitting tornadoes from the sky, rain so hard it dents the skin, a sky blacker than grief. Irene always chose the hellstorm.

Every. Single. Time.

Her choices shaped my world in dangerous ways. For years, I carried anger toward her, but now, finally out of her blast radius, I swim in a lake of empathy. Irene stumbled through life, dragging chaos into our home—Jean, Larry, French uncles—the pills—and I learned to call that chaos a friend.

It hurt me, and I resented her for years.

We hold onto resentment toward the parents who failed us, along with anger and disappointment that refuse to loosen their grip. If we aren't careful, it consumes us and turns us into what we fear most: them. Some days, I wish for a time machine—not to rewrite the past, but to stand in front of Irene and speak the truths I couldn't yet put into words. To slap some sense into her.

Maybe I just want to slap her.

But this is where forgiveness comes in. I didn't forgive her for her—I eventually forgave her for me. Carrying that resentment was like dragging her storm into every room I entered. She never needed to know she'd been forgiven—most forgiveness is private work anyway, a mercy we give ourselves. I didn't forgive Irene to excuse her behavior but to release the hold it had on me.

One of Irene's most significant lapses in judgment began the night she went to The Silver Dollar with her best friend, Linda. My mother was never good at making friends, let alone keeping them, because of her abrasive personality. Yet somehow, miraculously, she and Linda clicked the day they met at the French Club picnic.

Years later, Linda told me it was a warm summer afternoon when she first noticed my mother and remarked on how cute I was, zipping around on a sugar high from grape Kool-Aid, potato salad, and grilled hot dogs. I imagine Irene savored that moment; a compliment for me always felt like one for her.

That encounter reshaped Irene's orbit. The two bonded over their shared struggle as single mothers—Linda, who had three children (Billy, Sam, and Alan), and Irene, who was still recovering from Larry. Linda was the only one who helped my mother learn to walk again, emotionally, after Larry.

I'm grateful that Irene had at least one friend who breathed life back into her. We all need that friend who doesn't stand at the edge of the ditch but climbs down into the muck with us and pulls us out. That was Linda.

The Silver Dollar was a quaint bar tucked into Hartford's Frog Hollow neighborhood, less rowdy than The French Club yet just as saturated with escape. Bars aren't the real world; they're a shelter from it. The smell of stale beer drifted through a haze of tobacco smoke, while greasy hamburgers and French fries sizzled in the tiny kitchen, their scent wafting through the room like springtime pollen—comforting, oddly mature. Neon

Budweiser and Schlitz signs buzzed against the windows, flanking a heavy iron-fronted door that opened into an adult Narnia.

The bar shared its walls with a run-down boarding house of studio apartments and rented rooms for people barely hanging on. If my grandparents hadn't converted their attic into an apartment for Irene and me, we might have ended up there, too.

When Pépé's work took my grandparents out of town, or when Mémé finally put her foot down and refused to babysit, insisting that Irene look after her own child, she never sat at home. The thought of sitting alone with me in the attic apartment, staring at dull white walls, felt suffocating. Being surrounded by other people's noise and problems comforted her. Too young to be left on my own, I became her carry-on luggage, dragged into the smoky glow of her weekend refuge.

If it was a Friday or Saturday night and Irene was stuck with me, we were at The Silver Dollar. My seat was a booth in the back of the bar, a sticky vinyl booth that doubled as a babysitter. I can't recall how many times I fell asleep on that bench and woke up after last call, just that it was more than a few. After decades spent in bars, I now know there's a right time and a wrong time to be in one. If you have your underage child with you, it's the wrong time. Even at five, I knew I didn't belong.

But man, was it exciting going out with Irene. If I wanted to feel like an adult, being inside a bar at 2 a.m. fit the bill. A thrill pulsed through me every time we walked in. The bar was alive with alcohol-fueled aggression, whispered infidelities, screaming matches, fistfights, and slurred verbal assaults—a misinterpreted education in what I thought adulthood must be.

And the best part was that we were treated like royalty whenever we arrived. There was plenty of parking in the back, but we always snagged a first-class spot right at the entrance. I still question whether that paved strip was even meant for parking; it barely fit three small cars, yet Irene would glide in as if she held stock in alcoholism. The second we walked through the door, raspy smoker voices rose in unison: "Irene's here! Hey everyone, look, it's Irene."

And her cute son. Don't forget about me.

Irene grinned from ear to ear, glowing under the attention. After Larry, any scrap of validation became her fuel, an ego boost she mistook for confidence. It was all she needed to stroll back into a bar with her underage son in tow, using my presence as a prop to prove she was doing just fine, thank you very much.

When we walked in, the bar counter stretched along the entire left side of the room, lined with liquor bottles glittering under the bar lights—the rainbow-colored glass made drinking look magical. I wanted in on the magic long before I ever wanted the alcohol.

"A drink, Mommy," I'd demand before she even had a chance to set her purse down on the bar.

"Give me a second, Joseph. Go sit in the booth. I'll bring it over," she'd say, nodding toward Linda at the far end. Then she'd wave to her fans as they called her name. Miss Connecticut had nothing on Miss Irene.

Linda usually brought her youngest son, Alan, and the two of us would turn the bar into our own miniature Studio 54. He was my best friend, mostly because he never forced me to eat dirt. If he was spending the weekend with his father, I begged to go home the moment we arrived at the bar. But when he was there, I was ready to shut the place down.

Along the right-hand wall stood a large shuffleboard-and-bowling hybrid game, and Alan and I would play it for hours—the kind where a small metal puck glides over fine-grained sand to knock down miniature pins. You know the one. I was addicted. I'd beg Irene for quarters, and if she didn't hand them over fast enough, I'd ask any adult within reach. It wasn't uncommon for me to tug on someone's pant leg and ask, "Do you have a quarter?"

Like Oliver Twist, but for bar games.

Irene claimed the last barstool at the far end.

"Henry, can I get a Shirley Temple for the kid and my usual for me?"

By then, I was already trick-or-treating for quarters, enamored with those George Washington faces that felt priceless. I appreciated everyone's open wallets, though I realize now they were paying us to go away. Alan and I would bat our eyelashes, make the rounds, count our haul, burn through it, and head back for more.

One particular night, while Alan and I built our own small universe within this adult one, a man approached Irene and Linda. He rented one of the rooms attached to the bar, and Irene looked smitten even before he greeted them.

His name was Melvin.

Black hair slicked into a pompadour, a trimmed full beard, a brown snap-button cowboy shirt, faded jeans, and scuffed boots—he looked like he had swaggered in straight off the Gunsmoke set. Tattoos crawled up and down his arms and across his hands, but the one I remember most was the word MOM inked across three fingers. To Irene, it wasn't a warning; it was a love letter.

Red flags didn't slow her down. They were an invitation to speed up.

Within days, we were going to The Silver Dollar during the week, not just on weekends. Any excuse to see Melvin became our plan. Irene even stopped begging Mémé to babysit, determined that Melvin and I should bond.

He gave me quarters—handfuls of them. He bought me Shirley Temples. He picked me up and set me on his lap at the bar as if I *belonged* to him. Melvin wrapped us in a quilt of promise, and we needed that warmth; we had been freezing for a long time.

Frank and Larry had been drafted as potential saviors. Melvin was different. This time, she wasn't just trying to save herself; she believed she was saving me, too.

I overheard her on the phone with Linda one night, after a few weeks of Melvin cozying up to us. In no particular order, here was her justification:

"I need Joseph to have a father.

"He needs a male figure to guide him, to show him right from wrong.

"I can't be both his mother and father.

"I want better for Joseph.

"Melvin is terrific with him."

He needs a father. A mantra Irene repeated until she believed it, gaslighting herself into abandoning all reason.

THE PERFECT FAMILY

Within days, I was calling Melvin Daddy. Within weeks, he was living in our apartment. It might have been just a week. All I know is that it was swift, and a man who had been a stranger was suddenly part of our daily life. My grandparents were wary of Irene's quick decision, but she invested everything in Melvin's stock, expecting it to shoot straight to the moon.

Linda was convinced first. She'd met Melvin the same night Irene had and saw nothing wrong with him. He checked every box for a single mother perched on a barstool, downing her fourth cocktail, looking for hope in male form. Soon after, Mémé fell in line, and then everyone in Irene's cloudy orbit decided Melvin was a keeper.

All except Pépé.

In Irene's mind, she had struck gold. Melvin was handsome and told her exactly what she wanted to hear. He was a professional charmer. I've met countless men who float through life with that skill: pure forgery. Melvin attached himself to me immediately, eager to become the father figure she believed her son needed. He didn't just step into our lives; he steered them. Irene was blinded long before she realized he'd slipped the blinkers onto her, guiding her around Hartford like a mare on a rein. He led her now. He led us.

In her mind, she was no longer a single mother; she was part of a family.

One morning, as Irene helped me get dressed for school, Melvin stepped out of the bathroom and into my bedroom.

"Let me help him with that, dear," he said. "He has a father now." They called each other dear. It still makes me cringe.

Father? He was a stranger who, until recently, had rented a room behind a bar. I don't recall whether he even had a job, but employment isn't required to become an instant dad—no background check required.

Without thinking, she stepped away and handed me over to him—an agreeable sale with no request for a receipt—then walked toward the kitchen, calling back, "Let Daddy help you get dressed."

"Can you make me another cup of coffee?" Melvin asked as he gently helped me out of my *Star Wars* pajamas and into my school clothes. It was picture day, so he dressed me in a dark blue turtleneck and light grayish-blue jeans, then parted my long hair to the side. I have to admit I looked quite adorable.

Melvin swiftly consumed our apartment. It was no longer only Irene and Joe fighting her demons; now it was Melvin, Irene, and Joe—the Perfect Family.

We all lived together for a few years before the wedding. Then, a few days before Irene and Melvin were scheduled to stand before the justice of the peace and exchange rings, Irene went out for what she called her "final night out" as a single mother.

On that final night at The Silver Dollar, Irene planted herself on her barstool and spent the evening talking with Melvin's younger brother, John. Even as a young boy, I thought John was sexy. He was easily the handsomest of Melvin's brothers. And I hate to say it, but some of Melvin's siblings looked like the gene pool had been drained to kiddie-pool depth.

But John, or Johnny, as everyone called him, had black hair styled just right and a thick Tom Selleck mustache. When I was a teenager, I often wished Irene had married Johnny instead. I had no idea what I really wanted. He died in the mid-to-late '80s; they said it was cancer, though there were whispers it might have been something else.

Johnny was different from the rest of his family. While Melvin's mother and other siblings spent their lives defending and shielding him from consequences, Johnny did the opposite; he tried to warn my mother. She told me about it years later, when I was a teenager.

"There's something you should know about Melvin," Johnny said, ordering another drink, his posture heavy. "This is difficult to say. He has a history with children, specifically little boys."

"What do you mean?" Irene asked, instantly defensive.

Johnny described Melvin's questionable history with minors. Irene listened, but she fought the urge to believe him. Almost instantly, she threw up emotional walls, anything to protect the fantasy she'd built around Melvin. In her mind, anyone who spoke ill of him wasn't warning her; they were trying to rob her of happiness and steal her dreamboat. She refused to allow even a hairline fracture in the picture she'd painted of him. The world had always felt stacked against her, and she wasn't about to let anyone, even his brother, take away the family she thought she'd finally secured.

When someone's comfort zone includes driving while intoxicated with a child not in a seatbelt, reasoning becomes a foreign language. If Irene had taken Johnny's warning to heart that night, our lives might have unfolded differently, maybe better, maybe simply different. I've tortured myself with that question because, even though Melvin was the monster who moved into our lives, there is always a darker version of my story that could have played out.

It took me decades to understand this truth: it can always be worse.

Irene should have listened to Johnny. Melvin had a dangerous history with young children, a past buried and protected by his family for decades. Sadly, Irene already knew what he was capable of. She just pretended she didn't.

But she knew. She always did.

That frightening night, when Melvin called me from my bed, I ran downstairs to my grandparents. Irene came home from the bar, smelling of cigarettes and stale breath. I sat on Mémé's sofa, scared, and told her what had happened. That Melvin had touched me. He put his calloused hands between my legs and rubbed me there. The words hurt to say.

For a moment, I thought she believed me. Then she lit a cigarette, shook her head, and said I was confused. Melvin wouldn't do something like that. He was teaching me how to be a man. He loved us.

She ignored my confession and what Johnny tried to tell her.

I will never understand why Johnny broke that family loyalty to warn her, but he did, and I'm grateful he tried, even though it wasn't enough to stop Irene from welcoming the beast into our den.

In a May 11, 1968, write-up in The Hartford Courant, Melvin was arrested on two charges of moral indecency brought by the father of a juvenile boy. According to the report, Melvin waived examination of the charges of indecent assault and risk of injury to a minor. Whether he did so to avoid testimony, keep the details off the record, or secure a quiet plea deal, the effect was the same: he slipped right back onto the streets.

Who was that boy? Who was the brave father who reported Melvin? A friend? A neighbor?

Questions without answers.

Another article revealed that when Melvin was nineteen, he had already been arrested for endangering a child and later for the sodomy of a fifteen-year-old.

What the actual fuck. Reading the reports decades later, I found myself screaming into a past that would never hear me.

How could this be? How could someone be a serial pederast with multiple arrests—written up in the newspaper—and still have the freedom to saunter into a bar and build a life around unsuspecting families? Because there was no system to track these men back then. They slipped from town to town, slithering into children's lives and leaving broken ones behind.

That didn't change until 1994, when the Jacob Wetterling Crimes Against Children and Sexually Violent Offender Registration Act required states to maintain offender records.

A law written in a murdered child's blood.

In 1989, eleven-year-old Jacob Wetterling was kidnapped, raped, and murdered. His remains were not recovered until 2016, when his killer—Danny Heinrich—led authorities to the burial site as part of a plea agreement. Because he cooperated, Danny was never charged with Jacob's murder; instead, he received a twenty-year sentence on child pornography charges.

Ain't that some shit.

Before that law existed, it was open season on children. Men like Melvin were free to hunt them.

The pain Melvin inflicted on children was a fossil buried deep within his family, long hidden yet easily uncovered by anyone who bothered to look. Even decades later, as I sit at my desk writing this paragraph, I still scratch my head in disbelief that the prequel to my abuse was printed in plain black-and-white newsprint for anyone to read.

Nothing swayed Irene. Not Melvin's devotion to Popov Vodka. Not the MOM tattoo, which she read as tenderness. Not even Johnny cornering her in a smoke-filled bar to set off flares that she immediately extinguished. My mother had convinced herself she'd already survived the worst, so whatever came next had to be better.

On a warm summer day in June, Melvin and Irene stood before the Justice of the Peace in Hartford to exchange wedding vows. There were five of us in attendance: Melvin, Irene, Vinny, Sonya, and me. Vinny and Sonya's signatures appear on the witness lines of a card-style marriage certificate. My grandparents were absent.

The day we walked into the judge's chambers replays in my mind: brown carpet, two chairs, and a small table where Melvin and Irene stood between their witnesses. I sat in an oversized, overstuffed chair in the corner, watching Irene's smile crack her face with pure joy and delirium. Her dream came true. A wonderful husband and father, wrapped in a fucking pompadour, cemented together with two cans of Aqua Net.

Everyone was happy. Even I was.

The ceremony officially began. "Do you, Melvin, take Irene to be your lawfully wedded wife?"

His yes echoed through the small chambers, loud and eager. Irene followed with her own soft "yes," wrapped in relief, not romance.

After the formalities were completed, the Justice of the Peace announced, "By the power vested in me by the State of

Connecticut, I now pronounce you husband and wife. You may now kiss the bride."

Everyone in attendance clapped loudly. I ran to my parents, and after their kiss and embrace, Irene pulled me in, as if to remind me we had won. The crossroads had led to Melvin, and for that moment, our fear vanished.

The five of us piled into two cars and drove straight to The Silver Dollar. Once again, I was ushered into my booth with a Shirley Temple and a handful of quarters while the adults celebrated at the bar.

"I've got this round," Melvin announced. "I'm a new husband and the father of my incredible son." He pointed toward me, though most of the patrons already knew me as Irene's boy. I'd hounded them for quarters.

Now I was Melvin's son, a gift handed to a predator on a silver platter.

Between Father and Son

I walked to Parkville Community School from kindergarten through fifth grade. I walked through rain, sleet, snow, or wind without thinking twice—an admission that makes me sound exactly like my grandfather. During kindergarten and first grade, Mémé walked with me. By second grade in 1980, I was on my own. No adult supervision. Just me, seven years old, navigating the world.

The commute was a straight shot down Park Street. There was never a time, morning or afternoon, sunshine or snow, when that stretch wasn't at least a little sketchy. In second grade, I complained about being harassed on my walk to school, so Irene pulled me aside. She didn't call the school; she taught me the *bras d'honneur.* One arm bent in an L-shape, fist pointed upward, the other hand chopping the bicep. A nonverbal way to tell someone *fuck you!* There's an Italian version—*gesto dell'ombrello*—but we were French, so we used ours. Irene's logic, not mine. A physical act of pure contempt aimed at whoever earned it. Nothing says childhood innocence like learning French profanity before multiplication. Irene could have just taught me the middle finger, but maybe she wanted me to offend with flair.

"You need to learn to stand up for yourself," Irene warned. "The world is full of sick people."

At the time, I thought she meant strangers.

Looking back, it feels wild that an elementary school kid needed a tactical strategy to deal with street harassment. Back then, it felt normal. The bizarre part is that the harassers weren't kids—they were full-grown men, probably with children of their own.

Irene taught me the *bras d'honneur* for the biker gang that held court outside a dive bar on my walk to school. Big bellies. Big white beards that grazed their belt buckles. The air smelled of motor oil as I marched past them. It never occurred to me to cross the street and avoid them altogether. To this day, I'm not sure it made any difference that a second grader felt confident enough to tell tattooed bikers to fuck off, but I was armed and ready. I recall a rumble of laughter, a nod from a giant in leather. I may have even won a few of them over.

It didn't seem strange to me that at eight o'clock in the morning, bikers were lined up outside a bar, harassing school kids trying to get to class. My parents drank Budweiser for breakfast, so interacting with intoxicated adults before lunch was the norm. Still, these men made me nervous. I knew they'd be there every morning, leaning against their hogs, yelling and laughing as I clutched my lunch box and pretended not to hear.

Irene wasn't worried about my welfare, either. She did her part; she taught me how to tell them off, then added, "And run your ass off."

Walking home was a different kind of stress. By afternoon, the bikers had disappeared behind blackout windows, their Harleys parked in formation like guard dogs. I would slow my pace, dragging out the walk. Home wasn't a destination; it was a place I stalled toward.

Even though I disliked school, there was structure there. Consistency. Teachers who spoke thoughtfully. They were beacons of normalcy, a safety I craved even if I didn't yet have the vocabulary for it. Coming home felt like a gamble: Would they be sober? Drunk? High? Usually, the latter. Now that I think about it, I really dreaded the school bell ringing.

The routine rarely changed: I'd walk through the front door, and Irene and Melvin would already be well on their way to intoxication. Sometimes I swear I could feel it before I even reached the backyard. The heaviness of being a child of alcoholics. You carry it with you forever. The tension was a loaded spring, aimed directly at my survival. Even if I stopped at Mémé's place downstairs, she'd eventually send me up, where my parents had been drinking since before I left for school.

But this day was different. I knew it the moment I walked up the driveway and saw our car was gone. Everyone's gone! My grandparents were out of town, and their apartment sat empty. From what I could tell, ours was empty, too. The entire house was mine. The calm that came with the silence felt like a reward. A latchkey kid, before the term had a name.

I climbed the three flights of stairs until I reached my front door. I paused there, rummaging through my backpack to find the single house key attached to a stretched red rubber band. I had planned to wear the key around my wrist, but I never did. Surprisingly, I never lost it.

Although today would've been the perfect day to do just that.

I fiddled with the key in the dark hallway. The overhead bulb was, as usual, burned out. Carefully, I slid the key into the lock and twisted it. The latch clicked, the door sprang open, and I kicked it, almost falling onto the linoleum floor. I slammed the door shut behind me and locked it fast, as if adults were chasing me up the stairs.

Freedom.

For the next stretch of time, however long it lasted, I could throw my school bag on the floor, make a peanut butter sandwich, and watch cartoons. I smirked, picturing the fantasy version: them outside, banging on the door and screaming threats about kicking my ass, while I ignored them and watched Bugs Bunny outsmart Elmer J. Fudd. I imagined sitting there, calm and unbothered, knowing they couldn't get in. Knowing I was safe. At least until the lock gave out. Yes, they had a key, but in this fantasy, unlike me, they had lost theirs.

I stepped into the kitchen, pulled out my social studies book, flipped to the chapter on Paul Revere, and set it on the table. I had it timed perfectly: the second I heard the clunk of Irene's engine coming up the drive, I could shut off the television and run into the kitchen, acting like I'd been studying the entire time. My plan was a calculated effort. Sneaky? Yes. Necessary? Absolutely. If I was going to outsmart Bugs Bunny, I had to be prepared.

After setting the scene, I took off my jacket and hung it in the hallway closet. That's when I heard it, a faint murmur of voices. Muted. Muffled. I couldn't make out a word. My chest rose and fell with slow, deliberate breaths.

Burglars? In our house? Our most valuable items were the living room television and a yellow ceramic cat that Irene could not live without. I worried about my Etch-A-Sketch. I stepped toward the hall entrance and listened more closely. The sound was the television.

Relief washed over me, then confusion. Why was the TV on if nobody was home? Something felt off, though I didn't know why yet.

The sound drifted down the hallway toward me. I strained to pinpoint its direction. The living room? Maybe. I stood there, my chest still tight, listening for voices that belonged to real humans, but I couldn't make out anything except the TV.

Someone was home.

I slowly walked down the hallway, expecting to find Melvin passed out on the living room sofa, the TV playing to no one. I didn't call out his name because if he was sleeping, I didn't want to wake the bear. If I had to be around Melvin when he was drunk, I preferred him asleep. I poked my head into the living room. Empty. The television was off.

Then I realized the voices were coming from my bedroom. It didn't feel right.

I stopped in the doorway between the living room and the hall. I listened again. Just the hum of the TV, the bickering of unknown characters bleeding into the silence. Still, someone must have turned it on. But that didn't make sense. If I'd left my TV on, one of them would have shut it off before they left.

Like walking blindfolded through a dark room, I inched toward my bedroom doorway.

At first glance, my bedroom looked untouched. I didn't step all the way inside, but I noticed my pajamas on the floor, peeking out from the other side of the bed. I reminded myself to pick them up before my parents got home.

Late-afternoon sunlight spilled across the room. My favorite time of day—even now. A Toys "R" Us commercial played through the TV speakers. I knew the commercial by heart—Geoffrey the giraffe on roller skates with his disco crew, selling G.I. Joe action figures and, the toy I wanted more than anything in the world, the *Star Wars* Death Star.

I took one step forward, ready to turn off the TV, when something stopped me. From where I stood, I could see only the bottom edge of my twin bed, about a foot of space. A prickly sensation crept over my tiny arms. My breathing, steady a second earlier, quickened. My chest felt heavy, as if a 10-pound weight were sitting on it.

Something moved.

Under my *Super Friends* covers.

I stepped farther into the room and stopped.

Melvin.

In my bed.

My body knew before my mind did.

Melvin stared back, grinning. Evil. He reminded me of Dick Dastardly from the Hanna-Barbera cartoons. I had always been drawn to villainous characters, but not when they were curled up in my bed. Melvin lay there, his head propped on my pillow, arms behind his head. The posture of relaxed power. The posture of someone who already knew he would get away with whatever he was planning. Melvin was in complete control. He knew it. Sadly, so did I.

The sun had slipped behind the trees, casting monstrous shadows across the wall.

In fact, there was a monster in my bed.

I'd spent years terrified of imaginary monsters, the kind that crouched under the bed or waited in closets. It was ironic, considering I could tell members of a biker gang to fuck off without blinking. But the truth was: anything that went bump in the night left me trembling. Before Melvin moved in, an unexpected thud sent me running to my mother's room; her bed was the second-safest place in the house.

But now, an absolute monster lay sprawled lazily and unbothered, making himself at home in my bed. A glass sat on the windowsill, ice melting into clear liquid. It was no surprise Melvin had been drinking; he needed that liquid courage to give him the confidence to do what he believed he was entitled to.

I assumed the TV was on to keep him company. He never cared for soap operas, so *General Hospital* was just background noise. It was tuned to ABC because I'd been watching *The Facts of Life* the night before. Maybe he left it on, so I'd know someone was home. Maybe he'd just fallen asleep after drinking all day. Maybe he wanted me to find him before I made my peanut butter sandwich.

No matter how many excuses I made up for why my father was in my bed, every possibility narrowed to the same sinking thought:

Please. Not again.

"Where's Mommy?" I asked.

The blanket was pulled up to his waist, just below his belly button. His shirt was off. That's when I realized I had put my pajamas away before school. The clothes scattered on the floor weren't mine. They were his.

He didn't answer me. He just stared. Not at my face, but through me. Past me. Into the hallway behind me. It was the kind of look people give mannequins in store windows. I was shaped like a person, dressed like one, positioned like one, but not real. He looked at me as if I were an object. A prop. Something that existed for his use, not his concern. And that's exactly what I was to him. Not a child. Not a son. Just something he believed he was entitled to.

"Daddy? What's going on?"

I silently prayed this wasn't real. My body reacted before my mind: my nerves buzzed, my stomach tightened, and sour saliva pooled under my tongue. I swallowed. It burned.

Reality felt distorted. I'd expected an empty house.

Melvin reached for the glass on the windowsill. He took a slow sip without breaking eye contact, then set it back in the same place.

"Come here," he said, patting the space beside him. It was a twin bed; there was barely any room. "Sit with me. I want to talk."

A bead of sweat rolled down my forehead. My face burned, and I started trembling.

"Where's Mommy?" I repeated. My voice was shorter this time. I wasn't asking for information. I was asking for rescue.

My body tingled from my toes to my chest, where my heart felt like it was trying to escape. It pounded so hard I could hear it vibrating in my ears. I wondered if he could hear it, too. The fear was sharper than on my first day of kindergarten. My legs twitched with adrenaline, and a strange pressure built behind my eyes and across the top of my head.

It felt like the moment right after waking from a nightmare—when you don't know where you are, what's real, or whether you're safe. Usually, after a few seconds, your brain catches up, and you exhale, relieved it was just a dream.

But my brain lagged.

I wasn't dreaming. It was a true nightmare.

I had worried about burglars, and in a way, someone had broken in, except that Melvin lived here. He sat at our dinner table. He wrapped Christmas presents. He kissed my mother goodnight. He tucked me in, checking under the bed for the monsters I feared. And now he wanted to take me somewhere in his twisted mythology, somewhere a child should never go.

Dread spread through my body like a countdown. I needed to get away. Run. Hide. Do anything but stand there and wait. Even if nobody was home to protect me, I had to protect myself. The only clear option was to leave. I started to turn away from him—

"Get the fuck back here, Joe."

I froze, my back to him. I wanted to believe this was innocent, that he was drunk and just wanted to talk. But this felt different. Menacing. The past tapped me on the shoulder: *I'd been here before.* Once, I'd escaped. Now I needed to escape again.

My vision blurred. The hallway seemed to shrink. Panic tightened around me. I was on my own. Nobody was coming. I turned to face him. My emotions split, fear on one side, something rare on the other: anger. But God, I was mad. My bedroom was my safe place. My Narnia. The place I ran to when Irene and Melvin were drunk and screaming about money, jobs, or my grandparents. And now he lay there as if he belonged, soaking my sanctuary in vodka fumes.

I loved and hated him at the same time.

Melvin knew I had nowhere to go. Years earlier, I had run downstairs and found safety. He learned from that mistake and recalibrated. He married Irene, locked us in his orbit, and waited. Patient. Calculated. And this time, before he struck, he made sure we were alone.

"Get over here. Don't make me fucking tell you again." His voice was a low growl.

He reached for his drink again and, whether by accident or design, dropped it. The glass didn't shatter, but I heard the small slivers of ice scatter against it.

"Pick that up," he commanded.

I knew I had to. My fear wasn't vague anymore; it had shape. Edges. I didn't know what he'd do if he got out of that bed. Slap me? Grab me? I forced myself to move. The TV buzzed in the background, but the pounding in my ears drowned out everything except him. Something electric hung in the air, like static just before a shock.

By the time I reached the bed, I was only inches away. I knelt to pick up the glass.

In one swift motion, Melvin wrapped his arms around my waist and lifted me off the ground, rolling me toward him. The glass slipped from my hand. Suddenly, I was on top of him.

He stayed under the blankets. The warmth of his chest made some part of me want to believe, just for a second, that this was normal. Like when a newborn is placed on a parent's skin.

No, Joe. This isn't love.

I tried to roll off him, willing my body toward escape. If I could just hit the floor, I'd be outta there. I didn't know where I'd go. His grip tightened. Escape was a joke.

He laughed, as if this were a game, and placed his rough hands on my stomach. He poked me once, twice, then rubbed my belly—*for good luck, my son*—before tickling.

I hated being tickled. It made me lose control, lose myself. Squirming and laughing when you want to scream is its own kind of hell. Tickling feels like a cruel joke, mixing pain with laughter. Involuntary giggles burst out of me. I couldn't help it. My body betrayed me, responding to something my brain knew was wrong. He thought I was having fun.

"Daddy, please stop," I managed. "That hurts."

My small body rested against his chest. For a moment, he stopped. His hand lay on my stomach, like a boyfriend's might while lying on the couch watching TV. The giggling faded. I caught my breath. We sat in suspended time—no words, no movement, no air. The television carried on in the background, too ordinary for what was happening.

Then everything shifted. Melvin's hairy, tattooed hand slid from my stomach to my crotch. He began rubbing. It wasn't playful. It wasn't harmless. I pushed and twisted. A trapped animal. I tried to slide off him, but his grip tightened.

"Relax, Joe. Stop fighting me. I'm not gonna hurt you," he whispered.

His arms tightened, not comforting, but claiming. I felt something hard against my leg, something under the blanket. My whole body reacted. Every nerve lit up with warning. If he desired my body, I didn't like it anymore. I prayed to myself, frantically: *Please God. Please Jesus. Please let Mémé walk through that door.*

Nothing changed. It became clear that I wasn't going to escape.

Melvin didn't ask for permission. He was taking what he wanted. All the fight drained out of me. Instinct knew what my mind couldn't: there was no winning. My brain scrambled, like a radio stuck between channels. Being in bed with my father was so fucking wrong. I knew it was wrong. Did he? I had no words, no tools, no roadmap to guide me— nothing to prepare me for this encounter.

Children aren't born knowing how to confront a parent who blurs every boundary. Parents should be the definition of safety. This was dangerous. And Irene, whether through denial, fear, or willful blindness, had given him authority over me long before this moment.

"Are you going to run if I let you go?" he asked.

I shook my head not because I didn't want to run, but because I had no idea what he'd do if I tried. Melvin loosened his hold, and I slid onto the narrow strip of mattress beside him. His breath hit my face. I swallowed back the nausea.

"Are you crying?" he asked, noticing a tear slide toward the sheets. His expression shifted, almost wounded, as if my fear insulted him. As if lying beside him like this should have comforted me.

He reached up and wiped the tear away with the back of his hand. His voice softened, rehearsed: "I'm not going to hurt you. I'm going to love you."

With the care of handling a baby animal, he rubbed my back slowly. I tried to swallow the moment, but the tears kept coming, uncontrolled. He wiped another tear from my cheek, almost warmly, lovingly, then slid his other hand back to my private parts, pulling me even closer.

"I want to go watch TV in the living room," I mumbled. Part of me hoped that asking something innocent would snap him out of it.

Instead, the hand on my back came up and smacked the back of my neck—quick, sharp, jarring. My whole body flinched. The shift from soft to violent felt like another violation. Melvin's mood snapped like a twig. Moments ago, he had spoken gently. Now he was slapping me because I wasn't playing his game.

Then came the words that made everything real:

"Take off your pants."

My sobbing became unhinged. There was no more pretending. Irene was right; the world was full of sick people.

"No," I cried. "I don't want to."

Melvin looked at me with certainty and entitlement and said the sentence that claws at me from the inside. "Yes, you do."

I refused, so he did it for me. It all happened fast. One second my pants were on; the next, they were balled on the floor beside his. My body went limp. I couldn't move. I kept crying, but he ignored it completely, as if I weren't even in the bed anymore.

It was the purest evil I had ever experienced.

His breath hit my skin as his hands moved across my legs, under my shirt, touching me in a way that didn't feel human. I shut my eyes tight and tried to disappear. I slipped into the fantasy version of the afternoon. In the fantasy, I was in the kitchen making a peanut butter sandwich, watching TV, and excited that no one was home. Safe. Innocent.

I kept my eyes closed until I felt his weight shift. When I opened them, he was on the floor, kneeling and pulling me toward the edge of the mattress.

What happened next didn't feel real. Not then, not for years. I didn't have words for it. Only sensation. Shame. Silence. His confidence terrified me, the way he acted as if this were common and expected. Deserved.

I became motionless. Still enough to survive.

Melvin had his mouth on me. Wet. Sticky. My mind had to leave the room, so I thought about Paul Revere and my homework, sitting on the table. He let out a sound I'd never heard before, a mix of joy and pain from deep in his throat. Then he collapsed forward, his face resting on my chest. I could smell his sweat and Aqua Net. His weight made me feel smaller. He was shivering.

When he finished, I opened my eyes. He stared at me as if he expected gratitude. Was I supposed to high-five him and congratulate him for destroying me? I stared up at the popcorn ceiling, then turned my head toward the TV. The *General Hospital* credits rolled—almost four o'clock. Irene would be home soon.

Melvin stayed there for what felt like forever. His breathing slowed. Finally, he lifted his head. Sweat dripped onto my stomach. He pulled himself up, leaning back on his legs.

"Go get me a towel."

I slid off the bed robotically and ran to the bathroom. When I returned, he was standing, pulling on his shirt. I handed him the towel, keeping my distance. I avoided looking at his private parts. I kept one eye on Melvin at all times, a new rule for my survival kit. I'd always have to be prepared. I could never let my guard down again.

He took the towel, wiped himself off, and pulled his pants up.

"Get dressed. And clean up this bed." His voice was flat, as if we'd just finished cleaning out the car.

I put my pants back on, numb. The tears dried up; they were worthless. My childhood was short-lived. Gone. I felt my innocence leave me. The saddest part was that my body didn't feel like mine anymore. A foreign skin holding pain I hadn't known existed until Melvin introduced it to me.

I'm bad now.

As he walked toward the door, he turned back and said without emotion, "This is between us. If you tell your mother, she won't believe you."

Then he left the room. Just walked out, as if nothing had happened.

By the time Irene came home, I was at the kitchen table, pretending to read about Paul Revere. I couldn't focus. It felt as if my brain had been unplugged and plugged back in the wrong way. There was the boy who walked into that bedroom, and then there was the one sitting at the kitchen table afterward. I didn't yet understand the shift; I just knew something permanent had changed.

Everything in the house felt artificial, like a prop version of my life. Melvin sat in the living room, watching TV. Irene walked in, dropped her keys beside my backpack, and went straight to her man. I heard her kiss him and tell him she loved him. I listened to Melvin's voice—soft, casual, ordinary—finally sober—as he asked what was for dinner.

His warning—*This is between us*—echoed long after he

spoke. I lived between two realities: the child who wanted a father and the child who knew he was the monster. Saying anything felt pointless. The greatest gift Irene ever gave him was believing him over me after his first attempt.

That's why most survivors stay silent. Our truth is often dismissed.

At seven years old, I learned I was living in a house full of monsters. After that day, when I feared monsters hiding in the darkest corners of my room, they weren't the imaginary ones under the bed.

It was Melvin.

Pulling Mommy
from the Bushes

After Pépé kicked Vinny, Sonya, and my troubled cousins out of the house, they moved into a second-floor apartment down the street, a five-minute walk away. Pépé never forgave Vinny for the chaos he caused the night he put his head through the garage window. Maybe I learned to hold a grudge from my grandfather.

At certain times of year, Melvin would travel to Canada to visit his brothers and his mother, Lillian, whom I was encouraged to call Gram, though I never wanted to. She disliked me because I wasn't related to Melvin by blood, and I disliked her because, when she acknowledged me, her abrasiveness turned me off. I didn't need her. I had a grandmother, Mémé. That was enough for me.

During most trips to Canada, Melvin, Irene, and I would pack the car and drive to Saint-Jean-sur-Richelieu for a long weekend. I vaguely remember disliking Quebec and Melvin's extended family. At Lillian's apartment, everyone over fifteen would spend the day chain-smoking odd-smelling hand-rolled cigarettes in the kitchen. Most of his family depended on government aid; their main activities seemed to be drinking and rolling cigarettes. They mostly spoke French. I only knew a few phrases, my favorite being "ferme la porte" whenever someone left a door open.

Insecurity set in because I didn't understand what they said, especially when my Canadian "cousins" spoke in French and then pointed at me and laughed.

I enjoyed the car ride through New England, especially the eight hours of scenic views across Massachusetts's lush hills and into Vermont's Green Mountains. Not surprisingly, my favorite part was stopping for dinner at a truck stop in White River Junction. I appreciated being somewhere different, surrounded by strangers unaware of us. Perhaps I found a sense of freedom by simply being away from our house and the usual routine of my parents drinking and arguing. Melvin and Irene appeared happier on the road, giving the impression that we were a normal family. I used to think that living near snowy peaks might bring us more happiness.

Sometimes Melvin went on these trips alone, and when he did, I became Irene's guardian—a role meant for an adult, not a child. My mother knew better than to drag me into a bar on a school night. Apparently, Friday and Saturday nights were acceptable for an eight-year-old to be in a bar, but midweek? That might look bad.

So when Melvin went to Canada without us and Irene didn't want to bring me to The Silver Dollar on a school night, we'd schlep over to Vinny and Sonya's apartment so she could drink, get high, and bond with her brother. While they sat in the kitchen listening to loud music, I was forced into Timmy and Tommy's bedroom to fend for myself. The smell of farts and old sneakers made me wish someone would open a window.

Although my cousin's bedroom was filthy, it wasn't the worst room in their apartment.

I don't believe Vinny worshipped Satan, but staring at the artwork he painted across their living room walls, you'd be hard-pressed not to think he'd cut off kitten heads and smeared their blood over his body in some underground ritual. Wicked enough to keep Mémé out of their apartment.

It was a Sunday night, the day before third grade, and I'd been playing in my bedroom. Melvin had gone to Canada for the weekend. God, I loved it when he left; I could finally sleep with both eyes closed. Irene walked in wearing her shoes and said, "We're going to Uncle Vinny's."

I asked if I could stay with Mémé, but Irene yelled no from the hallway. I put on my sneakers, fastened the Velcro, and grabbed a light jacket.

The autumn afternoon breeze followed us as we zigzagged through the neighborhood and up the cracked sidewalk to their building—a white, three-story house that looked a little like my grandparents'. The crooked, worn stairs to their landing always left a sick feeling in my stomach. I hated walking into that apartment and always stayed close behind my mother. The first thing I saw was a floor-to-ceiling painting of the devil, larger than life and unavoidable.

Honestly, the art might have scared the gay out of me.

"Joseph! Let go of my fucking leg," Irene bellowed. I clung to her pant leg like my life depended on it, because at that moment, it did. Vinny's apartment felt like the gateway to Hell. I didn't need to worry about seeing the Devil in the mirror; I was already in his house. Not even a hurricane-force gust of wind could have torn me from Irene. She pried my fingers apart one by one, but the second she'd let go, I'd latch onto her again, because some part of me still believed she was there to protect me.

Vinny's artwork was the scariest shit I'd ever seen: glowing red eyes, green reptilian scales, and bulging muscles barely covered by a brown loincloth. Props to Vinny; the Devil looked like it could peel itself off the wall at any moment. Satan's smirk followed me wherever I went, no matter where I hid. Those long black fingernails looked ready to slice a young throat. If that thing escaped the wall and came after me, I'm pretty sure I would've climbed back inside Irene.

"You scared of the big bad Devil, boy?" Vinny laughed, the sound ricocheting off every wall. He yanked me away from my mother and shoved me toward the kitchen, then toward my cousin's bedroom. I whined—instinct, not strategy—and that didn't sit well with him. Whiners were babies, and he didn't allow babies in his house.

Even when I tried to act tough, everyone saw it was just that—an act. Vinny never took me seriously because of my softness, my feminine edges. Like most straight men, he found a pansy boy uncomfortable. It didn't sit right. So he handled me the only way he knew how: by banishing me to the bowels of my cousins' bedroom, hoping they'd toughen me up.

Any sign of cleanliness stayed outside on the front lawn. As an adult, I can confidently say our apartment above Mémé's was much more livable. I didn't realize that at the time, but I do now. If the show *Hoarders* had been around in the late '70s, my aunt and uncle's apartment would have been an unforgettable pilot episode.

Clutter covered every surface. It was the kind of place where you had to move something just to set something else down. In reality, it wasn't a home, more of an abandoned storage unit. Nothing in that space felt warm or cozy. The apartment reminded me of an unorganized closet where five people were trying to function. Sure, the place needed paint, bleach, and maybe an exorcism, but when the people living there didn't care, imagining anything different was a waste of energy. It seemed Vinny and Sonya had simply given up.

Bookshelves sagged under dime-store figurines, chipped and dusty; ashtrays overflowed with lipstick-stained cigarette butts. Cockroaches felt less like pests and more like pets. Clean and dirty clothes were tossed everywhere, on equal footing and without discrimination.

The path from their front door to the kitchen felt like an obstacle course. You didn't step over things; there wasn't room. You just stepped on whatever was in your way. Vinny and Sonya had no choice but to put their bedroom in the middle of the apartment: three kids, two bedrooms, simple math. Timmy and Tommy shared one room; Bonnie had the other. The dining room became their bedroom the day they moved in. Calling it a bedroom was generous; it was more like a sad thrift store, with everything on the shelves under a dollar. With no designated closet, they didn't separate clothes from where they slept; they just merged the two. Proof that disorder lived there.

After navigating Vinny and Sonya's unmade bed in the center of the room and the odd, mismatched furniture scattered everywhere, it felt refreshing to finally push through their dark bedroom and step into the bright fluorescent light of the kitchen. It was the only room with natural light, which only made things worse, spotlighting the grime bleeding across the walls. Everywhere else, the curtains were always drawn. Always. I never understood what they were hiding from, but even when the sun was welcoming outside, their apartment felt more like a secret than a home.

Although the kitchen was the brightest room, it didn't feel safe; it looked like a drug den. The four-chair round table was just large enough for a few beers, a magazine filled with weed seeds and stems, and a couple of ashtrays. Timmy's Algebra 1 book was there too, balancing rolling papers and a cigarette lighter like a makeshift centerpiece. An old wringer-washer rattled on the uneven linoleum like it was dancing without music, and Sonya—cigarette dangling—fed dripping clothes through the press into that antique beast. Sonya loved that machine, maybe more than she loved her kids. When it hiccupped or choked on a pair of jeans or a heavy sweater, she'd stroke it until it settled and started purring again: loyal, predictable, unlike her children.

"Get your ass in the room with the boys," Sonya muttered. "They're waiting for you."

My cousin's bedroom was a shock to my system. It made the rest of the apartment look like it had been scrubbed with Pine-Sol. I itched when I went into their room. They didn't have pets, but I wouldn't be surprised if they had fleas. I used to wonder if I was really related to these cousins; nothing about this room reflected my life. *Sesame Street* wallpaper covered my walls. Theirs were plastered with crooked KISS posters, and their furniture was held together by masking tape, ready to fall apart if one of us sneezed. I've always questioned whether I truly belonged in this family, and standing in that disaster zone didn't help the argument.

No adult ever set foot in that room, and I understood why. If I were Sonya and walked into that dilapidation, I'd have ripped out my fallopian tubes and flushed them straight down the toilet. Maybe I'm being too harsh on my cousins. Did they ever have a chance? Their mother once forced visitors to remove their shoes upon entering her house; now she had forgotten how to operate the vacuum. Their lack of housekeeping was clearly a family trait. Timmy and Tommy's twin beds sat across from each other: one shoved against a wall, the other tucked under a curtain hanging from two bent metal rings. No chairs. No desk. No dignity. One bed didn't even have sheets, just a single pillow and a crocheted afghan Mémé had given Tommy before Pépé evicted them all.

"Get outta here. We don't want you here." Tommy snapped, glaring at me over a heavy-metal magazine. "Highway to Hell" blasted from their black-and-silver boombox so loud my ears rang. Their music, along with the adults' music in the kitchen, was competing for the title of the worst music being played. I wanted to ask them to turn it down, but I knew better; that kind of request would've earned me a mouthful of something worse than dirt, possibly dirty underwear. I hated that music. I would've killed for Olivia Newton-John or *Grease*. Something joyful. Something with choreography.

"Aunt Sonya said I have to," I muttered, closing the door behind me. I didn't want to be there any more than they wanted me, with them or in their filth, but being behind enemy lines still felt safer than sitting in the living room with green Lucifer staring me down.

"Get *out*!" Timmy shouted, already halfway off the bed.

I stuck out my tongue and spun toward the door, ready to bolt. The only thing that kept me from having the back of my head yanked back was the disaster zone between us: dirty clothes, old food, and empty Pepsi cans carpeting the floor. There wasn't a single clear path for him to run fast enough to catch me. Thank God they were slobs.

At least the entire apartment was consistent.

I slammed the door and turned back into the kitchen. By then, the weed had been picked apart, rolled, and lit, leaving a hazy gray cloud drifting above Irene and Vinny. I disliked that pungent, skunky smell. Still do. The fact that they smoked openly in front of children felt negligent. Adults choosing themselves over the kids who relied on them. Maybe they didn't think it counted as "real" drugs because nobody was snorting lines with a rolled-up dollar bill. To me, they were just smoking weird, extra-stinky cigarettes, like Melvin's relatives in Canada. I hated anything burnt: weed, cigarettes, even the sulfur sting of matches just blown out.

"Why aren't you in the room with the boys?" Irene choked out, taking a drag, then passing the joint back to Vinny.

"They don't want me in there."

Sonya yelled toward the hallway (not that her sons could hear her over AC/DC), "Goddamn it, boys, I'm gonna kick your ass."

That was as far as her parenting went. A weak threat with no follow-through. Thankfully, she didn't force me back into their purgatory, and I wasn't about to argue with her.

"Mommy, can we go home?" I asked, trying to climb into her lap.

"Irene, take him to the living room and turn on the TV," Vinny suggested without looking at either of us.

I didn't want to go into the living room alone. That's where the Devil waited. I had convinced myself Satan enjoyed it when little boys were left unsupervised. Irene peeled herself off the kitchen chair, stumbled, then steadied herself against the table. She took a sip of her beer, then led me into the living room. The air wasn't clear, but at least I could breathe easier.

She grabbed a blanket from Vinny and Sonya's makeshift bedroom. It was coarse and smelled of sour milk. I doubted it had been washed in months, maybe years. Perhaps it was too thick for Sonya's washing machine. Irene guided me to the sofa, tucked a cushion under my head, and draped the stiff blanket over me.

"If you fall asleep, I'll wake you when I'm ready to leave," she said, then turned on *The Dukes of Hazzard.*

"Mommy, I don't want to be here. I'm scared."

"Don't be scared," Irene said. "I'm right in the other room." She kissed my forehead, then returned to the kitchen.

Alone. Uncomfortable. The air felt heavy with an unknown wickedness. I could hear the adults laughing in the kitchen, their voices too loud, too careless. I pushed the blanket toward my feet, but otherwise stayed perfectly still. The green Devil watched from directly above. I tried to ignore its sinister grin, but it loomed over me, waiting for me to blink so it could drag my soul to Hell. I watched the TV, a safe escape and a comforting distraction. I loved Bo and Luke Duke, especially how they slid across General Lee's hood. After the "Greased Lightnin'" dance in *Grease*, it was the coolest TV moment I'd seen.

Years later, while walking through the streets of Madrid with my friend David, I attempted that exact move on a small car that looked like a Fiat and nearly cracked the pavement.

No matter how hard I tried to stay awake on Vinny and Sonya's uncomfortable sofa, forcing myself to focus on Daisy Duke teasing the entire cast with her statuesque body and perfect brunette hair, I couldn't keep my eyelids open. By the next commercial break, I was asleep.

I slipped into a familiar dream, the one that visited me often. In it, I'm standing in my grandparents' living room, staring out the window at the street below. It's nighttime. The streetlights cast film noir shadows along Prospect Avenue.

A yellow taxi pulls up. A gray-haired, medium-built man in jeans and a white button-down shirt steps out. He rounds the taxi and walks toward the driveway. Who is that? He looks up at me. We make eye contact. He smiles.

It's my biological father. It's Frank.

A spark of joy rises in me, and I lift my hand to wave, but then something shifts. Him. His body. His expression. One second, he's the man who has come to save me from everything; the next, he's transforming: cape, blood-red vest, sharpened fangs—a vampire. Dracula is stalking up the driveway.

My joy dissolves. I run through the house to lock the front door, but no matter how fast I move, he's faster. When I reach the kitchen, he's already inside, waiting. Blood drips from the side of his mouth. Irene lies motionless on the floor behind him.

I screamed until someone shook me awake from the nightmare. I sat up, my neck cold with sweat. Irene hovered. Nothing was in focus. In the shadows, with her swaying posture, she looked like the Devil from the living room wall, coming to life.

"Joseph. Let's go home. You're having a nightmare."

My eyes were wide. I panted. I stayed still until the room stopped tilting. I couldn't tell whether I was trembling from fear or if Irene was swaying. When everything sharpened, I realized it was her, drunk, rocking side to side.

Irene and I never spent the night, and thank God for that. First, there was no room for us. Second, ewww. I sat up robotically, put on my shoes, and made a beeline for the door.

Vinny was already passed out on his bed. Sonya followed us to the front door and locked it behind us after we left. I didn't know what time it was, but dawn was creeping in through the vertical windows in the stuffy stairwell, so I assumed most of the East Coast was waking up. I took the steps like a professional athlete fleeing danger, moving as fast as my tired legs would carry me.

"Wait for me. Don't go outside," Irene called after me.

I paused on the landing and watched her descend the staircase, like a toddler learning to walk: one step… pause… grasping the handrail… taking a deep breath… then another step.

At this pace, we'd be here until lunch. I had school in a few hours.

"Help me," Irene slurred.

I walked back up the set of stairs and let her lean on me as I guided her, step by step, making sure she didn't collapse and crush me. I focused on one task at a time: first, leave the building; then, go home.

Outside, the fresh, sweet air swept over us, but it didn't sober her. If anything, once we hit the street, her intoxication intensified.

"Hold on, I'm trying to walk," she complained, fighting gravity as if it were a bully shoving her from behind.

When Mevin wasn't around, I became Irene's default caregiver. Her stabilizer. Her best friend. The one person responsible for keeping her upright so she wouldn't hit the curb and knock out an incisor. It was an impossible job for a child; Irene needed an actual adult. Where the hell was Linda when you needed her?

I didn't choose this job, but as the child of an alcoholic, those responsibilities fall on you whether you want them to or not.

We passed the house on the corner, then inched toward our street. Her moaning cut through the eerie quiet of early morning. I whispered encouragement—"We're almost home, Mommy, keep moving"—and squeezed her hand as I guided her across the street, doing everything possible to keep her steady and on the sidewalk.

We moved in slow motion: a few steps on concrete, then a lean toward the bushes, then back onto the sidewalk. I kept talking, not sure whether I was keeping Irene alert or keeping myself calm. I couldn't tell you what I rambled about: school, the Devil painting, a McDonald's Happy Meal toy, anything to fill the morning air. She probably didn't hear a word. Still, we made it past a few more houses before things shifted.

I looked up at her face, and something was wrong. Her expression had changed—vacant and unfocused.

"Mommy? Are you—"

Too late.

Her eyes glazed over, her body went slack, and she stared forward as if making eye contact with something I couldn't see. Probably something that wasn't there. Then she began moving again, sideways, straight into the bushes. Before I could react, she toppled headfirst. I was no match for holding up a full-grown adult. Her face smacked into branches, then into dirt, her legs sticking straight across the sidewalk like a fallen mannequin.

Completely still.

I started crying. I wished to be brave, but the fear of losing my mother overwhelmed me. I knelt down and pulled at her arm, gravel pressing into my knees. She remained still. I shook her more forcefully.

"Mommy! Wake up!" I screeched, straining to drag her from the bushes. I tugged and twisted, but she didn't budge. At eight, my understanding of death was simple: stillness meant gone, like when she lay across our kitchen floor after taking the pills.

I observed her chest rise and fall slowly. Good—she's alive, just unconscious.

I didn't stop trying. I had no idea where I was dragging her, but seeing her half-buried in the bushes felt unreal. Last year, I'd learned in school that some ants could lift fifty times their own weight. I needed their help. My mother felt like a boulder. Why couldn't we be ants?

I had to wake her up before someone found us. The embarrassment of lying flat on the ground would piss her off.

I thought about running back to Vinny's and Sonya's, but they were the reason we were standing out in the street. Well, one of us was standing. They'd be of no help to me, and I didn't trust them. I had to blame someone for this mess, so I chose them.

I pulled on her hair, not worrying about the consequences. If she woke up angry, it meant she had woken up. I could deal with her rage later. When she first collapsed, I feared the neighbors would come outside to investigate. Now I prayed someone would turn on a porch light. I needed an adult.

I can't believe I'm saying this, but I needed Melvin.

Finally, a sound. A low groan. Then, slowly, her limbs twitched awake.

I stepped back to give her some room. Like a robot rebooting, Irene pushed herself up. Her color returned. She reached for my hand. I grabbed it, but when she looked into my eyes, she didn't seem to recognize me. Then, slowly, she did. She let go and placed her hands on her face. I moved to the strip of grass between the sidewalk and the street. Good decision, because seconds later she heaved—loud, violent, erupting—and puked all over the spot where I'd been kneeling. She stayed there awhile, moaning, then lay back down in the dirt.

"Let's go home, Mommy. Let's—"

She whispered so softly that the wind almost carried the words away: "Wait… a minute."

I wanted to be home, safe in my bed, but instead I found myself crouched beside bushes at dawn, waiting for my mother to recover from poisoning herself. I didn't understand why she couldn't control her drinking. Why did she need alcohol? Why did she need weed? Why did she need nights like this?

Time blurred. Eventually, after more coaxing, Irene pushed herself to her feet. Honestly, she reminded me of a child, and I was one. I gripped her hand again, as tight as possible, ready this time if she fell. Thankfully, she didn't.

We walked the rest of the way home, slowly and unsteadily, dipping into bushes twice and nearly colliding with a chained fence. To this day, I don't know how I pulled it off, but we made it to our driveway and into our home.

I did everything I could to get Irene inside quietly, but it was nearly impossible. Drunk people can't be quiet; their senses are so off that loud sounds seem quiet. Seriously, she clomped up each step as if she wanted Mémé to wake up. We made it up the first set of stairs, and, to no surprise, when we reached the landing on the second floor that opened into Mémé's kitchen, she appeared, wrapped in her rose-colored robe, peeking into the hallway.

"He should be in bed, Irene. He has school today."

Seeing her eight-year-old grandson support his thirty-four-year-old mother broke Mémé's heart. Irene ignored her, likely because she lacked the energy to argue. Neither of us looked at my grandmother as we went upstairs. Irene avoided her out of shame, and I avoided her out of shame for being Irene's son.

I guided my mother into her bedroom. She collapsed face down on the bed. I pulled off her shoes and set them neatly beside the closet. She'd need them when she woke. The nightlight glowed softly, and dawn light seeped around the curtains.

"Roll over, Mommy. You need to get under the blanket."

She mumbled into her pillow, "Leave me alone."

I pulled the blanket up around her, unable to tuck her in completely. The blanket meant comfort. And if I could give her one small comfort, maybe this night would end better for us.

I leaned in and kissed her cheek. "I love you, Mommy."

As I reached the doorway, she lifted her head just slightly. "Stay home from school."

"But it's the first day," I said softly.

No response. She began snoring; I left, feeling I had done all I could.

In my room, I changed into pajamas and climbed into my twin bed. The clean sheets smelled fresh and safe. I rolled onto my side, facing the blank TV screen, then out the window, gazing at the giant oak tree, its branches stretching toward the house.

My eyes grew heavy. The last thought I remember was: I can't wait to meet my new teacher tomorrow.

BLOOD-STAINED KITCHEN

Voices quickly escalated, and the atmosphere in the kitchen soured; a word that I didn't understand at age eight comes to mind: vitriol. When Melvin and Irene fought, their verbal abuse tore through the apartment like a tornado. At first, it was calm conversations and friendly banter, then suddenly—*whoooosh*—came vocal attacks meant to cut someone in half. Melvin excelled at cutting people down; he was rarely challenged. He was a bully, and his victims were his immediate family.

Nothing about their loud voices really caught my attention at first. Fights like these were common. In fact, it was unusual for their evening not to end in what sounded like a barroom brawl. Whenever I spied on adults, I giggled at how clearly the curse words came through.

Then Melvin said something that pulled me completely away from watching *Magnum PI.*

"Go ahead, you stupid bitch. Do it. I dare you!"

I leaped from the sofa and ran to the living room threshold as quietly as possible, listening.

Irene's voice boomed through the apartment. "I'll do it, motherfucker. I will!" A crack of splintering wood split the air, followed by the crash of shattering glass. I'd soon learn that Melvin had thrown one of the wooden chairs across the kitchen, knocking cocktail glasses to the floor.

I raced down the hallway, my oversized padded pajama feet flopping on the floor as I slid to a stop before the kitchen. Just as I was about to turn right into the doorway, Melvin loomed over me. In my peripheral vision, his youngest brother, Louie, stood. He'd been sleeping on our sofa for a few weeks until he could get back on his feet. Having one of Melvin's brothers on our sofa was normal. He had many brothers, and they always needed a helping hand. Melvin grabbed me, flung me over his shoulder, and carried me back to the living room, kicking and screaming.

"Stop squirming." Melvin plopped me back onto the sofa. "You stay in here and don't leave this fucking room."

Standing in the living room doorway, he yelled down the hall, "Goodnight, whore." Then, with all the malice you'd reserve for an enemy, he taunted, "I hope you do it!"

He turned back toward me. "I'm warning you, Joe. Don't go into the kitchen. I love you." He turned and walked down the hallway toward his bedroom, then slammed the door behind him.

Melvin's reaction to Irene's threat to kill herself was too calm, even for him. Did he want her to die? Was he simply calling her bluff? Those questions have stuck with me; they surface every time I replay that night.

Threatening to kill herself gave Irene power over the situation. She rarely had power and felt comfortable exerting it only when she was drinking. Melvin didn't like it when someone else held the reins. King Melvin sat on the throne. Whatever his reasons for goading her that night, no matter how horrible the argument was, his response and actions added up to one truth: he didn't really care whether she lived or died.

I can't recall exactly how quickly I ran toward the kitchen, but it was surely within moments of Melvin shutting their bedroom door. I rounded the corner and paused at the doorway, and what I saw is something my brain will never let go of.

Blood. Irene's blood.

The only time I'd seen that much blood was when I'd secretly watched *Friday the 13th* with Alan. The kitchen scene could have come straight out of a horror movie. Time paused. I felt like my heart did, too.

I must have screamed. A swift pressure tightened in my stomach. My lungs filled with air. A tingling sensation washed over me, goosebumps. Irene stood by the table, her eyes locked on mine. I thought I could feel her pain: anguish, betrayal, defeat, and a desire not to live another second in the life she had created.

A mixture of hot tears and cheap mascara dripped down her cheeks. She held a fragment of broken glass in one hand, and the shades of her blood coating it burned into my eyes. The shard slipped from her fingers and crashed to the floor, shattering into smaller pieces. One of Irene's wrists had been sliced open, the white meat of her flesh darkening to red.

Louie dashed to the closet-sized pantry, rummaging for towels. He found a few and turned to tend to Irene. I wanted to run toward her, but I was afraid of her. This wasn't my mother. Who was this woman?

Yes, Irene had taken pills before trying to end her life—*how could I forget*—but to cut open her wrist while her son was in the next room? It was mind-boggling. Whoever stood in our kitchen was a wild woman. I had never seen her before in my life. Her eyes cried out as Louie tried to wrap a kitchen towel around her bleeding wrist. She looked over at him, not responding, simply accepting what was happening. The smell of rusty pennies filled the air.

"Go get another towel!" Louie shouted. I wanted to help. I *needed* to help. But I stood motionless, my brain struggling to catch up to the scene. I couldn't take my eyes off Irene as the blood trickled down her arm and pooled on the floor. She reached for the chair, but her knees wobbled, and she collapsed onto the floor like a stuntwoman.

Louie noticed I had frozen in place. He shrieked, "Joe, towels!"

"Okay." I snapped out of my daze and ran down the hallway toward the bathroom. As I approached the doorway, one thought looped in my head: How was Melvin in bed? Did he really not care? Sure, our house was constantly rife with toxic behavior, but this was beyond disturbing. He had upset her to the point that she sliced open her wrist. Irene's behavior that night was unlike anything I'd ever seen.

I rubbed the tears from my eyes and tried to focus on what I needed to do. Even though I was frightened by the woman sprawled in sticky blood, I desperately wanted to hug her and tell her everything would be all right. My mother didn't have to die because I would be there to protect her. It didn't matter. She was covered in blood, and I thought she was dying on the kitchen floor. I pulled the towels from the vanity and heard her cry out, a thin, needle-like sound that seemed to carry the very essence of the glass that had sliced her.

My panic and tears didn't stop me from helping Irene stay alive. I had one goal: be brave. Be the son your mother needs. I ran down the hallway toward the kitchen, thrusting the towels at Louie. She was now lying on her back, hands at her sides. Louie grabbed the towels and worked quickly, removing one soaked towel and replacing it with a dry one. He tossed the blood-marinated towel to the floor; it slapped as it landed, splashing the linoleum with more gore.

"Mommy, I love you." Sobs erupted from deep within my confusion. I tried to catch her attention, but she seemed transported elsewhere; her eyes were fixed on the fluorescent tube lights hanging above our heads.

"Go wait in the living room, Joe," Louie said gently.

The only way I was leaving was if Irene told me to or someone dragged me away. I wanted my mother to know I was there, that I loved her, and that she had me. She'd always have me. Even if she was fighting with Melvin, she didn't have to die. Why wasn't I enough to live for? I kept talking to her, nothing remarkable, just begging her not to die.

Irene turned her head and sputtered, "I love you, too. Don't cry." She wearily closed her eyes again as Louie kept pressing towels to the wound. They soaked through quickly. She'd need to go to the hospital, right? I'd gone to the school nurse for much less.

I had to distract my mind, as I had when Melvin and I were alone. With Louie in full nursing mode, I grabbed the broom from the hall closet and started sweeping up the glass around Irene. I didn't want her to cut herself again. I maneuvered around their bodies on the floor, trying not to step in blood. I went to work, the broken pieces clinking as they dragged across the floor. I thought of Mémé. Where was my protector? She'd do everything in her power to stop Irene's pain. The broom's bristles left red streaks across the linoleum, making me whimper as I tried to hold back my childish emotions.

When all the large pieces of glass were swept away from Irene, I propped the stained broom by the sink and knelt beside her. Louie glanced at me; he didn't tell me to leave. He knew we needed each other. I put my hand on her shoulder, leaned in, and kissed her sweaty forehead.

"Should we call for help?" I asked, but Louie didn't respond.

At school, a lady had told us that if there was an emergency and no adults were around, we should dial 9-1-1. Those three numbers would alert the police or firefighters, and help would be on the way. Even though I was in the kitchen with two adults, 9-1-1 felt like the only clear option. But Louie wasn't telling me to call. No police. No ambulance. No sober adults. I understood that his primary focus was on stopping Irene from bleeding, but where was the direction to call a professional? He wasn't a nurse. He wasn't a professional at anything, except maybe a couch surfer.

Irene opened her eyes again. Barely. "Joe. Don't call for help. Uncle Louie is helping me." Then her eyes shut again, as if she were resting after a long day at work. My grandparents were gone. Melvin was most likely snoring. I was stuck in this predicament with Uncle Louie. Just three of us. Nobody else. It felt like we might all die together.

Louie and I sat on the floor with Irene in silence for what felt like hours. I can't remember how long it was, only that it was long enough for the bleeding to stop and for some color to return to her cheeks. She had been so pale. I held her hand. Louie held the other. He kept urging me to go to bed, but each time he asked, I only grew more resolute. I wasn't going to abandon my mother until I knew she wouldn't die the moment I fell asleep.

More time passed. Irene grew stronger, alert and present, insisting on "getting up," using her uninjured hand to push herself upright. The kitchen looked like a crime scene. In my young opinion, she'd lost a lot of blood, yet she was using all her might to reclaim her dignity.

Louie shifted, seating himself behind her on the floor, giving her support as she leaned against him. "Joe, go get some tape from Melvin's tool chest in the closet," he said.

Louie knew precisely what he was doing. I had doubted him, but he was proving he was in charge. I did as I was told.

He used the gray masking tape as a giant bandage, wrapping it around the towels that had become Irene's makeshift sutures. I hurried to the sink with an empty glass. So helpful, I thought. Carefully, I washed the dried blood from my hands; I noticed a few drops on my pajamas. I filled the glass with cold water and rushed back to Irene.

I knelt beside her and handed her the water. With her good hand, Irene grabbed the glass and took a few large gulps. She smiled at me in appreciation, then passed the glass back. A deep sigh escaped her as she leaned back against Louie's chest. One of his hands combed gently through her hair. Tears streamed down his cheek, while his other hand gripped her wound tightly. Louie loved my mother in a way that transcended the bond of in-laws. I understood their love for the first time that evening, when she tried to kill herself. It bothered me that they could be secretly in love; now I'm glad my mother had him. And I'm so happy he loved her the way he did. If Louie hadn't been there that night, Irene might have died. I'm sure I'd have called 9-1-1 at some point, but it might have been too late.

"Don't cut yourself on the glass, Joe. Mommy was stupid tonight."

"I'm sorry," I said, apologizing for something that wasn't mine to carry. "Are you going to die?"

"No, everything's fine. Why don't you go to bed?"

I didn't want to leave her on the floor, but my eyes were heavy, and the clock on the wall showed it was almost morning. I'd have to miss school again. With her good hand, she wiped the tears from my cheeks and told me she'd be going to bed soon, after resting for a few more minutes.

I was slightly confused, and remain so to this day, that just a few hours earlier she had been jabbing her wrists with broken glass, and now she was telling me everything would be fine. Not only that, but she was heading to bed. At that age, I guess I expected it was normal for her to go to bed with her husband. In fact, I didn't question it at all. I had to lie next to Melvin when I didn't want to, too—just another aspect of family life, sleeping with the enemy.

"Don't say anything about this to Mémé. I don't want her to find out," Irene said.

Stunned, I couldn't look away. Not tell Mémé? Was that even possible?

She continued, "I'm serious. I'll be mad if you tell her. This is our family's business."

She pulled me close and kissed me on the cheek. I stepped away, leaving her with Louie. I heard their whispers as I walked into the living room to turn off the TV. Normally, I'd have eavesdropped, but I was too tired to be nosy.

I peeled off my pajamas and dropped them into the hamper. My mother's dried blood made me uncomfortable; I didn't want to sleep with it on me. I lay under my sheets, shivering with fear. Irene would live. That was a relief, but then a new thought arrived: What would happen tomorrow morning?

Questioning it was silly because I already knew what tomorrow would bring. The mirrored response that happened every morning after one of my parents' blowout fights—they dismissed it, swept it away like shattered glass. And I never understood whether their reaction was positive or negative. As an adult, it is absurd to ignore something as traumatic as an attempted suicide. But as a child, it was fantastic, because the drama ended as quickly as it started. The screaming and cursing from the night before vanished with the rising sun. Peace returned for a moment, though the sight of the sliced wrist was now part of my permanent collection of memories.

The morning might go something like this: we'd all wake up at different times. Irene might still be awake from the night before. Melvin next. Me after. Louie passed out on the sofa until the afternoon. I'd walk into the kitchen, and there they'd be at the table, Melvin and Irene, talking over coffee and cigarettes as if the previous night had been a hallucination. Irene's wrist was freshly wrapped in clean bandages. She'd offer me a bowl of cereal, and the three of us would sit together, as if nothing had fucking happened.

Melvin and Irene twisted my reality. I'd wake up braced for more fighting, but the calm tone of their morning-after interactions left me disoriented. The level of rage in their fights became normalized. I got used to it. Sure, I hated their violent streaks, but with this latest stunt, it felt like we were living through an active family war, and I'd eventually learn to dodge their explosive outbursts.

What I lived through was a family barely held together, with adults hating each other and a child watching. They didn't love each other, but they also wouldn't leave. Melvin wanted me; Irene wanted her fantasy. We were all firmly planted in our familiar roles: Irene, the damsel in distress; Melvin, the hero.

And me, the distraction. The punchline. The kid who learned to perform so no one had to admit what was real.

IMPACT

Despite the comfort of the hospital bed, the steady beeping of machines and unfamiliar noises pulled me from a deep sleep. The pungent smell of gasoline hung in the air. The harsh glare of fluorescent lights made my eyes water. Disoriented, I tried to piece together my surroundings. I knew I was in a hospital, but what had happened? My memory had more blank spaces than story. As my eyes adjusted to the light, I shifted to sit up, only to be hit with a wave of gnawing pain in my left shoulder.

The room was large, about the size of a classroom. I was in a hospital ward. My bed was closest to the exit, with a window to my left overlooking the hallway. A small boy cried out from behind a curtain in the bed to my right. Across the room, three beds lined the opposite wall. The boy directly across from me had a metal stand with a TV on it, like the one my teacher used to roll out for movie day. The boy next to him slept soundly, while the third bed, by a window with a view of Manhattan, sat empty.

I remember seeing the Empire State Building out that window for the first time, a building that seemed tall enough to touch heaven.

The ward door opened, and a young nurse glided into the room, heading straight for my bed. "Good afternoon. I see you're finally awake. I'm Mary, your nurse today."

I rubbed my eyes. "Where am I? Where's my dad?"

She inspected the intravenous needle taped to my left arm. "You're in Jacobi Hospital in the Bronx. Your dad was discharged this morning." Nurse Mary adjusted the IV fluid bag hanging from a metal hook attached to my bed. "He sat by your bed all day yesterday," she added.

Staring at her, I shifted and grimaced. Pain radiated down my arm.

"Are you having any pain?"

"Yes," I grunted. "My shoulder hurts." It hit me then: I was alone, surrounded by strangers.

"Where's my mom?"

"Your mom will be here tomorrow," she said, adjusting my blankets. "Do you remember what happened?" She paused, then added, "You were in an accident. Your collarbone is fractured, which is why you're wearing a sling." She picked up the cup of water from my bedside table and filled it. "You should drink some water. Dinner will be coming up soon."

I took a sip. Nurse Mary was kind but focused on her tasks. "I need to check your vital signs," she said, walking around the bed and placing a small blood pressure cuff on my right arm. "Please stay still, Joey."

"Joe," I corrected.

"What was that, dear?"

I winced as the cuff tightened. "I go by Joe."

She ignored me and looked down at her watch. I tried to get her attention again. "Where are my clothes?" I asked.

Nurse Mary counted to herself under her breath. The release of the blood pressure cuff was a relief. She slid it off my arm. "Your clothes are in the bottom drawer of your nightstand," she said. "They're ruined."

Nurse Mary walked to my left and opened the bottom drawer of the bedside table. The stench hit me all at once. That's when I realized the intense smell of gasoline was coming from my clothes.

"They're soaked in gasoline," she said. "We were going to throw them away, but we're waiting for your mom to arrive."

I stared down into the drawer at the plastic bag, my fuel-soaked clothes balled up inside. I didn't know what else to say. My mind went blank. No questions. Just one urgent truth: "I have to pee."

She closed the drawer. "Of course. Here, let me help you." She unhooked me from the IV fluids and capped the IV catheter.

There was no urinal or restroom in the boys' ward; the only bathroom was in the hallway. With care, Nurse Mary pulled the blankets off me and helped me swing my legs over the edge of the bed. I was wearing a hospital gown, and I worried it would open in the back. She tied it tightly, helped me slip on skid-resistant slippers, and steadied me as I stood. My legs turned to jelly, and I sank back onto the bed.

"I can't walk," I squeaked, looking from my legs back up to her. She must have heard the distress in my voice.

"Don't worry. That's because you've been in bed for two days. Once you start walking, you'll be fine." She slipped her arms under mine. "Okay, on three. One, two, three. Lift. There you go."

Nurse Mary slowly helped me to the door. I didn't touch the handle, but I could tell it was heavy. Everything in the hospital seemed gigantic; I had never spent the night in one before. The restroom was across the hall, a few doors down. She guided me along the pristine hallway. My room was quiet, but the hospital corridor was alive with patients, doctors, and machines bristling with wires and tubes. The noise was exciting yet bizarre. I remember loud voices from the nurses' station a few feet away.

Nurse Mary stopped in front of the men's room. She opened the door and stepped aside. "I'll wait for you out here."

It felt strange that my nurse didn't come in with me. My right arm was in a sling; my legs felt as if they had no bones holding them up. I had been asleep for two days. Oh, and I was only eight. Having an adult with me in the restroom seemed responsible.

I held the wall, using my good hand to inch toward the urinal. Pain in my arm pulsed through my petite frame, but I had to pee so badly that it was all I could think about. I propped myself up against the urinal and finally let my bladder go.

Back in my bed, Nurse Mary reattached me to the IV bag and tucked the covers around me. I didn't have my mother at my bedside, so the tender care I received from Nurse Mary made a difference.

"Here is something for your pain," she said, handing me my plastic water cup and a small pill. I swallowed it and finished the water. I hadn't realized how thirsty I was until then; it was as if I were becoming aware of everything slowly, in small moments. When I set the cup back on the bedside table, she refilled it and set the pink water pitcher within my reach.

"Is there anything else I can get you? My shift is nearly over," she said, smiling warmly. "You'll have a new nurse tonight."

"Can I get a TV?" If I had to wait for Irene to bail me out of the hospital, I needed something to keep me entertained.

She frowned. "I'm sorry. The television costs five dollars a day to rent. Your father didn't leave any money."

That seemed odd. Couldn't the hospital add it to my bill? The rationale still doesn't make sense. I didn't have money for food, IV fluids, or skid-resistant slippers, but I had been given those items quickly. Nobody had asked me for cash. How did all this work? Why make me suffer more? I was a child, alone in a strange hospital, and nobody could spot me a fiver so I could watch my soap operas. It seemed unkind, thoughtless.

The boy across from me leaned over. "I'd let you watch mine, but my mom said I'm not allowed to let anyone else watch it."

Why did his mother care? What was wrong with these people in the Bronx?

I nodded and looked out the window. Anyway, TV was just a distraction; there were more pressing questions, like what I remembered from the accident. Nurse Mary had confirmed that Melvin had kept vigil by my bedside while I slept. I could picture him sitting there, but the images felt like a dream. Whether he had really been there or not almost didn't matter; in my mind, Melvin had stayed by my side.

While some of the events are lost to memory, many of the details leading up to my hospitalization with a broken collarbone are clear. For starters, Melvin hadn't had reliable work in months. I'm guessing Irene's loud complaining echoed through the house enough that my grandfather finally stepped in. Pépé had been a longtime employee of Gem Mayflower Moving Company. The hype around the company in my grandparents' lives reminds me of the buzz around JetBlue Airways when I worked there. Their lives revolved around the company; Pépé wore his green shirt with the company logo even on his days off. I can still see that green-and-yellow tractor-trailer with the company name stretched across the side.

To help out my parents, mainly to help me, Pépé secured a part-time position for Melvin as a driver's apprentice. His main job was to help unload cargo from the trailers upon arrival at their final destination. Grunt work for a man with a ninth-grade education.

It was the end of summer, and Melvin drafted me to tag along on this short, cross-state road trip. The job was to transport a massive church organ from one church to another, an organ like the one at Our Lady of Sorrows. I jumped at the chance to join Melvin because riding in a tractor-trailer cab for hours sounded like more fun than anything I'd done all summer. This type of adventure was perfect for me, and, strangely enough, I did enjoy spending time with Melvin when he wasn't drinking. Or when we weren't alone. That's how I ended up in the cab with him on the day I almost didn't make it back home.

It was August 24, 1981. Melvin turned on my bedroom lamp at 4:30 a.m. I'm sure I was already awake. Knowing me, I hadn't slept much that night. After a quick breakfast, the two of us loaded up in Irene's car and headed to Gem Mayflower's offices on the other side of Hartford. Typically, drivers were discouraged from bringing guests on trips. But because Pépé was a senior driver and my grandmother often traveled with him, I'm sure he only had to give the scheduler a passing nod when my name came up. Just like that, Melvin was allowed to take me along on this fateful trip.

We pulled into the parking lot. Rows of trucks sat in the dark, their lights asleep, but ours glowed, its engine roaring through the early-morning silence. I buzzed with excitement. As we walked toward the cab, though, the mood began to shift. Four people stood clustered on the passenger side by the steps: the driver, Konstas, his wife, and his two young daughters.

Being careful not to offend Konstas, the short, round, hairy driver, Melvin asked, "Did you get approval for your family to ride along? I have approval for Joe to come with us today."

Konstas responded kindly but gruffly. "Eeet's fine. This is my family," he said in a heavy Greek accent. I barely understood him and simply nodded whenever he gestured my way.

The organ had been loaded the day before, so all we had to do was climb aboard and drive off. The six of us hoisted ourselves into the tractor-trailer cab. I went first. Melvin lifted me onto the first step, and I pulled myself inside with help from Konstas, who was doing pre-departure checks in the driver's seat. I climbed into the sleeper cab. Next came Konstas' wife and their two daughters. Finally, Melvin pulled himself up and closed the door. A few mismatched old pillows were flung onto the mattress. Gross to think about now, but cozy in 1981. The bed in the cab felt like a fort in the woods, enclosed, dark, slightly mysterious, the sort of thing I'd generally have loved, but with three children and an adult packed back there, it felt claustrophobic.

I positioned myself behind Melvin, leaning against the cab's wall. Bouncing around in the back felt like an amusement ride. I probably chatted and played games with the two daughters. I gazed out the window at the highway as we crossed the New York state line. It was the perfect kind of day. Konstas' wife, quiet and demure, sat behind him, speaking only to her daughters and to him. Her native language was Greek, and she didn't speak fluent English. Another bonus, since she wouldn't try to parent me. You know, the motherly eye that watches over all children. The last thing I needed was some Greek lady I barely knew telling this American boy what to do.

By mid-morning, we'd arrived at our destination somewhere in New Jersey, across the Hudson River from New York City. Within fifteen minutes, boredom set in, and I was ready to get back in the truck and bounce around for a few more hours. There was a park to play in, but the girls stayed in the truck's cab most of the time. I tried to keep out of Melvin's way, but not hard enough.

Whenever I noticed him stop for a break, I'd run over. "Are you almost done? I'm ready to go home."

He smiled. "Soon. A few more hours."

A few more hours felt like days.

My weariness began to weigh on Melvin, so it was a relief to everyone when Konstas finally pulled the air horn cord, and the blast signaled it was time for us to leave. I was the last in the sleeper cab, climbing over Melvin and launching myself onto the mattress. I'm sure the girls were annoyed. Honestly, I think they'd been annoyed all day; they hadn't expected me to be there. They were our surprise, and I was theirs. The truck huffed and puffed as we slowly pulled out of the church parking lot and into the late-afternoon traffic.

A steady rain shower began after we stopped for a quick bite at a fast-food restaurant. The pavement was slick, black, and shiny. Steam hovered over the hot parking lot. The long day had exhausted the four of us in the back of the cab. Konstas' wife curled around her daughters in a protective embrace, while I leaned against the wall, covering myself with pillows. We traveled along the highway. Melvin said we were crossing the George Washington Bridge. The bright lights from northbound and southbound traffic blinded me as raindrops streamed upward across the flat truck windshield. I closed my eyes. I wanted to be home. Splatters of water hit my arm. For some reason, Melvin had the window rolled down, his arm resting on the edge of the open frame.

"Daddy, the rain," I whined.

Melvin ignored me, so I whined again. He told me to be quiet. I leaned forward and looked out the front window of the cab. The rain came down in sheets, turning the outside world into something like an impressionist painting. I think Melvin was focused on Kostas's driving. As we inched along in the middle lane, a smaller moving van, a U-Haul-type truck, sped past our driver's side at an alarming rate. He might even have been driving on the shoulder.

Even if the sun had been shining, the box truck driver was going too fast. Konstas huffed, "Ah hope zat guy gets into an accident," his Green accent thick with irritation.

Then Konstas changed lanes. The blinker clicked loudly, each tick like a small gong in the dead quiet of the cab. His wife shifted. One of the daughters sat up. My gaze moved from the blurry road to Konstas.

As if in a dream, the tractor-trailer tilted from right to left, as if trying to regain its balance. Everything around me moved in slow motion. We rocked a few more times. I slammed into the cab's wall, and one of the girls landed on top of me. The pillows around me became a kind of shield, a protection I hadn't known I would need. The truck tipped farther to the right; my stomach flipped. I felt the impact as the truck tipped onto its side and slammed into the highway.

"Hold on, Joe!" Melvin screamed.

Everything went dark.

Aftermath

Over time, I heard bits and pieces about the accident. I learned from Irene that I was the last to be pulled from the wreckage. The emergency responders were afraid to go back inside the cab for fear of an explosion. Melvin, surprisingly alert, told the paramedics I was still inside. A brave stranger jumped into action, climbed into the cab, and pulled me out. I think about that often, how I escaped death because of a stranger. Not everyone did, though. A young man had been killed. Decapitated. I found that out by listening in on many adult conversations months and years after the crash. What happened that rain-soaked afternoon was far worse than I had heard, but I wouldn't discover that until I sat down to write this memoir. In a Gannett Westchester newspaper article dated August 25, 1981, I found details that finally filled in the gaps that had remained for decades.

At approximately 4:25 p.m., as Konstas merged into the left lane, he lost control of the 18-wheeler. The trailer jackknifed, swinging sharply behind the cab. The rig went airborne, cleared the median, and skidded to a stop, blocking three southbound lanes of the New England Thruway. The young man I had heard about growing up was twenty-six-year-old Greg, driving a Trans Am. The tractor-trailer landed directly on top of him, shearing off the roof of his car and killing him instantly. The police said it happened so fast that Greg wouldn't have known he died. Our truck and Trans Am weren't the only ones involved. Another tractor-trailer, trying to avoid our wreckage, slammed into a Buick, which then crashed into a disabled van on the side of the road. A Volkswagen Rabbit and a Plymouth plowed through the debris, finally coming to a halt inside our overturned trailer. In all, seven vehicles were left scattered across the highway, like toys on a living room carpet.

***

Back in the hospital ward, I had drifted off to sleep, only to be awakened by city lights filtering through the windows. Night had fallen. The Empire State Building's spire shone like a beacon. The pain medication the nurse had given me for my collarbone had knocked me out. I slept through dinner delivery, any medical procedures, and the noise and movement when the boy in the next bed was discharged.

The lights above each bed were bright, except for mine. My bed was in the shadows. I wanted to sleep again, but my stomach growled at the clang of utensils from the other patients eating dinner. There were two buttons next to me: one for the light above my bed and another to alert the nurse. I turned on my light. My meal tray taunted me, sitting just out of reach. The pain in my shoulder returned. Pulling myself into a seated position, I sneered at the preteen across from me. His rented television was angled just enough to block my view. Jerk. While he stuffed his pie hole with hospital food, laughter echoed from his bed. Then another eruption of laughter from the TV speakers as Jack Tripper acted like an imbecile on *Three's Company*. That's when I really started to dislike that kid for refusing to share his TV experience with me.

I pushed the nurse's button. A loud voice boomed from the speaker above my bed. "What?"

"I can't reach my food, and my arm hurts," I said. The man on the intercom sounded grouchy.

Silence.

Then I heard a heavy tread approaching. I turned to look out the window into the hallway, and a blur of white passed by. The ward door flung open, smacking into the wall. We all turned. A woman in white scrubs and a hat, like Bobbie Spencer wore on *General Hospital,* marched toward my bed. I sat back, realizing there was no man on the other side of the intercom; it was NurseZilla.

Without a word, she kept her distance and gave my overbed table a slight shove. It slid a few inches closer, but still just beyond my fingertips. Then she turned toward the door. As she grabbed the handle, she paused to address my television nemesis. "Turn that down. This isn't your house. Lights out in thirty minutes."

Was she just going to let me starve? "Can you help me? My arm hurts." I whimpered, staring at my food tray, unsure what mystery dinner I'd been given.

NurseZilla ambled over to the overbed table and hovered above me. Her commanding presence unnerved me. She was nothing like Nurse Mary. Slightly out of breath, she said, "You'll have to learn to use one hand for a while." She opened my carton of milk and peeled the lid off the dinner plate.

Salisbury steak with French fries and a small bowl of chopped fruit stared back at me.

I grabbed a French fry and shoved it into my mouth, no time for ketchup. I hated Salisbury steak at school, but this questionable meat would have to do. Being picky about food was not an option. This place felt more like a boarding school for wayward children than a functioning healthcare facility.

NurseZilla pulled a small bottle from her apron pouch. "Here. Take this for pain. It will help you sleep." After I swallowed the pill, she left the room. I slowly finished my dinner. Sleep overtook me again quickly; the last thing I remember was the music from the ending credits of *Three's Company* in the distance. There's a chance I fell asleep with a French fry dangling from my mouth.

My introduction to the night shift had just begun.

Waking up in the middle of the night in a strange hospital brought a different kind of pain. I yearned for my mother. Where was she? Even though Melvin had been discharged, why had he left me? He should have kept camping out in the chair next to my bed. He should have been there to open my milk cartons and help me get to the bathroom down the hall. It was confusing to me as a child. A caring mother, whose only child was in a hospital in New York City by himself and not even close to being a teenager, would have jogged from Connecticut if she had to. But that wasn't the case. My mother unlocked a new level of abandonment. I felt lost and forgotten.

I rang the call bell again, hoping that NurseZilla was off duty.

"What?"

Nope. NurseZilla was working a double shift.

"I have to pee."

The stomping of her feet down the hall sliced through the silence. My shoulder kept throbbing, and I wanted more of the special pills that made me sleepy and pain-free. The door opened, and NurseZilla swept toward my bed. She shut off the call bell and shoved my overbed table out of the way. Then she stepped aside. "Okay. Swing your legs over."

"My legs still don't wanna work."

"They work," NurseZilla snapped. "You have to move them. Come on."

I grabbed my left leg and dragged it over until it flopped off the edge of the bed. I stared at NurseZilla; she stared back. I slowly moved the right leg, with no help from my right arm, until both legs hung over the edge. My body felt damaged in a way I'd never known.

NurseZilla started walking away. "I need help," I called after her.

She snickered. "You have to walk by yourself. You can't go home until you walk."

Going home? I'd been wondering whether I'd ever see my family again. I tried one more time. "The other nurse helped me."

NurseZilla grabbed the door handle and swung it open. "I'm not that nurse." She propped the door open with a wooden wedge, then disappeared.

That bitch!

I sat there for a moment, trying to make sense of my predicament. A soft snore from one of the beds reminded me I wasn't alone in the room. I gripped the side of the bed with my left arm and tried to stand, but my spaghetti legs gave out, and I dropped back onto the mattress. The idea of pissing all over myself crossed my mind, but the embarrassment of that pushed me to slide down to the floor.

Still no urinal. Why hadn't I asked for it?

I crawled, with one arm in a sling, across the cold linoleum, through the propped-open door, and into the hallway's obscene brightness. To this day, I have no idea how I managed it, even though the memory is as clear as a summer day. I continued across the recently mopped hospital floor toward the men's restroom.

As I crept across the floor, I noticed how empty the hallway was. A few beeps here and there, an occasional moan from somewhere I couldn't see. I kept my eyes down; looking up at the lights made me dizzy. I finally reached the restroom door. It took me a moment to figure out how to push it open. Soon, my hand found the cool tile just inside. As I inched into the bathroom, a pair of large hands closed around my hips. I had no chance to fight; strong adult arms lifted me to my feet. I twisted around and was greeted by a smile from a maintenance man.

"Lean on me. Do you need the urinal or a stall?" he asked. I nodded toward the urinal, my words lost to pain, humiliation, and the shock that NurseZilla had let me crawl across the floor like an animal.

I hated the night shift.

This angel of a man helped me to the urinal and held me up while I peed. Then he walked me to the sink to wash my hands and guided me back to bed, even pulling the sheets up to my chest. And then he was gone.

There have been times in my life when I've wondered whether this man was real or if my imagination had created him to protect me from the truth: my parents had left me to fend for myself with a nurse who thought an excellent bedside manner meant letting an eight-year-old drag himself across a hospital floor with one usable arm. Was this man real? This superhero in green overalls with a kind face. A man who may have had children of his own and found it ruthless that his employer trusted NurseZilla as a caregiver.

The next morning, Nurse Mary was back. I instantly felt safer. I had to get out of here as soon as possible to avoid another night shift. With a bounce in her step, she entered the room to discharge my TV nemesis. A staff member eventually wheeled his television away. I'm sure it was taken to another child, one with five dollars in his pocket, to fight off the burdensome boredom of sitting in a hospital, staring at the walls for multiple days.

I learned to use one hand. My legs worked better. Nurse-Zilla was right, which gave me yet another reason to despise her.

After I finished breakfast, Nurse Mary came over to me. "Good morning. How's your pain?"

"It hurts a little."

She handed me another pill with a cup of water. I swallowed it. *My precious.* I loved those pills. They turned anxiety into calm, pain into ease, and made me shrug when I thought of Irene. "Is my mom coming today?" I asked. I set the empty cup on the overbed table.

"Your mom is on her way. She'll be here shortly." Nurse Mary handed me a warm towel to wash my face. "You're being discharged today," she added. "And then you get to pick a toy to take with you."

This news thrilled me. A toy meant things were finally turning around. My mother hadn't forgotten me; I'd be going home. Daytime was much better than the night in this hospital.

I nodded off again and woke to the sound of Irene and Vinny entering the room. By then, all my roommates had been discharged; the room was mine.

"There's my baby," Irene slurred, stepping toward my bed, Vinny right behind her. "Are you okay?" she asked, leaning in to kiss me and brushing my bangs from my eyes.

Nurse Mary came in, likely happy to see I hadn't been forgotten. I'd pestered the staff. I'm sure my maintenance man friend would have to replace the call bell after I left. I called the nurses' station about every five minutes, asking about my parents. Maybe I was asking for pain meds. I really can't be sure.

There was a flurry of activity around my bed. Vinny flirted with my nurse. "I hope my nephew hasn't been a pain in the ass," he said.

She giggled. "Joseph has been a delight. He even made it to the bathroom and back in the middle of the night."

I did not correct her.

"Let me get the paperwork ready, and we'll get him on his way home," she said to Irene, then turned toward the door. "I hope you brought him some clothes, because his are soaked in gasoline," she added, walking out into the hallway.

Irene opened the bottom drawer. "Jesus Christ. They're soaked with gas. We didn't bring any other clothes."

"I thought you grabbed something for him," Vinny replied.

"I fucking forgot. Get off my case, Vinny," she barked, pulling the gasoline-soaked clothes from the hospital bag and tossing them onto the bed. The fumes burned. "I guess you have to wear these."

Irene began unraveling the bundle just as Nurse Mary reentered. While Irene signed the discharge papers, Nurse Mary removed my IV catheter, then foraged around and found a T-shirt and a pair of shorts another patient had left behind. The clothes were oversized, but I wore them anyway. Anything was better than marinating in gasoline for two hours.

The orderly wheeled me down the hall, and I recalled crawling on the floor and the kind maintenance man who rescued me, which gave me a feeling of being cared for, even though he was a stranger. Two different strangers had come to my rescue, one pulling me out of the truck's cab and the other helping me stand when the pain medication left my legs barely usable.

At the nurses' station, Nurse Mary held out a large bag that looked like a beat-up sack Santa might carry. "Joseph, pick out a gift."

I reached into the bag with my good hand and pulled out a Mork from Ork figurine. It was Robin Williams as Mork, trapped in his plastic packaging: shaggy brown hair, crimson jumpsuit with a large silver triangle and suspenders, standing beside an oversized egg that showed how he arrived on planet Earth in the sitcom *Mork and Mindy*.

I kept that toy for years.

THE LUCKIEST BOY
IN CONNECTICUT

Irene scurried around the house as if Ed McMahon had just knocked on our door with a check for $10 million. It was July 21, 1983, my adoption day, the day Melvin would finally own me. My mother tried to envelop me in her happiness. I needed it; I was melancholy. For Irene, today was a milestone, a reward for all her past decisions. A pledge she had made to me while I was still in her womb, to stop at nothing to find me a father. Frank didn't want me. Larry didn't want me. But Melvin, well, he wanted me in all the wrong ways. Irene had every reason to cheer; she had fulfilled her promise. I wish she had broken it.

"Joseph! Are you ready?" she asked, a cigarette in one hand and a green ceramic ashtray in the other, as she passed through my bedroom. "Come on. We have to go. It's your big day."

I sat on my unmade bed, staring at the wall. I wasn't looking at anything in particular; I didn't have the energy. I felt like a gas tank with fumes, barely enough fuel to get through the next few hours. As I quietly wasted time, Irene and Melvin chattered in the kitchen. I couldn't make out what they were discussing, but I assumed it was about me. It usually was.

Sitting on my bed, I imagined running away for the first time. It became a fantasy that kept me grounded—the hope of escape. It sounded exotic, chic, and fun: the chance to make my own choices instead of living with adults who spent most of their waking hours drunk. I knew I'd likely have to live outside, which seemed tough in winter, but even the fear of freezing didn't stop me from dreaming of this life. Even at a young age, I sensed that living with Irene and Melvin wasn't sustainable. Oddly, many kids in the 1980s were running away. Missing children appeared on the news and on milk cartons. Running away brought fame, and even though childhood TV stars intrigued me, I didn't want my face on a missing-child poster in the post office.

Truthfully, I never had the guts to run away. Once, as a teenager, I jumped on my bike and "ran away." I pedaled as fast as I could until I was about three miles from home. That's when the crushing realization hit: I'd be sleeping behind a Kmart dumpster. I turned back in a quick, desperate return. But the idea kept me excited. In that moment, waiting to leave for the courthouse, I wished I had the nerve to slip down the back stairs, sprint out the front door, and escape into the warm summer air. I had no plan, no destination—except to start looking for my biological father, Frank. He hadn't wanted me when I was born, but I thought that if he understood the gravity of what Melvin did to me when Irene wasn't home, he'd protect me. I told myself Frank was bound to show up eventually.

"Joseph! I don't want to have to call you again," Irene yelled from the kitchen. I couldn't bring myself to get up and go to her.

There were a lot of moving parts to this adoption that had to be sorted out before our court date—namely, Frank. When Irene and Melvin decided to proceed with the adoption, Melvin's lawyer, Willie, informed them they had to place an ad in the Hartford Courant's classified section, searching for

Frank and asking him to step forward and either claim or disown me. He had thirty days to respond, and until that clock ran out, Melvin couldn't legally adopt me. My parents had to give Frank a chance to be involved in my life. I've watched a lot of soap operas in my time; it wasn't out of the realm of possibility that this man might knock on our door one day. The ad in the newspaper made me realize I was nothing more than a worn-out sofa placed in the want ads.

While we eagerly awaited those thirty days to end and our scheduled court appearance before the judge drew near, Irene asked me daily, "Do you want Melvin to be your real Dad?" Her eyes sparkled whenever she asked. I couldn't break her heart. She wanted this more than anything. Honestly, the last time I'd seen her this happy was when she thought Larry was going to marry her.

During dinner or randomly while we watched TV, she'd pressure me, unprovoked, "If you don't want him to be your real daddy, you just say the word, and we'll stop."

I don't know whether she was lying to herself or to me, perhaps both, because we knew the truth. Melvin would never allow these proceedings to stop. I was his winning lottery ticket, and he wasn't throwing that fortune away. The fucked-up part was that she'd ask me this right in front of him. I had no choice but to say yes, emphatically. There was no other option. I was being adopted whether I liked it or not.

I prayed that Frank might see the article in the paper. With each passing day, I'd come home from school and open our apartment door, hoping my bio dad was sitting at the kitchen table, waiting to take me away. My imagination ran wild. I'd envision Irene and Melvin standing in the kitchen, yelling at this stranger in a black suit, a crisp white shirt, and shiny shoes, in which I could see my reflection. I'd know who he was instantly, even though I'd only ever seen him as a vampire in a nightmare. I imagined reaching up to hug him; his mustache tickling the side of my face. His arms wrapping around me became an instant cure for all my suffering. My life instantly got better. Frank was there to take me away from the bullshit that plagued my life.

Sadly, Frank never answered the newspaper ad. He never responded. He never came to save me.

While I sat on my bed, daydreaming about Frank, Melvin caught me off guard. I jumped when he walked into my bedroom. He looked inscrutable, uncomfortable with the idea that I might be harboring thoughts without his input.

"What are you thinking about?"

"Nothing, Daddy."

He walked over and sat next to me on the bed. He mimicked, "Nothing, Daddy." Then he rested his hand on my back. "I hope you're not lying to me."

His touch felt like poison. A disease with no cure. I knew his fingerprints were all over me; if only I'd trusted anyone enough to let them dust me. There was never a time when his touch was welcome. Even when it was innocent, if that was even possible, his hands felt like a stranger was groping me. The kind of stranger Irene warned me about when I walked to school. Irene reminded me to stay away from creepy men and never to talk to strangers, but what was I to do when the creepy man was living in my apartment, making me call him Daddy, and sitting two inches from me on my bed?

And I was about to become his son.

"Are you happy?" Melvin asked, now rubbing my back in slow circles. I stiffened. He went on, "Why are you so tense?"

Even now, as I write this, I still can't believe he didn't understand that his touch was an intrusion. Did he not know, utterly consumed by his desire? Did he know and simply not care? Or did realizing that his touch made me want to burn my skin only intensify the game?

"Yes, I'm excited," I said, still staring at the wall. I wanted him to go away. To find a new wife. A new family. A new son. But that was more far-fetched than believing Frank might swoop in and carry me away. Melvin had become an unwanted tattoo, an imprint no laser, no matter how powerful, could remove. He hovered over me, always present. A shadow that followed my every move.

"That's not very convincing. You're hurting Daddy's feelings." We sat in silence. I could hear Irene putting away the clean dishes. When I didn't respond, he beamed. "I love you so much. After today, you'll belong to me. My son. This is a special day." He smiled, and it looked bogus. "Now, stand up so I can fix your tie."

I stood up mechanically and gazed out the window. Melvin leaned forward, shifting me into position between his knees, and began fiddling with my tie. My tie didn't need adjusting; he'd already helped me with it earlier. Controlling my movement was another excuse to touch me, to be close to me, to prevent any separation between us, to remind me that I was a marionette and he held my strings.

"You look so handsome." Then an awkward pause. "Kiss Daddy."

Melvin pulled me even closer, and when he leaned in to kiss me, I turned my head to the side so his lips landed on my left cheek. He stayed there, his wet lips slicking the side of my face. I felt his grip on my arms tighten. He pulled away and turned my face so I looked directly at him. The heat from his touch crawled through my body, an invading virus.

He cooed, "What is that? I want a real kiss," even as Irene was in the next room.

He held my head in place and gently kissed me on the lips. I zoned out. I wanted to scream, but he had my voice locked away. I didn't have the key. My silent prayer: Just let him kiss me, and maybe then he'd leave me alone for a few hours. None of this felt right, but it was reality. I quickly learned that, even though I hated these moments with Melvin, it was best to let them happen. At least my pants were on. He didn't move his lips. They lingered softly against mine. Then I was caught off guard. He tried prying my mouth open with his tongue. It slapped against my lips, reminding me of eating spaghetti. Sloppy. Messy. Trying to kiss me with his tongue was new for him; he had never attempted it before. I kept my lips shut as tightly as I could, an involuntary safety measure baked into my head: Don't open your mouth when your dad is trying to French kiss you.

Then Irene started down the hall. We both heard her high heels clicking on the linoleum. Closer and closer to my bedroom. I felt his intensity ease. I knew he'd have to stop; he was probably mad I hadn't opened my mouth, perhaps even madder at Irene for interrupting. I had won this battle. By the time Irene rounded the corner and stood in my doorway, Melvin had slid over and pushed me away.

Irene grinned. "Look at my two favorite guys. Are we ready to make this official?"

Melvin nodded at me, and I forced out the smile I had perfected.

My mother disappeared down the hallway. Melvin held my shoulders as he guided me down the hall behind her. She grabbed her purse, opened the front door, and started down the staircase. We followed closely. Melvin let me walk in front of him so he could slap my ass and give it a little squeeze. He did that often. I've seen sports players do it. I'd seen adults do this to each other, a signal of love or affection. Ownership. Perfectly all right for adults in a loving relationship or for footballers after a touchdown. Cringy for a father to do to his son.

As we drove to meet Willie at the courthouse, I sat in the backseat, holding onto a shred of hope that Frank was waiting for me in the parking lot. I knew he wasn't; the thirty days had passed, but believing he was there eased the rumbling in my stomach. I had mastered controlling my facial expressions, giving off the aura that I couldn't be happier. Still, my insides felt like firecrackers, one exploding after another, as if it were about to be a new year. Fireworks are usually a sign of celebration, but my stomach wasn't celebrating; it was internal-izing my stress until, in my forties, I'd be up at night with acid reflux.

Melvin sat behind the wheel. The radio was tuned to Country 92.5 FM, the only station my parents listened to. Tammy Wynette belted out her hit "Stand By Your Man," a song about sticking with your man no matter what he does. Great message, Tammy. Irene tried to sing backup, and an awkward sense of glee filled the car. Jesus Christ on the cross! Was I the only one who wanted to hurl myself out of the car and run and hide behind bushes? Her enthusiasm was palpable. Looking back, I'll give it to Irene; she always stood by her man. Through sickness. Health. Abuse. In the rearview mirror, I watched Melvin smile. He looked like the cat who ate the entire fucking nest of canaries.

When the song ended, Irene chirped, "Are you excited, Joseph? Can you believe you're going to have a father?"

"Yes. I believe it," I mumbled, keeping my eyes locked on the buildings we drove past. As I spoke, I knew it sounded unappreciative, with a bitchy undertone. I had trouble watching my mouth; the threat every child hears bounced off me. Watch your mouth, young man? Yeah, that was never an option for me. I was muted today, trying to process why Melvin had tried to make out with me before he adopted me, but on a typical day, I barely shut up. I talked a lot. And when I spoke, I was a smart ass. I was almost ten and had found a tool I used often: sarcasm. Sarcasm tasted better than a glass of cold milk and unlimited cookies. My number one offense was shit-talking under my breath. I'd get a slap across the face without warning. It always felt like a thousand ant bites, but the pain was worth it. If I were miserable, I wanted Irene to share some of it with me. And nothing made my mother more miserable than when I was being sarcastic. With Melvin, I showed respect, but Irene received the full brunt of my sardonic tongue. I thought talking back was my superpower. If I had no autonomy over my body, I'd own my voice.

But often, my mind raced through the many disasters that might be waiting around every corner. I did whatever I had to do to give my brain a rest. Even when Irene was around, and I was technically safe, my mind raced with thoughts of protecting myself.

One thing that helped was learning to quiet the negativity around me by playing mind games to distract myself from my internal monologue. I figured that if I couldn't make sense of anything, I'd ignore it. I had to quiet the noise. It grew even louder as my body became a vessel for a deplorable man. So, on the ride to the courthouse, I played my favorite car game. As we traveled down the street, my eyes followed the houses as they passed. I'd whisper the different facades to distract myself. Softly, I'd say, "Brick, green, stone, brown—"

"Joseph, stop. That's fucking annoying," Irene interrupted.

"Sorry." I had no idea she could hear me over Hank Williams Jr.'s music.

I didn't stop, though. I kept counting the houses and repeating the words in my head. It was a way to be defiant, exactly what I wanted. Defiant sons are unadoptable. Untouchable.

We parked in the garage beneath the probate court. The building looked like a jail, fitting the occasion. Irene opened my car door, and I knew the inevitable was upon me. Melvin told me to pick up the pace as I followed behind them. I tended to wander, so when they reached the top of the steps, and I was still meandering behind them, they were not smiling.

Irene walked ahead toward the waiting area. Melvin stood with the door propped open. As I approached, he leaned in and whispered, "Don't act up in there. Do you fucking understand?"

I understood. When Melvin molested me, if he thought I'd been a good boy, he'd only give me oral sex. If I had been a bad boy, I'd get a spanking, often authorized by Irene, and then he'd still give me oral sex. The sexual act itself was never negotiable. Of course, it was all for my own good. So I tried to stay on his good side to avoid the spanking. My goal was always to survive: make it through the day's family fiasco, deal with it, and be ready for the next twist.

The large metal door closed with a clang; I jumped. My skin tingled. My stomach wanted to let go; I was afraid to fart. Irene was at the check-in desk with the clerk. My breathing sped up, my body reacting as it had when Melvin knelt before me. I started swaying back and forth involuntarily. Sometimes I didn't realize I was moving until a teacher pointed it out or Melvin slapped me on the back with his open palm.

During the previous school year, in the third grade, my teacher, Miss Kerr, called a parent-teacher conference with Melvin, Irene, and the school counselor. Whenever I stood in class for more than a minute, I'd rock back and forth. I couldn't stand still. I had to make a conscious effort not to sway. If I was sitting, I was fine, but the moment I stood up, especially when I became anxious or uncomfortable, my body fell into a rhythmic pattern that calmed me. This is common among sexually abused children. We sway because it's self-soothing. Comforting. I didn't realize it at the time, but the movement helped me regulate my emotions.

Melvin hated it. It drove him up the wall that I had this tic—this imperfection. Whether he knew he was the cause, I'll never know. Do pederasts understand that they damage children? That their selfish acts stay with the victim well into adulthood? That the crimes against our bodies seep into most of our future relationships? Nevertheless, I believe they do.

"Are you a fucking retarded?"

One of his favorite insults. I looked up at him and said nothing.

"Stop fucking swaying!" he seethed. There was an empty bench next to us, so he pointed for me to sit. I followed his order, realizing I was slipping into bad-boy territory. But my feelings were hurt, and tears welled in my eyes. Irene approached us, but I focused on the freshly mopped floors. Melvin acted casually, as usual. The mood was somber; Irene felt it. I'm sure the clerk did, too.

"What happened?"

"Nothing," Melvin said as he put his hands in his pockets and looked down at me. Without looking up, I felt his gaze on me. I knew I had to pull myself together. I forced back the tears. I thought I was good, but a tear escaped and slid down my face.

"What did you say to him? This is supposed to be—"

"He was swaying back and forth, looking like a fucking idiot. I'm tired of it." Melvin barked at her, making it clear he thought she was beneath him. He pulled a pack of cigarettes from his pocket and headed for the front door. "I'll be outside having a cigarette. You stay here with the pussy and make him stop crying."

Irene looked stunned. She sat next to me, but I didn't look at her. I stared at the floor instead. She didn't say anything, though the tension radiating from me was impossible to miss.

The joyless vibe of the entire situation hung between us. Was Irene really that blind to my detachment?

"Why were you crying?" she asked, shifting her purse to the other hip and sliding closer to me.

I wiped my face. "Just leave me alone."

Irene didn't want to hear the truth. She didn't want to hear that I didn't want Melvin to be my father. I wanted my birth father, the one who didn't want me. The laundry list of negatives I had about Melvin was dismissed. I stopped confiding in her because whenever I shared something with her about Melvin's verbal or physical abuse, she'd go right back and tell him. It never felt like she was defending me; it felt like she was protecting her world. To me, Irene was often as untrustworthy as her husband was.

Before she could respond, loud footsteps drew our attention. We both looked up. It was Willie, walking toward the clerk. Then Melvin appeared at our side. Willie waved for us to follow.

The adults escorted me down a long corridor and into a small waiting room. The room's décor was bleak, like my future. We filled the four chairs, all of them uncomfortable, lumpier than Irene's mashed potatoes. Willie began to brief my parents on what to expect as we sat before the judge. Occasionally, he looked over at me and asked if I understood. I had no idea what he was talking about. I knew I was the "minor child" everyone discussed, the one without a father because "his whereabouts are unknown." That left me, the bastard child, open for adoption. But the rest of their conversation didn't interest me. I sat there, watching my life play out, unable to change the channel, the main character of this story yet just an afterthought.

The double doors to the judge's office opened. The four of us filed in, one after another. I shuffled between Irene and Melvin, a position that left me no chance to dash outside. A placard hung to the right of the doorway, the judge's name emblazoned in black ink: The Honorable Judge James H. Kinsella. To my child's eyes, the room was massive. Impressive. Judge Kinsella's office had a better decorator than the waiting room. I was surrounded by masculine tones and furnishings that brought the entire room together. It calmed me. I still wonder if that was the intent: to relax criminals before their sentencing. Dark mahogany wood and paintings hung strategically throughout the chamber. A large wooden table sat in the center of the room. Two empty high-backed chairs on one side and four leather chairs for us on the other. It felt serious. Too serious for a little kid. My parents wore feigned smiles. I tried to follow along.

Melvin sat me down between him and Irene. Willie sat at the end of the table, next to Melvin. I held my hands in my lap so no one could see they were trembling. A silence fell over the room as we waited for Judge Kinsella to enter. The clock ticked loudly. It read 10:15 am.

Irene grabbed my hand. "It'll be over soon."

My silly mother. I wanted to tell her that this was only the beginning. Again and again, when Melvin and I were alone, he reminded me that once I was legally his son, Irene could never take me away. She didn't have the confidence to leave him. He said it with pride, with conviction, as if adopting me voided any claim Irene had on me. Sadly, he wasn't wrong. Melvin made me believe he'd loom over me for the rest of my life, trapping me under his weight. He controlled my entire experience of the world. As a child, I thought this would last forever. I never considered that I'd eventually grow up, become an adult myself, one who didn't have to live with him. But at ten, I didn't think too far into the future. I had to live in the moment.

My attention returned to the proceedings as Judge Kinsella and a woman I assumed was his court secretary entered and took their seats across from us. The judge smiled at me; I returned the gesture. Maybe he wondered why it was so hard for me to form that smile. He didn't notice. The woman with him looked stern, and I instantly disliked her. She reminded me of what Sister Nun might look like without her religious habit. There was a brief pause as papers were shuffled and eyeglasses adjusted, then an instant eruption of debate. I zeroed in on the Muzak softly echoing from the ceiling speakers.

Then his touch. I was pulled back into the meeting when Melvin placed his hand on my thigh. A light squeeze, a reassurance that he'd take care of me now. The adults controlled the narrative about why Melvin should be allowed to adopt me. My biological father was absent. Irene and Melvin were married. He was practically my father already. They just needed to explain all this to the judge, sign a few pieces of paper, and we'd all live happily ever after. A question for Melvin here—Irene there. The back-and-forth at the table sounded like white noise, the machine-like hum I fell asleep to, the fan in my bedroom. I tried to keep up, but everything seemed to be happening around me.

I was too young to put this together then, but now I can see how sitting in that judge's office felt like being the main character in H.G. Wells' *The Time Machine*. The Time Traveller sits inside the cockpit of his homemade machine and zips into the future. While he sleeps, the clear globe he sits inside reveals the passage of time. Buildings rise and then are razed. Countless sunrises and sunsets, darkness turning to light on repeat. The action happens all around him; he's a mere bystander.

Sitting in Judge Kinsella's chambers, I felt like the Time Traveller, watching the world shift and change, yet unable to pull the brakes.

There were some laughs and jokes across the table. I sat fidgeting until Judge Kinsella finally acknowledged me: "This is a big day for you. I've seen many little boys like you adopted by loving, caring parents. You're a lucky boy." Then came the question I'd been dreading all day: "Do you want Melvin to be your father?"

I remembered Melvin's threat, and I nodded.

Judge Kinsella laughed. Nobody noticed my disengagement, my inability to show any happiness about being adopted. Incredible. I was slumped in my chair, weighed down by the same heavy sadness I'd felt, wondering if Irene had forgotten me in a New York City hospital. I wanted to answer honestly, to say, "No," but I was too afraid, afraid of the aftermath of that simple two-letter response.

With time running out, the judge's voice rose just slightly. "Can you say yes or no out loud?"

Melvin squeezed my leg. Irene looked over at me, concern spreading across her face.

"Yes," I said, forcing volume into my soft voice.

I spoke loudly to feel powerful, to give my fear a way to escape. I looked at my new father. He patted me on the leg. *That's my good boy.* The adults in the room read my loudness as enthusiasm. The cheering came swiftly and loudly, like when your team makes the basket. Willie congratulated Irene with a hug. Handshakes were passed around the table. I'm shocked there weren't cigars. Melvin leaned in and gave me a peck on the cheek. Irene wrapped her arms around me, tight enough to steal my breath. Someone patted me on the head. I think it was Judge Kinsella.

Paperwork was signed. Irene shed many tears. Before the signatures dried, my name was changed. I no longer bore the surname of Irene's ex-husband, a man I'd never met and who had no biological connection to me. All the talk about me being a bastard was in the past. Aunt Juliette could choke on a communion wafer. A father wanted to give me his last name. What more could I ask for?

Within weeks, I received my new birth certificate, which erased all records of Frank abandoning me. Frank was gone. Any chance of his coming to find me evaporated from my mind. From that day forward, my father was Melvin. Always and forever. Melvin's name replaced the "Unknown Father" on my original birth certificate.

I became the luckiest boy in Connecticut.

I climbed into the backseat. Irene rolled down her window and lit a cigarette. The halo of smoke curled from her lips, hit the rushing air, and was driven back into my face. I choked. How poetic. They didn't ask where I wanted to go. It didn't matter. My adoption celebration was Irene and Melvin's day; I was just occupying space. Anyway, I knew where we were going. It was our usual spot for good news— the very place where this entire shit show began.

The Silver Dollar.

PART 2

WAKEFIELD CIRCLE

Four months after my adoption papers were signed, we were moving into a new home.

The move didn't come out of nowhere. In the two years since the 1981 accident, our lives had been measured in paperwork, forms, signatures, and settlements. Weeks after I was discharged from Jacobi Hospital in the Bronx, Melvin's neck pain didn't let up. It got so bad that he couldn't work. He couldn't even get off the sofa. By the grace of God, though, he could still drink, so all was not lost. When alcohol and weed failed to dull the pain, he finally drove himself to the emergency room. That late-night visit revealed what no one had noticed at Jacobi: his neck was broken. Melvin sued the hospital and won. The settlement didn't fix everything, but it bought the next chapter: a new address and the illusion that we were starting over.

Melvin's neck injury and the resulting settlement gave my parents something they'd never had: a glimmer of hope. We lived hand to mouth. There was usually food on the table, but whatever money was left bled into the Silver Dollar or the corner package store. On Prospect Avenue, I remember Irene counting pennies, then sending me to the gas station on the corner, where a curmudgeonly older man sat behind stained plexiglass and sold me a pack of cigarettes for fifty-nine cents.

The settlement allowed my parents to move out of my grandparents' attic apartment, the only home I'd ever known.

By then, tensions between Pepé and Melvin had turned the house into a two-story war zone. Anything Melvin said got under Pepé's skin, and their fights didn't stay contained. Harsh words traveled easily between floors.

My grandparents never liked Melvin, but, like many Catholic families in the 1980s, they prized appearances over honesty. Even though Pepé despised my new father, he still vouched for Melvin, helping him secure the Mayflower job on that fateful trip with Konstas.

By the time the settlement check arrived, we were facing eviction. Mémé and Pepé couldn't bear the thought of throwing their daughter and grandson onto the street. It felt un-Christian. But then Mémé found Irene's cannabis plants on the back patio, and whatever shred of peace we had left finally collapsed.

Not long after that, in November 1983, just after I turned eleven, Melvin and Irene bought a two-story condo at the Berkley Condominiums on Wakefield Circle in East Hartford. They bought it from Willie, Melvin's lawyer. I was a kid, so I can only assume my parents got a deal.

The news hit like whiplash. I came home from school and walked into a party mood, with beers and cigarettes already in their hands, their faces lit up as if Irene had hit it big on a scratch-off ticket. They told me they'd bought a new place and that we were moving the following weekend. I didn't know what any of it meant, but their happiness was contagious. I bounced up and down the hall anyway.

I don't remember the exact date, only a flicker from our last moments on Prospect Avenue: Irene and Mémé on the back steps, holding each other as if they might never meet again. The women and the child cried; the men were happy not to see each other every day.

When I replay it, I wonder what Mémé was really grieving. Technically, she'd already lost Irene to drugs, alcohol, and Melvin. But having Irene upstairs, close enough to monitor and intervene, was its own kind of comfort. Now we were leaving her line of sight.

Worse, Melvin had the wheel. No guardrails, no safety net, just the world according to Melvin. Mémé knew it.

Wakefield Circle felt like a dream. At the end of Penny Drive, tucked into a quiet dead-end street, the late-'60s neighborhood exuded calm. No speeding cars. No dodging bikers on the walk to the school bus stop. None of that chaos here. Picture a street from *Stranger Things*, and that was Wakefield Circle.

The front doors did it for me first. Every unit had its own color, as if the neighborhood had decided to be cheerful on purpose. After school on Friday, bicycles lined up neatly in front of a red door. On Saturday, it was a yellow door. On Sunday, it was green. Beyond the condos, the lush Northeastern woods stretched out, offering adventures from sunrise to sunset. My favorite was building forts. Most of the kids in the neighborhood were young Gen Xers, eager to stir up trouble at any hour, rain or shine.

Wakefield Circle was a preteen utopia, a place where the world felt safe and boundless. People moved there to rebuild and start fresh. We fit the profile perfectly.

Moving gave us a sense of upward mobility. We owned something now. Renting was behind us. Melvin made sure we understood what it meant, too. "This is only the beginning," he said. "We've arrived." The three of us were stepping onto the staircase toward our perfect future. Because Irene and I didn't know any better and were grateful for Super Melvin, we wrapped ourselves in his story like a winter coat two sizes too big.

The excitement we felt upon entering our first home was like unwrapping a gift wrapped in sticky fish paper. Irene and I didn't fully grasp it yet, despite our history with Melvin. Still, the joy was authentic. I genuinely felt it—similar to the thrill of beginning a new relationship, the hope that this time everything will be better, that this time it will turn out differently.

My mother and I thought we were getting a happy ending. All the demons and monsters that lived in our past, under my bed, and inside Melvin's pants, seemed to evaporate in real time. And if a good relationship can rot, we convinced ourselves that a rotten one could heal.

But the best part was my new bedroom. On Prospect Avenue, I slept in a pass-through bedroom. On Wakefield Circle, I had a room with a door that closed, giving me privacy for the first time in my preteen life.

Then Melvin asked, "What color do you want for your bedroom?"

"Purple," I said, "with a white stripe through it."

By the end of the week, my bedroom walls were a vibrant mix of violet and plum, with a six-inch-wide white stripe circling the room. It was the most amazing bedroom a young gay boy could ask for, even if I didn't yet know what I was.

But in Melvin's world, even paint had a gender. Would he have painted it pink if I'd asked? Never. Like Irene, he was deeply homophobic. Like many straight men of his time, he believed homosexuals were an abomination, a threat to the moral code, and a danger to children. Irony has a funny way of showing itself. He compartmentalized what he was doing to a child and let that hatred point outward toward an imaginary villain. To him, that was acceptable. But the possibility that his son wanted a pink bedroom? That might have been the kind of "wrong" that earned bruises.

Purple was safe. Manly. He didn't mock me for it. I was obsessed with the color and grateful to him for the room. I went from childish wallpaper to a designer bedroom in a week. Boxes were stacked everywhere in the condo, but Melvin prioritized my comfort. I loved him for it, because I didn't know what else to do with a man who could be kind to me and still harm me.

Honestly, my parents deserved some good fortune, a hand to lift them out of the hellscape. Well, Irene did. But it was Melvin's broken neck that opened the door to something new for us. Both of them had struggled their entire lives, even when things weren't objectively bad. If Irene and Melvin could make a situation worse, they excelled at it. Much of their hardship was self-inflicted, yet they lacked the tools and understanding to escape it. When someone lives in constant turmoil, they stop noticing it. Irene and Melvin lived so comfortably in the turbulence they created that it felt normal, like the static hum of the TV you don't notice until it shuts off.

***

The Monday after we moved in, Irene enrolled me in Pitkin Elementary School. Overnight, I had a new school, a new bus stop, a new hallway full of strangers. The expectation was clear: make friends. The problem was, I didn't know how.

I had friends already, technically. My cousins Timmy and Tommy. Linda's son Alan and his stepbrother Will. But those friendships were preinstalled, inherited through family and bar stools. I didn't know how to approach a kid and become someone he wanted to pull into his circle.

To make friends, you need confidence, the sense that you belong wherever you land. I hid so much of myself that

191

I barely knew how to act around kids my age. Often, I walked with my head down, afraid they'd see the pain behind my eyes. And my laugh, high-pitched and screechy, didn't help. It was the kind of laugh that got you clocked in the arm.

Within days, I learned that making friends didn't come naturally. I didn't have the knack for it. I had a knack for being bullied. I wanted friends to play with outside, so I learned to avoid the bullies and attach myself to a small group, the kind of kids I would do anything to impress, anything to make them accept me.

I needed to be liked. Acceptance was the drug of choice for preteens.

Wakefield Circle had children from every corner of childhood. There was an eight-year-old posse that tried to start fires in the woods. There were the preteens in loud T-shirt patterns, slowly going deaf from blaring Def Leppard through their Walkmans. Then there were the mid-teens, disturbed beyond recognition, including Curtis, the kid who shoved pencils into a cat's anus while the other delinquents crowded around to watch her run in frantic circles, trying to escape what had been done to her. I saw it from a distance and ran home, crying.

The older crowd, late teens and early twenties, had already graduated but were still living at home, spending hours parked along the street in beater cars. They smoked skunk weed and groped their girlfriends while someone's mother drowned herself in Pinot and burned the pot roast.

All this played out around the circle while my parents stayed locked inside, fighting with the windows open and the liquor flowing. I didn't care which group took me in. The goal was acceptance. Thankfully, it was the Cyndi Lauper kids.

School was another battlefield.

At Pitkin, it was midyear. When the guidance counselor walked me into my new homeroom and welcomed me to the class, dozens of unfamiliar eyes looked up from their math books. I swayed back and forth. It was the first day of the rest of my schooling, and it could go either great or horribly wrong.

I should have known.

By the end of the day, I was called a fag more than my actual name.

Living in the suburbs might have offered my parents better opportunities and status, but from my eleven-year-old perspective, too many kids my age were hardcore bullies. In Hartford, bullies slammed you against a locker, tripped you in the hallway, made you nervous about being in the boys' bathroom with them, and then forgot all about you. Most of those assholes picked on kids in younger grades. Kids in the same grade defended each other. We protected our own.

At Pitkin, the tyrants sat next to you in class. They messed with you quietly, in plain sight, as if they could bend the room around you and make you feel crazy for reacting. They'd steal your pencil, hide your book, and slap you on the back of the neck, then look away. Spitballs were always aimed at your head. The intimidation cut your soul in two. It made you doubt your existence and question how you looked and sounded. Sometimes it felt like they wanted you to die.

Within the first week, I befriended two girls in my class, Gwen and Dory. We sat together at lunch, a *HUGE* deal for a sixth grader, and I let my guard down. I thought I was making them laugh with me, not at me.

One day, as I rushed into class before the final bell, I stopped short and tripped over my own feet. Dory was at the chalkboard, facing away from the room, drawing a massive whale outlined in chalk, with the letters J O E written underneath.

Yes, I had love handles, but that's common for a boy my age. What kid didn't shop in the Husky section at Bradlees? But that whale, taking up half the chalkboard, made something inside me implode, as if my new friend had harpooned me.

As she stepped back from the board, my classmates erupted in laughter. Kids bent over their desks, howling at my expense. What could I do? As everywhere else in my life, it felt like me versus them. I trudged to my seat, humiliated. Dejected.

Why didn't I erase the board? Why didn't I storm out of the classroom, drop out of elementary school, and join a cult? There's only one answer: I didn't have the courage. I didn't have the confidence. I didn't have whatever it took to make friends.

When our teacher walked in, she demanded that whoever did it come forward and erase the board. Nobody moved a muscle. They stared straight ahead at the chalkboard, at my abomination.

I refused to be a tattletale. I hoped that silence might earn me some respect. After a beat, our teacher grabbed the eraser, wiped away my embarrassment, and began the day's lesson. I fidgeted in my seat and glanced at Gwen, her head down, and at Dory, who looked triumphant. I felt like a gutted fish, gasping for air, as the teacher wrote right over the ghostly outline of the whale. I didn't know whether Gwen had been involved in my embarrassment, so I pointed all the blame at Dory.

Gwen lived just a few brick buildings away from me on Wakefield Circle. Dory lived miles away, so I saw her only in class, which suited me fine. Dory reminded me of a young Shelley Duvall in *The Shining,* only upside down. Instead of being terrorized by a psychopath, she was the one doing the terrorizing. She wielded words like an axe, hacking at the door of my confidence, trying to splinter me.

Without Dory in Gwen's ear, Gwen and I connected in the neighborhood. We even became friends, despite Gwen's friendship with Dory, the chalkboard artist. Gwen became one of my closest friends during that era.

Dory? Not a chance. She harassed me every day until she moved out of the school district.

***

After school and on weekends, no matter the temperature, I wanted to be outside. I roamed the circle and the woods beyond it until I found another kid trying to escape the inside of their house the way I was trying to escape mine.

I had a reason to be outside. A few weeks after we moved in, the initial joy that had vibrated through our condo faded. My parents' drinking returned to its previous level. Once the boxes were unpacked and the walls were painted, boredom drew them back to the bottle. The bottle brought back the same fights and discomfort we'd endured on Prospect Avenue.

And Melvin, after a short sabbatical, went back to abusing me. I believed things would be different when we started over. That's what Melvin said. He lied again. Irene got stir-crazy and started staying out late again at a new bar, even closer than the Silver Dollar.

The inside of our house became a loop of sameness, a lazy Susan of slaps, screams, and broken bottles on the counter. When I heard "D-I-V-O-R-C-E" by Tammy Wynette blasting on the turntable at any time of day, I knew emotions and blood-alcohol levels were high. Tammy became a bat signal, telling me to stay away. I'd be turning the corner toward our front door when I'd hear Tammy's voice seep through the cracks in the closed doors and windows, with Irene joining in:

"Me and little J-O-E will be going away." I'd then quickly turn around and linger outside until the street lights came on.

My heart breaks for Irene because she refused to believe she deserved better than crying into her beer and listening to Tammy Wynette, while making excuses for Melvin, who wielded all the power.

It still maddens me.

Relief came from living on Wakefield Circle. Yes, the tormentors were hard to avoid, but I learned to live with the name-calling and roughhousing. Being bullied by wild kids was easier than what I endured at home.

There were always kid-led activities happening somewhere along our street. The neighborhood felt like a childhood fair that never closed. Bikes. Dungeons & Dragons on patios. Games invented on the spot. Girls played with Barbies on the hill behind my building. God, I wanted to play with them.

Sometimes a few of us tagged along with Gwen, walking the circle until the streetlights flickered on, pushing her two-year-old sister in a stroller because Janice, their mom, was on her second box of Franzia and couldn't be trusted to care for a houseplant.

When I wasn't in the mood to hang around Gwen and her sister's stroller, I drifted toward the boombox group, especially Pete Armstrong, whom I quickly claimed as my best friend. I don't know whether the feeling was mutual. Pete and his older brother, Paul, lived across the street on Penny Drive, not on Wakefield Circle, but close enough to count.

We'd hang out under a weeping willow in front of my condo building, listening to Prince, Michael Jackson, or Madonna while we played kickball. I liked kickball. With kickball, I could use my legs. No bats to swing. No need to jump. Swinging a bat and jumping were boy talents that skipped me.

Although I had a few friends, I approached friendship all wrong. Instead of being honest and letting them see the kind, funny friend I could be, I thought I had to perform. So I lied. I fibbed constantly, and "fib" makes it sound harmless. It wasn't. Lies slipped out of me like water through a sieve.

And these weren't cute kid fabrications like "Hey, I once had five cats." Some were meant to charm, to get a laugh, to make me seem more interesting. I was giving people what I thought they wanted. But many of my tales weren't harmless. In today's world, you might call them "alternative facts." In any era, they were just lies.

Most of my stories were easy to debunk, but nobody had Google at their fingertips. Still, the biggest lie in my childhood vault is one that makes me hang my head in shame.

Did I want those neighborhood kids to like me that badly? Yes, I did.

One late afternoon, standing under the weeping willow with an audience, I launched into a dramatic monologue with no basis in truth, and I never thought to stop.

"The reason we moved here is that my grandmother died," I said. "She was flying to California to buy me a gift. She loved buying me presents because I was her favorite grandchild. The plane crashed. Nobody survived.

"Anyway, they sold her house, and my mom got a lot of money. That's why my mom doesn't work, and my dad barely gets up before lunch. They're retired. Yeah. It's cool."

A couple of kids fell quiet. Pete's eyes widened. I ate up the attention.

Exaggerating didn't seem that bad. Everyone stretched the truth, right? My parents did it all the time. I found lying fun, even though I sucked at it because I always went too far. I didn't know when to reel it in. I always yanked the line until it snapped.

"That's bullshit, Joe." Paul turned down the boombox's volume. "You wear hand-me-downs. You don't have money." He glared at me, almost amused. He refused to believe a word of it.

I started swaying. "Yes, it is. I double-swear it's true. The plane… it hit a mountain in Kansas or something."

Paul didn't miss a beat. "There are no mountains in Kansas. You're lying."

"I'm not." Panic flooded me. "She burned up in an airplane. I swear to God she's dead."

Paul smirked. "Come on, Pete," he said, grabbing the handle of his boombox. "Let's go ask Mom if Joe's grandmother died in a plane crash."

I knew the jig was up. Paul was going to check the story, figure out I was lying, and then call my mother. If Irene found out, I'd be trapped inside for weeks.

"No, don't ask your mom," I pleaded.

One by one, the group dispersed, but not before one of them came over and shoved me into the dirt. I remember thinking I deserved it. I sat there and watched them shuffle away, shame bubbling inside me.

I wanted them to like me, and I thought the road to popularity began by painting a picture of my life that was the exact opposite of the truth. I didn't want to be the kind of kid who felt he had to lie about his grandmother's death to be liked, but that's who I was becoming.

Lying wasn't my choice. It was my training. Melvin taught me that the truth was dangerous and handed me alibis to replace it. After we were alone, he'd rehearse them with me: "We were out fishing." "We were just cleaning out the storage unit." So when Irene asked, I didn't answer as myself; I answered as Melvin.

When your home runs on denial, telling fiction starts to feel like the only language anyone speaks. Irene's love felt performative. Melvin's protection was a forgery. My happiness was a circus act. In that world, being dishonest didn't seem immoral; it protected the truth. It was functional.

And if everyone around me was pretending, why couldn't I make my life seem more thrilling, more daring?

I lied to protect the truth when I should've told the truth to expose Melvin's fraud. After my tall tale about my grandmother, lying stopped feeling like protection and started feeling like poison. Sitting in the dirt, ashamed that I'd told people Mémé was dead, I realized how easily my words could destroy my credibility.

Masking the truth was good sometimes and bad at others. At eleven, with parents who'd wrecked any resemblance to honesty, it felt impossible to sort out. After Paul called me out, I started keeping my stories shorter and closer to the truth. I edited myself in the other direction, cutting out the dishonesty before it left my mouth.

Then, as if Heaven had been keeping an eye on me, at the end of 1984, Irene's best friend, Linda, sold her Hartford house and rented a condo in our neighborhood. She arrived with Alan and his stepbrother, Will. Something shifted. Alan knew my history. He could check my stories against the facts. More than that, he gave me a reason to stay honest.

A few weeks later, a moving van pulled onto Wakefield Circle, bringing Alan and Will. For me, it was another chance to start over. Another chance to get it right. Another chance to get it wrong.

New Kids On The Block

The day Linda's moving truck pulled into Wakefield Circle, the neighborhood became a teenage spectacle. New kids meant a sprint for information. Gossip ran laps around the circle, a cruel game of Telephone. By the time it reached anyone under fifteen, the original truth had been stripped, distorted, and reshaped into fiction, the kind I'd once been proud to call my own.

Before Alan and Will arrived, the rumors were that they were asylum-level crazy, so beware: Hartford maniacs who would trip you to the ground before introducing themselves.

All of it was bullshit.

Until about a week after they arrived, I realized one of them might actually be unhinged.

Linda rented a condo within a three-minute walk of my home. It felt surreal that my Hartford world had crash-landed on Wakefield Circle. I'd talked about my life in Hartford, tall tales stacked on top of one another, and suddenly having actual people from my past move into the circle gave me a false sense of popularity, as if I were about to become somebody.

In the weeks before they arrived, I started building buzz. I oversold them. If the local kids knew I had bad-ass friends, I'd earn the respect I wanted and thought I deserved. Whenever the older kids were in rare form, and I felt cornered by their words, I'd start praising Alan and Will.

"Wait until Alan and Will move here," I'd say. "They're so cool. They're my best friends."

"Joebosity. You're a fucking nerd. I'm sure all your friends are nerds," Paul howled, insulting me from the willow tree across the parking lot from my condo. Gwen and Pete listened as I squirmed. Bullies always attack for an audience. The shitty part was that, in private, Paul knew how to act like a human being. But when other people showed up, he pulled on his bully mask, and I stood there, swallowing his poison.

"Yeah," I said, raising my voice to a high pitch at Paul. "Just wait, Alan and Will are awesome."

I threw my head back to cackle, my mouth wide. A gnat hit my tonsils. My gag reflex fired before I could breathe or comprehend the moment, and I sprayed vomit across the grass. All in front of Gwen, Pete, Paul, and whoever else was camped out under the tree.

"Joebosity ate a bug!" Paul danced around. "Joebosity is like Mikey. He'll eat anything."

The universe rarely gave me a break in the 1980s.

Alan and Will were a force to be reckoned with the moment they stepped out of their condo and onto the sidewalk. In Hartford, they were free-spirited, carefree, and constantly balancing trouble. The boys lived to avoid Linda's parenting.

Don't cross the street for trick-or-treating. They crossed.

Don't curse. They cursed.

Don't stay up too late on a school night. They never went to bed.

I followed like a puppy seeking affection.

Like most of us in the '80s, they were blue-collar kids raised by a single mother and largely self-taught. I knew they were tough, but I'd adjusted to it. I was afraid of everything. They weren't scared of much.

On day one of moving to Wakefield Circle, Alan and Will were cautious, like someone starting a new job. Calculating. Careful. Sizing up the local competition. As I walked them around the circle, pointing out who lived where, they casually flexed their muscles, trying to intimidate anyone who crossed our path. I introduced them to whoever we bumped into as we wandered. A proud weirdo with his cool friends, a couple of new toys I wanted to show off to anyone who wanted to play with them.

As we approached my place, Alan noticed a few kids sitting in the willow tree.

"Who's that?" he asked.

I tried to ignore Paul and the other kids perched high in the limbs. Alan stayed curious and started toward them. Will followed. I hesitated. I had a feeling this wouldn't end well for me. Paul had warned me he wouldn't rest until he learned the truth about my grandmother.

Once I introduced everyone, Paul didn't mince words. "You've known Joebosity for a long time."

It was only their first day, and my nickname was already being delivered like a rotten welcome basket. Alan laughed at it, the sound sharp and unsettling. I swayed back and forth, my sneakers pulling me down. A cold sweat broke out across my forehead. Paul smirked, savoring his control.

Please don't bring it up, I pleaded silently.

Paul didn't hesitate. "He told us his grandmother died in a plane crash."

Alan looked at me and rolled his eyes. "That's not true. His grandmother lives in Hartford."

Paul glared at me in disgust. "I knew it. Joebosity. The fat liar."

I tried to keep things moving. After we stood there for a beat, I steered Alan and Will back toward my place, fighting the urge to hang my head. I tried to act like I didn't care; everyone lies sometimes. But I had promised myself Mémé was off-limits.

Alan and Will hung out for a while, giving Linda time to unpack her kitchen and get dinner together. I showed them my purple room, but they weren't impressed. When the sun began to dip, I walked them back to their condo. I couldn't risk them bumping into other kids without me there to filter the conversation. An unsettling feeling lingered that more of my storytelling might surface. I had preached false sermons so often that I'd lost track of the landmines I'd buried, and I dreaded the possible explosion that could follow.

Will trailed behind us in silence, watching.

Alan offered his solution. "You need major help, Joe. Now that I'm here, I'll be your therapist. You gotta stop lying."

Alan was only two years older than I was, but he might as well have been twenty.

I laughed it off. "I don't lie anymore. I don't need your help."

"Yes, you do," he protested. "But my shit ain't free. I'm charging you twenty-five cents an hour."

Then he grabbed me by the waist and flung me to the ground. I screamed like a girl. He jumped on me, playfully slapping my husky boy boobs. Will joined in. A heap of childhood fun, wrapped in an adult world of cruel words and judgment.

The truth was, despite Alan being fourteen and knowing very little about the world, I desperately needed his help. He'd been here for less than a day and was already considered cooler than me, even though I'd lived there for over a year. It's hard to convey how much bravado a fourteen-year-old boy can have, but trust me, Alan exuded it. He seemed impossibly cool. I, on the other hand, did not.

The storm hit a week or so later. It started with Curtis, the kid famous for shoving pencils up a stray cat's bunghole. I can't remember the spark. Back then, preteen violence ignited over mundane disagreements, like the wrong look or the clothes we wore. Hand-me-downs were an odd thing to fight over. In 1984, every kid with an older brother wore used school clothes.

Without warning, as a large group of us loitered on the sidewalk, Will launched into the air and collided with Curtis. In an instant, they both hit the ground, skin slapping skin. The vibration of Will's fist striking Curtis's jaw felt feral. Teeth gnashed. Pleas escaped Curtis as Will stayed relentless.

I planted myself next to Gwen. Fists and legs were melding together in front of us. We both watched with amazement. The chanting, "Fight! Fight! Fight!" echoed from the wall of kids hovering over two young bodies thrashing around.

The crowd was already taking sides: Alan and Will, who had started exciting scuffles that would be talked about for weeks, or Curtis, the established kid nobody really liked because he abused animals. Even though the clash captured the moment, we were all slightly surprised because nobody, and I mean nobody, messed with Curtis.

Will stood up and kicked Curtis in the stomach.

"Get up, piece of shit," Will ordered. "I can beat your ass all day."

Curtis folded in on himself on the ground, both hands clamped over his gut, blood seeping from his split bottom lip. He couldn't get air. When he didn't respond quickly enough to Will's threat, Will struck again. We all stared, watching in real time as whatever grip Curtis had on the neighborhood evaporated.

Instant karma for those defenseless cats.

Paul slithered over and parked himself beside Alan, picking a team as if he were choosing a lunch table.

"Damn," he said, grinning. "You guys are cool."

Alan smiled. He never got his hands dirty. He was too handsome to be punched in the face. I'd have called it a teenage travesty. He winked at me, like, *Relax, Joe. We're running this now.*

Then Alan sauntered up and tapped Will, not even a pull, more like a remote-control pause button. Not because he felt bad, but because Curtis's bruises were drifting into the *Run-somebody's-mom-is-coming* territory.

Honestly, Curtis never had a chance.

Alan turned to the crowd, all those kids staring as if they wanted seconds. "My brother is unstoppable," he warned. "He's like the Terminator."

Will grunted, eyes still on Curtis. Alan laughed. Gwen smacked my arm.

I figured my life was over.

Alan and Will knew exactly what they were doing. They were quiet for the first week, considering friendships and feuds, observing the hierarchy, and taking inventory. Alan did, anyway. Will cared only about violence.

Will knelt beside Curtis, as if deciding whether to hit him again, then stood. The crowd's enthusiasm curdled into mania, swept up in boy-brain bluster. Alan patted Will on the back. Paul giggled maliciously. He'd been waiting for someone else's pain to serve as entertainment on Wakefield Circle. Alan and Will were gifts Paul never asked for, but he took them anyway.

How the hell was Paul already chummy with my friends? I didn't like it at all.

I stood on the sidewalk, watching it unfold, thinking, *What have I done?* I assumed every kid in the neighborhood would hate Will. And my stupid plan to become popular was shrinking with each blow he landed on Curtis's face. Will fought like a prisoner whose cigarettes had been stolen. The violence played out like a routine, something rehearsed on the bus on the way home from school. Alan was the brains. Will was the brawn.

When Curtis tried to sit up, Will coiled, ready to pounce. "Whoa, man. Cool down." Alan grabbed Will by the shoulders. "You see, when Will gets mad, I'm the only one who can calm him."

Will stood there, breathing easily now, positioned beside Alan like a loyal animal on a short leash.

Bruised and cursing under his breath, Curtis limped home, a few kids clustered around him. I swear one or two of his friends hesitated, as if reconsidering which camp was safer. As Curtis shuffled away, the Wakefield Circle's ranking system recalibrated. Money, nice clothes, and brawn rose to the top. Girls, on top. Skinny, pretty kids stayed protected in an invisible bubble.

Me? I lived in the social mud. I was the Husky-sized kid in used clothes, with drunk parents and a head full of confusion. I thought I was cute and fun. The rest of the kids had reached a silent, unanimous agreement.

I was neither.

That's why Will's violence felt like a grenade. It didn't just beat Curtis. It shook the order I'd been losing my whole life.

As the crowd began to disperse, Gwen leaned in and said, "Alan is totally hot."

I smiled and shoved my hands into my pockets. "I guess."

Somewhere beneath my denial, I knew exactly how hot Alan was. I just hadn't named it yet.

"His brother is scary, though," Gwen said as we reached the parking lot outside her building. "What's wrong with him?"

"I don't know," I said, kicking at the grass. "I've never seen him act like that before."

Gwen lowered her voice. "Curtis is gonna want revenge."

She was right. A come-to-blows like that never ended. It was only postponed. Not surprisingly, Curtis challenged Will a few more times. That was great news for Will. Wakefield Circle gave him plenty of chances to defend himself, and he almost always won. Then one day, Curtis and his goons moved on to new victims and stopped caring about cats, Will, or me.

Gwen turned toward her front door. "Yeah, Will makes me nervous. I'm glad he doesn't go to our school."

I left her and headed home. I cut between a few buildings and ended up standing in front of where the brawl had taken place. I told myself there was nothing to fear about Will.

I crushed on Will, hard, violent streak and all.

STORAGE UNIT #9

"You don't belong to me," Irene sang from her kitchen chair. "You were Lana's kid. She didn't want you, so I took you."

The woman I called Mom said it like it was funny. Like it was nothing. Whenever she said those words, my face went hot, and my love for her whittled down to a painful sliver. I didn't understand why she looked so happy to watch me break.

Lana was Irene's cousin near Washington, D.C. I'd met her when I was little. I don't know whether I really remember this or whether Irene told it so many times it became mine, but I see it anyway: I'm a toddler in Lana's house, spilling nail polish onto her coffee table. It bleached the wood and ruined it.

After that, they stated Lana no longer liked children. I wasn't sure if they were joking or blaming me.

Irene told me for years that Lana was my birth mother. She said it like a threat, like a fact I was supposed to swallow dry. I'd start crying, and she'd look disgusted. The next morning, she'd offer a careless apology, trying to erase the damage her unloving words had done to me.

In the first few instances, I believed she was sorry. But she kept repeating the hurt, one drunken night after another, until I saw the truth: her "sorry" wasn't sincere. It was permission to do it again. She never took the words back. She just hoped her choreographed mockery would smooth me over until next time.

I'd retreat to my room and cry into my pillow, asking myself the same question until it felt like a bruise: *What if*

Irene's right? My biological father refused to claim me. And if Irene was telling the truth, neither did the woman who gave birth to me.

What kind of mother says that to her child? Irene knew what it felt like to be hurt. So why did she do it to me? I wanted kindness from her. I wanted warmth. Instead, I got obligation: food on the table, a roof, and words that went for the softest part of me, again and again. She never touched me sexually, but she knew exactly where to strike.

Stop screaming like a girl. What's wrong with you? You're not my kid.

Her words bounced off the walls and lingered in my ears long after I went to bed.

During Irene's drunken benders, she often reminded me that I was lucky she hadn't aborted me, as my biological father had wanted. She hinted that Frank might have stuck around if she had. Hearing that made me feel unloved. I was a kid being abused by my adoptive father, flinching through Irene's insults and coldness. Some nights, it felt like the possibility of never being born was a mercy. I'm glad I'm alive now, but back then, I didn't know any other life to compare it to.

Melvin hurt my body in ways I learned to survive. Irene's words made me feel I didn't deserve to exist at all. I expected more from my mother, but disappointment was just another room in our condo, a room with no doors or windows, where they could always find me.

***

As expected, Melvin planned his attacks with precision. He cornered me away from Irene, preparing me for what was about to happen. It never failed. I could be doing homework or listening to "Like a Virgin" on my Walkman. None of it mattered to him. When he wanted me, there was no dodging him. The adoption decree paperwork was readily available, and he was prepared to show it if necessary. The grip he had on me was genuine—Melvin truly owned me.

My father's delivery was innocent enough, but the message beneath it dripped with menace. He'd pop his head into my bedroom. "Hey, I need you to help me in the storage unit."

"I was just about to ride my bike over to Alan's," I'd reply, making up a story to suggest I had a life outside of him.

"What did I just say?" he whispered. "Come downstairs when I call you. Don't say anything else."

Once my name echoed up the stairs, dread set in. I moved at a glacial pace anyway, because slowness was the only control I had. With Melvin, I used time to my advantage, just enough to avoid any unwarranted punishment.

People may say I shouldn't have cared about punishment at that point. But abuse rewires you, all of it. Sexual abuse doesn't just happen to your body. The abuser spends years training your brain until the impossible feels normal, until you start to believe: this is life, and this is what you do when Melvin summons you. Even when I hated what was happening to me, I didn't see a way out. I was trapped in that room of disappointment, the dark room where you think you know where the exit is, but every wall leads nowhere.

So I kept two lives. In one, I laughed with my friends, dodged bullies, and disappeared into my Walkman, pretending I was a regular kid. In the other, I did what I had to do to survive. The goal wasn't freedom. It was getting through this one. And the next one. And the one after that, until I could finally leave for good. I didn't know if I'd ever get away. Some part of me believed I never would. Another part kept getting ready anyway.

I think about the times I reached the landing and found Melvin holding the screen door open. I always went outside first. I stepped past him into the daylight, my eyes fixed on the doormat, refusing to let them meet Irene's. Melvin never let Irene's being home deter him from our ritual. He used the storage unit next door, his secret room, a room with unfinished walls, and stale air that mingled and circulated with my trauma.

I spent years trying to speak to Irene through my eyes. Words were dangerous. I kept hoping our blood connection would be enough for her to see my struggle, to sense that her child was being assaulted. I wanted her to feel my pain through telepathy. But if Irene didn't recognize the psychological trauma I carried from living with Melvin, she would never acknowledge it.

Maybe I gave her too much credit. Or maybe she moved through her life with cataracts she refused to treat. Either way, Irene didn't want to know. Throughout her marriage, she never removed the blinders, the same ones she kept by her bedside, ready to pull on whenever her choices were challenged. I imagine myself in Irene's shoes. There goes her wonderful husband, taking her young son to help reorganize their storage unit. Again. How did she not question that this was the third time in a month? How did she not question that we never had spare money to buy new items we needed to organize?

The storage facility was ten steps to the left of our front door. Each building had storage units for residents. On the first floor, the laundry room held two washers, two dryers, and a long folding table along the back wall. The door was red, a color that signaled danger. As we entered, the loud hum of the dryer filled the space, a noise Melvin found useful because it muted everything. The washing machines were to the left, and stairs to the right led to the storage bins. Robotic and emotionless, we marched up the stairs, me in front of him, a prisoner being escorted for my weekly discipline.

"Sit there, like you usually do." Melvin pointed to two stacked milk crates propped against the wall beside the staircase. From this spot, he could lean over the half-wall and watch for anyone walking up the stairs.

I protested, "Dad, I don't want to do this right now." I had recently turned thirteen and was thinking more clearly about his idea of father-son time, wondering when it would end. I asked a few times if we could stop. Melvin never allowed it. He acted as if he couldn't understand why I'd want to stop. He accused me of not loving him, and I apologized for hurting his feelings.

Our storage unit was number nine. Melvin sauntered to the chicken-wire door, unlocked the padlock with a key from his keychain, and after digging through a box, pulled out a stack of pornographic magazines he'd hidden for occasions like these, his way of turning me on. Always prepared. Always playing the role of a deceptive guide. All for an act that stole my soul and, you'd think, must have shredded his too. Or maybe not. Maybe the only thing a monster feels is the pull of his own desire.

"Do you want to spend the night at Alan's tonight?"

"Can I?"

"Yes, but we have to do this first," he said, already turning toward the crates. "You know how much it means to me."

"I know, Dad. I'm sorry."

He thumbed through the magazines. "You like this one, don't you?" He held up the cover of a porn magazine featuring a blonde woman, her breasts spilling across the glossy front. My throat tightened, but I learned to control my fear. Melvin didn't appreciate trepidation. He wanted me to be enthusiastic, happy that he'd chosen me. And his threat to find one of my friends to do this with him pulsed in my amygdala, the part of me that never stopped sounding the alarm.

I nodded. Truthfully, I didn't care about the magazine. I went along with it to please Melvin, to stay on his good side. I mastered going numb, separating my mind from my body. I only had to survive the next fifteen minutes and then go to Alan's for the night. That was the payment for receiving head from my father: a night when I could be a kid with my friends.

He told me to pull my pants down. I capitulated. Even though I knew what he wanted, I waited for him to direct me, letting him control the scene. Melvin's power. He handed me the magazine, and something deep within me went quiet. My brain played tricks to ease the burden: I was in the dark room again, unable to find the exit. He trapped me in here. My bedroom wasn't a prison; the darkness that consumed me when he got me alone was my prison, a purgatory of waiting for his unwanted touch. There was no escape, so I focused on getting through it once I was inside his world.

He knelt and placed his hands on my legs. "You like this, right?"

"Yes," I said, flipping through the magazine, refusing to meet his gaze. I had to tell him I liked it. Honestly, I hated it, but I had no choice. I didn't think I could ever stop him. When I tried to say no, he broke me with words that still affect me. The thought of fighting him off fizzled out as quickly as it had entered. Once he started the assault, I switched to autopilot.

"Good. So do I." He caressed me. "I love you."

I was still too young to ejaculate, so I played a game. Melvin had no idea I could manipulate him, too. This rebellious act gave me power I alone held. When we were in the act, I'd tell Melvin when I had "the feeling," and then he'd finish himself off, ending the session.

I used the idea of ejaculation to my advantage. I'd start to squirm: "Dad. I feel it. Stop. It's sensitive." I had to be careful with my con. I had to be equally calculating, and I'd succeeded in my deceit a few times before he picked up on my betrayal.

Melvin took my resistance as an affront to his advances. Once he realized what I was doing, he'd punish me for something unrelated, after he'd settled into his monologue about how this secret was the glue that held our family together. Melvin caught on to my trick quickly, and after a few harsh words and threats, I learned I had to endure his abuse for a set amount of time. After many years of this, I knew the perfect amount of time to let him have his way with me: fifteen minutes. Only then would I act like I had "the feeling" authentically. Then I knew I was safe until next time. He never stopped until I said my stomach tingled.

While he did his unholy deed, I stared at the naked ladies on the page and counted the minutes in my head until I'd shake my body and pull away, acting like I couldn't handle another touch. I drifted in and out of the moment, caught between two worlds: the one outside, where even the bullies felt safer, and the one inside Melvin's domain.

Then, a slight shift in the air. The laundry door opened, and the dryer's hum faded. Melvin didn't notice, or even hear the tap of shoes on the concrete stairs: someone was coming.

My stomach dropped, and my body prickled with nerves. We weren't alone. I knew it before Melvin did. He stood first, yanking up his jeans. As he moved aside, I lunged up. The porn magazine dropped to the floor. I fastened the button on my shorts. We didn't know who our intruder was, but we found out when the person reached the top step: her long brown hair came into view.

Irene.

She stood there for a moment. Melvin and I stared at each other. We weren't naked, and no genitals were visible, but the air was thick with accusation. Irene had finally walked in on something undeniable. Melvin knew it. She knew it. I knew it. The secret was out. The glue Melvin talked about, the stuff holding our family together, had been blasted with a heat gun. I had no idea what was about to happen. I was scared to be found out, yet relieved that the charade was over. It seemed inevitable that this would be Melvin's last night as my father.

My naive young mind believed the universe was about to implode.

He began to ramble. "Alright. Now we need to move these crates back into the storage unit." I shot him a glance, then looked at Irene. The thought in my mind at that moment was precise: *You're caught, Melvin. The jig is up. You're finished.*

Outwardly, I was calm, waiting for Irene to attack him. Would she kill him? There were countless blunt objects within reach that a mother might use to bash in her husband's brains, her savior, who had practically been caught with his pants down.

I had no idea. Inside, my heart rejoiced. It was over. I was about to be freed. Irene had working eyes, so she saw what was happening. I felt a surge of excitement: the truth was out; she would finally save me. She hadn't believed me when I was five, but she couldn't deny what she'd just walked in on. Melvin could ramble all he wanted, but there we were, standing in a position that wasn't about reorganizing a storage unit. Just three feet away was my mother, the woman I'd been desperately hoping would wake up from whatever trance Melvin held over her.

"Dinner will be ready in a few minutes," Irene said, met my gaze, then turned to walk down the stairs. Her slippers slapped against her heels as she descended. At that moment, I wished to God she'd fall down the stairs and break her neck. I hated her as much as the bullies at school, even more. At thirteen, I wished for nothing but an agonizing death for all of them.

All of this happened in seconds. Where was the screaming? Where was the outrage? Where were her arms, wrapped around me, apologizing for bringing this man into our lives? Nothing. She walked in on her husband and son in a compromising position, with a pornographic magazine clearly visible on the floor between them. She refused to face reality. Irene did what she always did: put on her blinders and embrace Anheuser-Busch and denial.

Irene completely failed me.

Melvin and I remained frozen until the laundry room door closed with a click. After a brief silence, he grabbed the porn and headed to the storage unit. "You can leave. We're finished."

I made my way toward the stairs. He stopped me. "You're happy about this, right?"

Why couldn't he just leave me alone? I remained silent, fearing that defending myself might anger him.

He threw the magazine into the cardboard box with the others, laid greasy, stained towels over them, covered the box, and kicked it to the far end of the storage bin. He closed the chicken-wire door and secured the padlock.

"Get out of here." He refused to look at me. "Go. You're a fucking wimp."

"What did I do, Dad?"

Ignoring my question, he delivered one last, harsh blow: "You can't spend the night at Alan's tonight. I've changed my mind."

Since Irene had thwarted Melvin's good time, he retaliated by taking away my night at Alan's. In Melvin's world, pettiness and pedophilia went hand in hand. Without a fight, I turned and descended the stairs, then stepped outside and walked past our front door. After wandering Wakefield Circle until dinnertime, I returned home to find my parents seated at the dinner table.

I'd never be free of this childhood.

A few months later, the maintenance department installed a locked door in the laundry room that led directly to the storage bins. Now, if someone were being sexually assaulted upstairs, there'd be plenty of time to compose themselves, adjust their clothing, hide their porn magazines, and pretend to clean an organized storage bin.

Convenient, and too obvious.

Nipples

After the new year in 1985, when I was twelve, I took my first job as a paperboy for the *Journal Inquirer*, an afternoon paper based in Manchester. After school, I'd grab a quick snack and wait for the pickup truck to drop off three bundles of newspapers tied with string, bundles I always struggled to untie. In the warmer months, the job felt like an adventure. I'd sling the cloth bag over my shoulder, stroll the neighborhood, and tuck each paper neatly between the screen and the brightly painted wood of every door. Winter, though, turned the route into a treacherous trek through snow and ice, each step a gamble against a broken leg.

Even though I fought not to injure myself in piled-up snowbanks, those afternoons brought a serenity. I clipped my Walkman to my hip and bopped to "Karma Chameleon" by Culture Club, the crisp wind in my face, the small independence of earning my way. Those were memories I carried long after my childhood ended. Still, having my own money made every challenge worth it. Most of my tips went straight to movie tickets, to hours spent escaping into other worlds where laughter and adventure balanced the darkness waiting at home.

While I delivered the afternoon paper to Wakefield Circle, Alan delivered *The Hartford Courant*—the oldest newspaper in the United States—in the mornings before school. I could barely wake up and get to school, so an afternoon route suited me. Alan didn't seem fazed by a 5 a.m. alarm. The rules were strict: the Courant had to be delivered to doormats before subscribers left for work. Between Alan and I, it felt like we had a monopoly on whatever media income we could squeeze from neighbors eager for the daily news.

Alan's parents had been divorced for years before our mothers met at the Silver Dollar. Every other weekend, Alan's father pulled up in front of Linda's condo, his new wife and stepkids in tow, and whisked Alan away on a family adventure. My envy flared whenever he said, "My dad is coming to get me this weekend." I dreamed of a father coming to kidnap me from Melvin and Irene.

What stung even more was that Alan expected me to collect payments from subscribers and deliver his Saturday and Sunday papers while he spent the weekend at Riverside Park in Agawam, Massachusetts. The *Journal Inquirer* didn't publish a Sunday paper, which made Sunday my day off, so lugging Alan's stack on my young frame filled me with dread. On Sundays when I helped him, I'd make multiple trips back home to finish the route. A few times, I didn't finish until well past dinner, dragging the sack down the sidewalk and promising myself I'd never do this for Alan again.

By the time I was done, the front of our condo was littered with Stop & Shop flyers and Medi Mart Pharmacy ads. The wind swept them into the bushes, leaving the maintenance man to deal with them later. Most people never saw the ads. I didn't care.

"Come on, Alan. I don't want to."

"Joe. Don't be a dick. I can't trust Will to collect the money."

That made sense. Will was a loose cannon, and trusting him with cash or any responsibility could have gotten Alan replaced by a kid who wasn't whisked away on weekend adventures with his father.

My attitude changed when Alan offered to split his tips with me. More tips meant more movies. I had recently seen *Beverly Hills Cop* and needed the money to see it at least five more times. Most kids in the neighborhood smoked, drank, and made out in the woods to escape the damage their parents caused. I went to the Charter Oak Cinema and got lost in the storytelling on the big screen.

"Alright, but I don't want to collect from Nipples." The hairs on my arms tingled. "He freaks me out."

Alan sipped his Cherry Coke. "He's harmless, just a creepy fag. You'll be fine." He leaned in. "I'll take you with me next time I collect payments." He paused. "Just don't go into his house." He batted his eyes. "Seriously. You'll be sorry."

That scared the shit out of me. "Nipples" was the nickname the kids gave the gay man who lived in the neighborhood. As a teenager, he made me feel uneasy in a way I couldn't explain. I didn't even like seeing him. I was convinced he'd turn me gayer by driving past me on Penny Drive in his red Mazda Miata. And the way he sneered at me made it feel mutual.

Maybe he saw himself in me, in my gestures, my voice, the way I moved. Even though I didn't understand I was gay, I'm sure he knew the moment he saw me running and screaming down the street.

In truth, my jealousy deepened. I believed Nipples was obsessed with Alan. Alan was mine, just like kids assert ownership over their friends. Teens can be so complicated.

Confusion fogged my feelings for Alan. Part of me wanted to be him: the way he looked, the girls drooling over him, the guys admiring his masculinity, that Italian swagger that made people step out of his way. There was even a rumor, the kind girls whispered whenever he walked by, that he had a huge penis. How did they even know? I hated them for it. I'd never met a fifteen-year-old who carried himself so much like an adult. His confidence made me crave his attention. Even now, I can't tell whether I was in love with my straight best friend or just wanted to step into his skin and become him. Maybe it was both.

On the few occasions I walked with Alan as he collected payments and tips, Nipples answered the door with a smile wider than his nickname. And the nickname fit. Later in life, after enough time in leather bars, I understood why his nipples looked as if they'd been left out in twenty-degree weather overnight. Two pink flesh bullets jutted from his barrel-shaped chest, impossible to ignore. No piercings, just gravity pulling them farther and farther from his body.

I sometimes wondered if his nipples had minds of their own. They entered the room before the rest of his torso. No matter the season, after Alan rang the doorbell, Nipples answered shirtless.

Nipples tipped Alan well. Alan stood in the doorway, flashing that mesmerizing smile, and Nipples melted under it, pliable as Play-Doh in a sculptor's hands. He kept pressing bills into Alan's hand while uglier kids got coins, and he laid on the compliments adults had warned me about, the kind you expect from a greasy guy in a windowless van:

"Thank you, Alan. Oh, the paper was earlier than ever before, Alan. Want to come in for lemonade sometime, Alan?"

Alan knew his bread was buttered by his looks, and he smiled even brighter. "Sorry, but I'm allergic to lemons."

He wasn't. He liked saying things that sounded official. Then, as we headed to the next condo, he pocketed the bills.

"See, Joe? He's harmless. He's like the girls in the neighborhood. He just wants my sausage."

I shuddered. "You're disgusting."

"Just remember," Alan said, smirking. "Don't go inside, no matter how much you want his lemonade."

The first time I collected payment for Alan, my Nipples experience was the polar opposite. He opened the door expecting Alan, and his Cheshire grin collapsed into a scowl.

"Oh. It's you."

I smiled. "Good afternoon. I'm collecting for Alan this week."

No smile. No kindness. No invitation for lemonade.

"You missed my paper last Sunday," he growled, handing me the exact change. "Make sure I get it next time."

Stupefied. "That was Alan, sir. I didn't deliver last Sunday. I'm just collecting—"

He closed the door halfway, then decided to address me one last time. "Just make sure I get my paper. And tell Alan I like it better when he collects."

When Alan's dad dropped him off Sunday night, we met outside his condo building. I handed him his money.

"Nipples is an asshole. He was so rude and blamed me for not delivering last Sunday's paper."

"He's fucking with you, Joe. Nips doesn't like you." Alan cocked his head. "Did he tip you?"

My face flushed.

"No. He gave me exact change. I don't know what his problem is."

Alan grabbed his basket through his gray sweatpants. "You just don't have this, Joe. That's the problem."

Nipples made me nervous because the fear wasn't just about being gay. It was about being visible, about being known.

If the neighborhood kids already thought I was gay, was I destined to become a spectacle, a freak like Nipples? The thought was terrifying. I was an odd, girly boy, yes, but I didn't want to be him. I didn't want my shame to be apparent, or to wonder whether my own nipples would grow hard enough to poke out a paperboy's eye. The idea of being "like that," so fully exposed and outside the boundaries of acceptability, was my deepest fear.

Even now, despite understanding its complexity, I feel ashamed of my adolescent repulsion. I still think Nipples was too friendly with Alan. But that childhood shame, shaped by my fears and Alan's last crotch comparison, was straightforward: I desperately did not want to be gay. And I especially did not want pulsating nipples.

He Works Hard for the Money

A week after I finished seventh grade, Alan knocked on our door one Sunday afternoon. It was the start of the Summer of '85, a few months before I'd start my last year at East Hartford Middle School. Irene yelled upstairs for me, and when I bounded down the stairs, I opened the door to find him standing there, covered in dirt from head to toe, exhausted yet flashing his charming smile and dazzling me with his crystal-blue eyes.

"Do you want a summer job?" he offered casually.

We had both quit delivering newspapers, and Alan had taken a job at Futtner's Farm, a farm that stretched from Silver Lane to Penny Drive's dead end and abutted the property line of Paul and Pete's house. Today, there is no trace of the farm. The memories of male teenagers on their knees, picking peppers and pulling up carrot tops, are long gone, replaced by a large housing development with concrete sidewalks—new families with the same hopes and dreams that brought us to East Hartford.

"What? A job?" I frowned, then stepped outside and closed the screen. "I don't want a job. I'm enjoying the summer."

"Don't be a pussy, Joe. Working on the farm will do you some good." I stared at his white T-shirt, flung over his tanned shoulder. "The owner is looking for extra hands."

Alan confessed that the workday was long and exhausting. He said reading *Wuthering Heights* in high school English was easier. I didn't believe that yet. But he made more money working on the farm than he did delivering the paper to low-tipping neighbors.

I shook my head. "I don't think so. That doesn't sound like fun."

"Joe," he said, wiping his gross, dirt-encrusted fingers across his face. His fingernails looked like he had washed his hands in oil. "I think you should do it. What else are you gonna do? Be a couch potato and listen to Whitney Houston all summer?"

That was *exactly* what I had planned to do.

Then he picked his nose and tried to rub it on me. "People already think you're a faggot. This might show them you're not." A long pause hung in the warm air. "Unless you are?"

"I'm not like Nipples."

He grinned and gently kicked my leg. "Prove it."

The window to the kitchen was open, and Irene stood there, eavesdropping like a vigilante. "Do it, Joe. I don't want you hanging around the fucking house all summer."

Irene had picked up on my feminine side, evident in my music choices and in how I'd screech whenever I became overwhelmed with excitement, which, at twelve, happened hourly. Irene feared having a gay son, so she took every opportunity to nudge me toward manhood.

I yelled through the screen door. "Stop listening. Rude." I looked at Alan. His pearly whites stood out against the mud caked on his chin. I caved. "Sure, I'll do it. When do I start?"

He walked away, speaking over his shoulder. "I'll knock on your door at four thirty. Be ready."

"In the morning?" I stammered. "I-I-I'm not getting up that early. Are you crazy?"

Ignoring me, he continued with his list of demands: "And wear boots. Pack a lunch. Bring a hat. It's gonna be hot tomorrow."

I hated everything about this.

The next morning, the microwave clock read 4:30 a.m. when I heard a light tap at the front door. I slurped the last of the milk from my cereal, set the bowl and spoon in the sink, and turned off the light. Irene had prepared my lunch the night before—a favorite: peanut butter and grape jelly sandwich. I grabbed the small cooler from the table and stumbled to the front door, my eyelids crusty with sleep.

Alan was all business. "Come on, let's go," he ordered. "We're gonna be late."

He turned and headed down the sidewalk toward the path leading to the farm. The street lights only covered us until we stepped off the pavement of Penny Drive and onto the cultivated farmland. I caught up fast, nervous about walking even ten feet behind Alan, swallowed by the darkness in the fields' absence of light.

As I tripped over mounds of dirt, Alan peppered me with the ins and outs of how the day might play out on the farm. "Listen carefully," he said. "We'll wait at the farmstand with the other guys until Jim arrives. Don't scream. Don't laugh. Don't fucking cry. I'll beat you up myself. Anyway, Jim's the owner. Then we'll be divided into two groups. I don't know which group you'll be in, so just go along with it. You'll climb into the back of one of the trucks. I'll sit up front. It's gonna be rusty, so don't scratch yourself. You could die."

I scrambled to keep up and had already forgotten most of what he'd said. Alan moved fast; he dashed through the darkness with catlike precision.

Sweat had already pooled under my neck. "Why are we walking in the dark?" I asked. "Can't we start this after the sun comes up? I don't think I can—"

Ten feet ahead of me, he berated, "Stop fucking whining. No wonder Paul calls you Joebosity."

That hurt.

We walked along the wall of sweet corn lining the uneven dirt road that outlined the farm's perimeter. I had spent countless hours in this field, never imagining I'd be lumbering through it as a preteen day laborer. The farm was the quickest way to the Charter Oak Mall, Showcase Cinema, and Silver Lane. And there were a few nights when we snuck onto the farm for a heist of corn, onions, and any other vegetables we could pull up from the ground, then raced home. Irene knew because she'd prepare whatever I took for dinner. She didn't care that I had all the makings of a professional thief; she wanted cheap produce.

One of my fondest memories of the farm wasn't the toils of manual labor but the time before we were old enough to work, when Alan, Will, Pete, Gwen, and I built a fort deep in the woods and filled our "kitchen" with raw sweet corn. We'd play an odd version of house, with Alan assigning cosplay roles to each of us, then we'd lean against trees and talk crap about each other. Remarkably, we never fell ill with E. coli.

After fighting to keep up with Alan for about twenty minutes, we emerged onto Silver Lane. It was an easy dart across the often-hectic road, since we, underage workers, were the only ones awake at this ungodly hour.

"Try not to embarrass us today, cool?" Alan asked as I followed him, walking up to the farmer's stand. In the darkness, I made out five or six young boys lingering. I immediately saw the age divide; younger workers huddled together while the older teenagers, loud and confident, barked orders.

"You fuckers better pull your weight today, or else it's melon time," the tallest of the older teens exclaimed, prompting his peers, including Alan, to laugh.

Alan pointed toward the younger kids. "Go stand over there with them. Jim will be out shortly. We start at five."

I murmured, "Who is the tall melon guy?"

Alan smirked. "That's Brett." With that, he moved toward Brett, and I shuffled toward a few kids my age.

A petite boy stood in the deepest shadows. He wiped his sleeve across his nose. I noticed the dirt caked on his hands and arms. Already? Had he been working all night? What had I gotten myself into?

I broke the tension. "I'm Joe. What are your names?" I felt shy, and the kids were reticent, quiet, and frightened.

The one with the dirty hands answered, "I'm Gordon." Then he shrugged toward the other. "This is my brother Chuck."

Chuck had a black eye. I asked for details. "What happened to you?"

He leaned against the garage door and slid down into a sitting position. "I missed a catch the other day."

Missed a catch? Before I could investigate further, the garage door began to open. In one swift motion, Chuck leaned forward and leaped to his feet. Agile, way more athletic than me. I'd have taken much longer. The two creaky garage doors opened, revealing the farmer's stand inside. On my way to the movies, I'd meandered past this wooden building countless times, but this was the first time I'd seen the inside. The entire operation looked fun. Girls staffed the stand. I daydreamed about all the teenage drama and boy-crush conversations that took place behind the wobbly counter, while weighing a customer's squashes and flirting with hardworking adolescent boys.

"Good morning, boys," Jim greeted us as he walked out from the farmer's stand. He stood before us: tall, dark-haired, handsome, masculine yet welcoming, wearing overalls and a stained T-shirt. We all moved in closer, as if he were about to tell us a tale.

"Alright. It's going to be rough today. Hot and humid. We need to pick the melons and peppers, then start on the corn. Is this the new guy?" He gestured toward me. "Joe, right?"

Brett elbowed Alan, mouthing, *"Melon time."*

"Yes, sir," I answered.

"Sir? Oh, I like this guy," Jim joked. I glanced at Alan, who gave me an approving nod.

Jim continued, "Well, welcome, Joe. I hope you brought your energy today. You'll be with Brett, Alan, and Chuck, working on the melons." Then he turned to the remaining boys. "Gordon and the rest of you will go with Calvin to start on the peppers."

I leaned toward Chuck. "Who's Calvin?"

"That's Jim's nephew; he's in charge of all of us." He forced a smile. "Don't piss him off."

Alan and Brett went to work quickly, carrying the large orange water cooler and supplies toward the flatbed truck we'd been assigned to. Chuck showed me where to store my lunch in the refrigerator. Then we hurried over to the pickup, the smell of diesel fuel filling the air.

Brett and Alan jumped into the bucket seat of the old truck, while Chuck and I climbed into the flatbed. Brett was sixteen and had a driver's license. Before I could secure myself, he gunned it, sending us tumbling toward the edge. I grabbed the rope tied to the cab to keep from being tossed out. Chuck giggled, but it wasn't a happy one; it was nervous, like someone who knew the worst was yet to come. The air felt thick under my nose, and sweat dripped from my hairline as I fought to keep from becoming roadkill five minutes into my first day on the job.

I heard Chuck sniffle as the truck jumped the curb and sped quickly across Silver Lane, hitting the farmland that ran parallel to the street. The melons were planted at the far end of the farm.

"Are you okay?" I asked Chuck.

He tried to focus on me, holding onto the rope as our asses slammed together in a shared rhythm against the steel platform. "I'm good. I hate this job."

I wedged myself between the water cooler and the large crates. "Why are you here?"

"My mom needs us to help her."

I left it there. We were twelve-year-olds. I agreed to this Hell for money, to buy pizza at the mall and movie tickets, while Chuck had the responsibility of supporting his mother. At least Melvin and Irene hadn't asked me to pay rent. I figured pushing the topic any further might trigger a meltdown, and if Chuck went home, it would leave me alone with Brett and Alan. Frankly, Brett looked like someone who had bitten the heads off doves. Just then, the pickup came to a clunking stop. We'd arrived at the melon patch.

"You'd better wipe your eyes," I suggested. "I don't think Brett likes criers."

The sun began to peek over the trees; the sepia blankness of the landscape slowly faded. The melon patch stretched for what felt like miles, from the edge of Silver Lane to the far side of the farm, where it met the perimeter.

Brett bolted around to the rear of the truck, chugging the last of his Jolt Cola. "Alright, ladies, let's get to work." He noticed Chuck. "Dude? Are you crying?" Brett tossed his empty can at Chuck, and it bounced off his chest, landing in the dirt.

"No. You drive so fucking fast I almost fell out," Chuck protested. That was a version of this fearful kid that caught me off guard. In the world of teenage farm workers, it was survival mode, and standing up for yourself, even with nothing to back it up, was a power move.

"This tough guy," Brett mocked.

Chuck had a farmer's game face, ready at a moment's notice. When the going got rough, Chuck got tough. Would I have a game face? I had no idea.

It went like this: Chuck and I stood on the flatbed, surrounded by open produce boxes. Alan and Brett moved through the melon patch, large serrated knives in hand, picking only the ripest cantaloupes, cutting them from their vines, and tossing them to us. Chuck and I packed them into boxes, stacked them three high, and kept going. That first morning, we worked from 5:15 a.m. until 11:45 a.m., then took our scheduled lunch break. There were water breaks during the morning, but only when Alan and Brett needed them. If we slacked off, the names Brett hurled at us hit harder than catching melons. Alan went along with the denigration. If Chuck and I got too tired and slowed down, a rotten melon would fly through the air and slam into our small frames. The worst was when one of us stopped for a piss break and got hit with a hard melon because we turned our backs on Brett.

"Melon time!" Brett screamed. Then *SPLAT*—a rotting explosion of orange and green burst across one of us. If we were lucky, we'd spot the incoming missile in time to dodge it completely. Semi-lucky meant getting splattered with cantaloupe guts and seeds. But if we were unlucky, like

Chuck had been a few days earlier, it would explode in our faces. Thankfully, that never happened to me. Whenever one of Brett's bombs came flying, I'd duck and glance at Alan in disbelief. He'd ignore me. I figured out the pecking order quickly that morning. Alan and Brett were "friends," but what I learned was that Alan simply toed the line. He knew not to cross Brett.

By the time I climbed off the flatbed for lunch at the farmstand, I thought death was imminent. I used to complain about carrying newspapers for an hour every afternoon, but farm work had me questioning child labor laws. I also questioned how much I actually loved going to the movie theater. I'd just seen *The Goonies* and wondered whether getting smacked with melon pulp was worth seeing it again.

I began to lose faith. It suddenly made sense why Chuck had dirt crusted on his skin before we even started that morning. The kind of dirt you collect working in the fields doesn't come off. It finds its way into every crevice of your body, into your sweat glands, embedded in your fingerprints. Dirt from manual labor reminds you where you stand on the food chain.

After our half-hour lunch break, we returned to the field and finished picking and packing the melons. By 2 p.m., I had closed the last box, and a wave of relief washed over me. I asked Alan if we were done for the day. He threw a handful of dirt at me and told me to be quiet.

Next, we hopped back into the pickup and drove over to the acres and acres of green peppers. The pepper plants stretched into the distance. When my parents drove past Futtner's Farm, the fields looked miniature, manageable. But working inside the maze of vegetable plants and corn stalks, the square footage of the field seemed to triple. The phrase 'back-breaking work' sounds strange when applied to teenagers now, but in the summer of 1985, it was all the rage.

At the end of my first day, I realized I had to quit. I told Alan as I dragged myself behind him on our way home. He threatened me with bodily harm. Usually, I wouldn't have believed he'd kick my ass, but after seeing how easily he bent the knee for Brett, I took his threat more seriously. I'd love to say I was as tough as Alan and could handle the farming environment, but that couldn't be further from the truth. While the three older teenagers had bodies ripped with muscles and were as toned as full-grown adults, mine was soft—marshmallow soft, like a Pillsbury Dough Boy. Melvin often called me a wimp. Perhaps he was right. Even though I argued with him every time he insulted me, on that painful walk home after my first day, I started to wonder if he had a point. If being a strong male teenager meant working twelve hours in the sun for two bucks an hour, then yeah, I was a wimp.

THE GREENHOUSE

That first night home from the farm, I had no energy to eat dinner. My muscles screamed in protest. Pain shot through them with the slightest movement. They felt stretched and unusable. My goal was to crawl up the stairs and collapse into my bed without showering. Irene wasn't having it.

"What the fuck is that horrible sour smell?" she asked, elbows deep in dishwater at the sink, giving me a sharp look as I hovered in front of the refrigerator.

I guzzled orange juice straight from the carton. "It's me, Mom. It's me."

"Go take a shower. You're disgusting."

The next morning, Alan knocked on the door again. I seriously considered throwing myself down the stairs, but I answered it instead. A fractured tibia seemed more straightforward to manage than what I'd experienced the day before. Day two was no better than the first. We spent twelve hours picking onions. Onions! I'd never seen so many in my entire life. I'm pretty sure that's why I can't stand onions to this day. As much as I loathed being knee-deep in dirt all day long, I kept going back. Partly because I didn't want to let Alan down, and partly because I was determined not to be beaten by sweat, dirt, and demoralization.

By the fourth day, while sitting at the broken-down picnic table between the farmer's stand and the large greenhouse, I noticed how much fun the girls were having at the stand. I realized—that was my jam. They were in the shade. No one was chucking fruit and vegetables at their heads. Working in the fields felt like being a Christian in the Colosseum, thrown to the lions with no escape. But the girls at the stand? They were carefree, the Roman elite with the best view.

On the walk home, I found it hard to speak. My joints and muscles screamed with every step, and my jaw ached from yelling to Chuck across rows of onions. But something kept coming to mind. I turned to Alan. "So, do you think Jim would let me work at the stand?"

He cackled, then stopped. "Joe, are you fucking kidding me? Only girls work at the stand." We faced off, me trying not to blink. "Seriously? What's wrong with you?"

I let it go. We continued on our way home. He kept an eye on me, glancing over every so often and shaking his head in disbelief. The thought of even asking about working at the farmstand offended him. Curious. It made perfect sense to me. In fact, why wasn't this on every teenage boy's mind who wasn't built like He-Man? Working in the fields wasn't feasible, at least not for me. Time seemed to speed up in that field, picking beets from the earth in six inches of mud. By Thursday, not even a full week in, I felt I should've been starting high school in the fall, not the eighth grade. The summer of 1985 was supposed to be my *National Lampoon's Vacation*. Instead, it was *Children of the Corn*.

Alan knocked right on time Friday morning. I'd been parked at the kitchen table, waiting, like he was my personal alarm clock. I opened the door in my pajamas. Rain fell in sheets across the parking lot. He tilted his head, impatient. "Let's go, Joe. We were late yesterday because of you."

"I'm not going today. I'm sick."

"You don't look sick," he snapped.

I leaned against the doorframe. "Bite me. I have a hangnail. I can't work in the dirt."

"A what?! What the hell are you talking about?"

"A hangnail, stupid. It's infected." I held up my finger, then quickly pulled it back out of sight. "Tell Jim I'll be in on Monday."

Alan shook his head and left me behind. I watched his shadow fade at the end of the street. Satisfied with my decision, I closed the door and went back to bed.

By Sunday night, the decision was clear: I'd not be returning to the farm.

On Monday morning, Alan hammered on the door, his frustration evident in the force of his fist. So annoyed that he didn't care if he was yelled at for waking up my parents. I answered in my pajamas. Again.

"What are you doing?"

"It's raining. I'm not going today."

"Fuck, Joe!" His displeasure came through in his raised voice. "I got you that job. Now I look lame."

Shame tickled my earlobes, but I shook it off, letting the humiliation flow out with the wind and rain. I knew I was wrong and the bad guy in this situation. I had a responsibility to man up and go to work, but I had already spent hours kneeling in the rain, pulling potatoes from the ground as I sank into what felt like quicksand. That work was not for me. I had nothing else to offer my friend, who had gone out on a limb to secure this job for me.

"Just tell Jim I'm sick."

That night, Alan knocked before dinner. When I opened the door, he was already walking away. He didn't even look at me; he just spoke to the sky: "Jim said you're fired. Don't come back." He sauntered off as if we were strangers.

Being fired as a farm rat should've been the perfect conclusion. Instead, it taught me something I've spent decades trying to unlearn: if I don't want to do something or it's too challenging, I can vanish, sleep through it, and wait for the consequences to find me.

By the end of the week, I went to pick up my four-day paycheck. Gwen had recently been hired to work the stand for the summer, and as I approached, she reached into the accordion file folder and pulled out a white envelope.

"I'm sorry it didn't work out for you," Gwen said, handing me the envelope. "That looks like hard work."

My name was visible through the transparent window. That made me question whether I wanted to be fired. Seeing my name on a paycheck felt like an adult thing. I lingered by the counter. "It's bogus. And Brett's a poser."

Just then, Jim entered through the back door that led to the greenhouse. He ignored Gwen and the few customers, then approached me. "I wish you'd have worked out. I needed the help."

My neck began to heat up. The shame spread from my ears to my face and neck. "I'm sorry, Jim. I was sick. I don't think I'm good at this job." Then I went for it. If you never ask, you'll never know. "Do you need help at the stand?"

He pulled me aside, his voice a whisper: "Only girls work at the stand. That's how it's always been, Joe."

His kindness seeped through his overalls, surprising me. I kept pressing him, hoping I was special. That I'd be the first teenage boy to strap on a cute apron, smile at the produce-loving housewives, and leave the day with only a dusting of dirt on my softened hands. Break through the Futtner Farm glass ceiling.

"I'm a good worker. I'd do well in the stand."

As calm as my middle school guidance counselor, who told me not to scream in the hallway, Jim snapped me out of my delusion. "Joe, if you think the guys are brutal in the field, they'll destroy you if you work with the girls."

Jim was absolutely correct. If I worked at the stand, Brett would spend the rest of his teenage years making me regret being a pansy. I slipped the folded envelope into my pocket and thanked him. I started to leave, but he coughed and called after me from halfway across the parking lot.

"Listen. Come back in November. I might have some greenhouse work for you."

That November, during my last year at East Hartford Middle School, I took Jim up on his offer. He hired me to work in the greenhouse on the weekends—planting seeds and preparing for the next season. He showed me kindness, something that felt foreign. He could tell I wasn't like the other boys, not even the smaller ones with black eyes. Working in the greenhouse was a dream come true. Once I made it through the snow and bitter cold, the greenhouse felt like the Garden of Eden. I worked with Gwen and another girl—we laughed, worked with our hands, and listened to pop music, all while avoiding Brett. My Christmas wish that year was never to see Brett again. He'd caused me enough trouble.

At the end of December, before Christmas break, Jim informed me that my work was complete. In those two months, I earned more money than I ever had and learned that if I enjoyed a job's duties, I excelled. During those few months, I opened a savings account in my name and proudly kept the little bank booklet in my dresser drawer.

Earning money and having a bank account fit perfectly with the imagined reality I slipped into whenever Melvin and Irene's daily parenting became too intense. I deluded myself into believing I was real, while the obstacles around me were part of a TV plot—a soap opera. I had to act my way through it. That felt better than the truth. I imagined my bedroom was an apartment, and I was just renting a room from two crazy drunks who yelled a lot and mismanaged their lives. I rearranged my bedroom to look more adult and placed a cooler at the bottom of my closet, stocked with cans of New Coke. The top shelf of my closet held all the Little Debbie treats. I liked snacks. Still do.

When I confined myself to my bedroom, I'd envisioned myself as an actor. Everything inside the four purple walls felt like real life. I could be anyone I wanted to be without feeling the venom of vipers. Outside my bedroom, it was a different story. Outside my bedroom, it was showtime. The way Melvin and Irene treated me, the kids in the neighborhood calling me a fag and hurling melons at me—all of it was something I had to act my way through. Fascinating how our brains protect us from threats. Even when I didn't have the tools or power to protect myself from trauma, my subconscious did the heavy lifting, diffusing the distress in the only way it knew how by treating everything outside my bedroom as part of a plot I had been thrust into.

After the greenhouse, my next job was polishing brass at a furniture store in the mall. Buffing brass headboards and helping customers load their new purchases into their cars made me feel like a human being.

And no touching onions all day. I hated them.

WILL POWER

"Can Will spend the night?" I burst into the house and asked Irene, who stood at the kitchen sink, ready to light a cigarette. Before she could answer, I piled on details. I needed my case to be airtight. "It's Friday, there's no school tomorrow, and my birthday is next week."

She took a long drag from her freshly lit Winston 100. "I know what day it is and when your birthday is, smart ass. Is it okay with Linda?"

I bounced on my toes. "Yes. Linda doesn't care."

Irene crossed to the refrigerator, pulled out a Budweiser, and cracked it open. "I'm going out tonight. You'll have to ask your dad."

Whenever my happiness landed in Melvin's hands, it usually ended in disappointment. But to my surprise, when he finally came home from whatever he'd been doing, I barely had to beg him before he agreed. Real happiness, the kind I didn't have to perform, hit me all at once. I sprinted to Will's condo to pick him up for the night.

The sleepover took place the day after Halloween, 1985. All the candy I'd collected sat in a large bowl on the dining room table. We didn't have artwork, so the bright candy wrappers decorated for us. That year I went as a witch: black dress, black hat, black high heels. By the end of the night, I'd ditched the hat and pranced around the circle in full goth drag. Apparently, on Halloween, a boy can dress like that, and nobody bats an eye.

Thank God for Halloween.

A full year had passed since Alan and Will left their mark on the neighborhood, and most of the kids still avoided Will. Nobody wanted to end up like Curtis. Even a year later, we were still talking about how quickly he folded and hit the ground. Because many of our peers avoided me for being husky and Will for being crazy and dangerous, the two of us spent a lot of time together.

Yes, I had a few friends, but it bothered me that I didn't have more. Will didn't care. He had Alan. He had me. He didn't flinch at the noise, the jeers, the little cruelties kids tossed around like candy. If someone mouthed off to Will, he'd walk right up, punch the loose-lipped kid in the neck, and keep going. Calm as a nun with a grudge. I wish I'd had that kind of zero-fucks confidence ten days before turning thirteen. I still do.

After dinner, Irene and Linda got dolled up and headed to the Silver Dollar for a girls' night. Downstairs, Melvin parked himself in front of *Gunsmoke* reruns, newly thrilled by cable, sipping vodka and 7-Up. Every so often, he yelled a reminder up the stairs: "Don't get too rowdy, or Will would have to go home." The thought of Will leaving and being alone with Melvin again, especially with Irene gone, scared me more than finding an apple in my trick-or-treat pillowcase. Most weekends when Irene went out to the bar, Melvin and I were left alone, and once he slipped into intoxication, there was no mystery about what came next. But with Will there, Melvin couldn't get me alone. I clung to those borrowed, false moments of safety.

"We have to keep it down. I don't want you to go home," I pleaded. Will sat on my bed as I shut the bedroom door, a barrier to keep Melvin downstairs.

"Let's listen to music," I suggested, circling my unmade bed toward the tiny record player on the desk. I flipped it on and grabbed the 45 Irene had given me as an early birthday present. "Do you like this song?" I held up the sleeve. "It's the bomb."

Will shrugged, like he couldn't care less. "What song?"

"I'm showing you. Hello?"

He didn't even look up from picking at his fingernails. "What?"

"It's 'Oh, Sheila' by Ready for the World."

He stood, giving his fingernails a chance to recover. "Damn, Joe. You love that fag music. Don't you have any AC/DC or The Who?"

I'd been shoved into defensive mode. "This isn't fag music. It's good music."

Will stepped closer, snatched the 45 from my hand. "It's lame. You'll be a teenager next week. It's time to stop being a dork." Though he was six months older, he treated that like dog years. "You need better music, or I won't stay again."

He held the threat for a beat, then laughed and handed the 45 back. "Don't start crying. I'm kidding."

Will grabbed another record. "Wang Chung? Jesus. No wonder nobody likes you."

"Bite me!" I hurled my favorite insult at him. It bounced right off. So I tried something sharper, something that made us equals. "They don't like you either."

I snatched the record with laughable authority. Will shoved me against the wall.

"That's because I beat people up. You're just… gay."

"No, I'm not. Don't say that."

"That's what everyone says," he shrugged, acting like he'd heard it a hundred times. "But fuck them dickwads. I don't care." He scooped up the rest of my 45s, making a face at each artist's name.

I shrugged, but a pinched feeling remained. Paul could call me Joebosity for his amusement, but being called gay? Unthinkable. I knew I was different, but I was definitely not gay. The worst possibility was that I had terrible taste in music, a teenage-boy failure. I had "Shout" by Tears for Fears and didn't care what others thought; nothing was more manly than Tears for Fears.

We listened to a few of my "obviously gay" songs. Will declared that The Pointer Sisters, Wham!, and Billy Ocean were gay, even though he'd never heard any of them.

A few minutes later, he was over music entirely. "Like, let's crank-call people."

I shut off the record player and slid the 45 back into its sleeve. Then I sat down beside him on the bed, heat creeping up my neck. "No. I don't wanna get in trouble. We have to be quiet."

He snatched my Garfield phone off the desk. "Take a chill pill, Joe." He popped off the orange cat's back, revealing the dial pad, then shoved the receiver toward me. "Come on. Just one. Then we can do anything you want."

The phone sat in his palm. I refused to take it. "You do it. I'm not."

"You're such a chicken," he taunted. "Don't be a scaredy-cat."

My toe started tapping. I talked back to adults, but crank-calling felt illegal, and phone records could reveal us. We'd get caught; Will would go home, leaving me alone with Melvin.

But the real reason I caved had nothing to do with the phone company. Besides Will, Alan, Pete, and Gwen, nobody wanted to hang out with me. And when they did, it was usually to make me the punchline. If Will decided I was a total dweeb, I could lose him, too.

A soft voice answered a few moments after I dialed a random number. "Hello?"

I held the receiver out so Will and I could both hear. I lowered my voice and went with the first thing that came to mind. "Hi. Is Wang Chung home?"

The older woman's voice crackled over the line. "I'm sorry. What was that?"

"I'm looking for my friend, Wang Chung. He's about four feet tall. Is he there?"

Concern tightened the woman's voice. "Who is this? There is no Chung here."

I covered the mouthpiece and whispered, "She's old. I'm hanging up."

Will slapped my titty.

"Ow. Like, that hurt, you spazz." I laughed, forgetting there was still someone's grandmother on the line, probably marching from room to room in search of an English new wave band.

The woman cut in. "Who is this? I will find out and tell your parents."

I returned to voice-acting mode, saying, "I'm just looking for my friend." I signaled to Will to end the call. He mouthed "bogus," but I kept going. I couldn't hang up without his okay, or he'd think I was a poser. So I played along, trying to sound joyful—uncomfortable but adaptable.

"His name is Wang Chung," I teased, "and he wants everybody to have fun tonight."

As the last word left my mouth, I erupted into a high-pitched scream-laugh, pleased I'd managed to work one of my favorite lyrics into the prank.

Will yanked the phone from my hand. "Psych! You won't tell anyone about anything, ya old bitch," he snarled, slamming Garfield's receiver into the cradle.

Melvin opened the door as Will leaned forward to put the phone down. I jumped off the bed. Will and I faced him. Calmly, Melvin leaned against the doorframe and asked, "Why are you screaming?"

"Sorry, Dad. Will was being stupid."

Melvin grinned. "Stop being stupid, Will." He closed the door. Though inebriated, he seemed pleasant. Goosebumps ran down my arms. I pushed the chill out of my mind and turned to Will.

He grabbed his backpack. "Let's change and watch TV." He jumped from activity to activity quickly, and I kept up with his erratic suggestions to avoid falling behind.

Will peeled off his shirt quickly, searching his bag for a T-shirt. As I pulled mine over, I noticed the ripples in his arms and the flatness of his stomach. Mine weren't like that. My stomach was an outtie, while his was an innie. He was in prime teen shape, and I couldn't ignore it.

We changed into pajamas, and I turned on my 13-inch Emerson. My bedroom lacked cable, so only NBC and ABC worked.

"*Knight Rider* is starting. Leave it there. That car is killer to the max." Will slid back against the pillow on his side of my bed. "I'll have one of those one day." A declared promise, not a wish.

"You won't own a KITT. You're on crack," I shot back, settling beside him.

He caught me off guard. I was never ready for anything. In a split second, Will turned and started play-slapping my face until we toppled to the floor with a thud. I shoved him off and scrambled up, disoriented, trying to re-map the room after the impact. The fall was loud. I went still, listening, silently willing the noise to go away.

I hauled myself onto the edge of the bed. Will kept laughing, but my voice came out raw. "Will. If Melvin sends you home—" I trailed off, unable to finish. I believe he understood the distress, even if he didn't know what it meant.

The *Knight Rider* theme music pulsed from my speakers, synths and percussion building until the room felt wired. It sounded like menace with a beat, like trouble was approaching. We loved it. Then the voiceover: "Knight Rider, a shadowy flight into the dangerous world of a man who does not exist." The intro was my favorite part of the show.

Halfway through the episode, Will nudged me. "Check this out, Joe."

I kept my eyes on the TV. "Shut up."

"Come on. Look."

I turned. Will's grin showed he was testing my comfort; I didn't notice anything. "What?"

Will's eyes twinkled. "My dick is hard."

My eyes slid down his chest to his gray pajama pants. He was right. His dick was hard, and the outline in his gray pajamas reminded me of a hidden banana. A haze rolled through my mind. I didn't know what to expect. I just knew I had to be ready.

"Gross. Don't be dumb." I returned my gaze to the TV. Will had a hard-on in my bed. Aside from my interactions with Melvin, I didn't think much about sex. Somewhere deep down, I thought boys were cuter than girls, but the idea jumbled in my mind. Confusion led me to compartmentalize these odd thoughts, unlike those of everyone else my age, sex, and gender.

His demeanor changed. He aged. "Do you want to touch it?"

Astounded, I replied, "In your dreams. My dad might come up any minute. Stop."

He threw the blanket over his crotch. I couldn't take my eyes off him. His voice soothed me. "There. It's covered. Touch it."

I hesitated, staring at the television, but my face flushed. The truth was, I did want to touch it. My curiosity grew, and I realized I liked Will. I thought he was strong, rugged, crazy, handsome, and flirty. Dumb as a box of candy corn, but I felt protected around him.

"Okay. Sure."

He pulled the blanket back again. There it was, hidden beneath his pajamas and underwear, bobbing up and down—bait to catch a gay fish.

I reached over and touched him, tentative at first, with no real idea what I was doing. I went through the motions, as if a genie might appear if I kept at it. People might think my history with Melvin made me experienced. It didn't. It made me compliant. It made me a service animal. And hello, this wasn't an adult in my bed. Will was my age, which might have made it feel safer, but it left me unmoored. The silence between us roared. The TV kept talking, and I kept listening for sounds downstairs, terrified that Melvin had sensed the shift in boyhood innocence upstairs.

Will pushed me back. We locked eyes. Then he spoke, as if changing the channel. "Go get me some Halloween candy."

For a second, I couldn't make sense of the words. Candy? The request didn't match the moment, and that mismatch made me question. "What? Candy?"

"Yeah." He grew impatient. "Your Halloween candy. Downstairs."

Completely invested in where this was going, I forced Melvin out of my thoughts for a moment, hopped off the bed, and headed for the door, tugging my shirt down to hide my enthusiasm. I'd barely reached the hallway when Will added one more condition.

"Bring me a Snickers."

I sprinted down the stairs, two at a time, and burst into the dining room. Melvin was on the sofa, watching the same show we'd been watching upstairs. I grabbed candy without checking, hoping Will would let me continue our game. In my head, it had turned into a stupid, dangerous fairy tale: do what he asked, and maybe I'd get a wish.

Melvin didn't look away from the TV. "I'm going to bed soon. Are you guys sleeping down here?"

When I had a sleepover, we often camped out in the living room so we could talk and giggle all night without disturbing the adults.

"We're sleeping down here, Dad," I said casually, "Just grabbing some candy."

I bolted back upstairs with a fistful of fun-size chocolate bars. I eased the door open and shut it quietly behind me. Everything felt like a secret, but I'd grown adept at keeping them, so it was easy. For a moment, it even felt fun, which made me think of the other secret I kept with Melvin, the one that was never fun at all.

I hopped over Will, took my spot, and handed him the candy. His face tightened, but he said nothing. His expression said it all: not enough.

A few minutes later, the candy I'd brought upstairs was gone, with empty wrappers littering my bedspread. He brushed the trash aside and pulled away from me as if my touch had suddenly turned hot. "I wanted a Snickers."

"I don't have any," I managed, embarrassment rising in my face. At the time, I didn't fully realize Will was stripping me down, piece by piece, every time I tried to keep him happy. Alan had turned Will into a trained fighting animal, and now Will was training me too, teaching me what I had to trade and how quickly I'd do it.

"Then I guess we're done." He rolled over, left my bed, and stepped into the hallway.

What the hell? I should have known better. Will's actions weren't a surprise. This wasn't my first time in Will's circus, performing humiliating tricks for his amusement.

Alan and Will's white three-story house in Hartford sat near dense woods, with the Trout Brook River below. The woods offered space for mud, hide-and-seek, and forts. The river was too far to reach from the house, making it a perfect, enchanting escape.

Because Will was six months older, he became the de facto leader when Alan wasn't home. I often spent weekends at Linda's house, feeling safer there. Once, when I was about seven or eight, Will and I stomped through the woods like they were ours. We headed to the new fortress we'd built, using the finest materials we'd stolen from the garage or scavenged from the woods.

Will paused. "I have to pee."

"Me too." We stopped, and I turned away from Will to hide my shame.

"Hey," he whispered, even though no one was around, "I'll show you mine if you wanna see it."

Ignoring him, I zipped up my pants. Will was a prankster who couldn't pull that with Alan, so he did it to me. I turned, and his pants were around his ankles.

He smirked. "Show me yours. Don't be a baby." His words matched Melvin's coercion. I didn't see that then.

I unbuttoned and pulled down my pants.

Will guffawed, then yelled, "Fag!" and shoved me, pushing me into the shrubbery. I scratched my arms and fell into red-and-green leaves. He pulled up his pants and disappeared into the foliage, his laughter echoing.

I forced myself up, eyes burning with humiliation. After fixing my pants, I brushed off the dirt and went to Linda's house. Inside, Linda watched over a big pot of soup, and Irene sat at the table to take me home.

"Have you been crying?" she asked as I climbed into the car.

"No. But Will's a jerk."

She backed down their long driveway, waited for clearance, then merged into traffic. "You have to stop crying in front of them, or they'll always pick on you."

I stared out the open window in silence, her advice evaporating with her cigarette smoke.

By dinnertime, the faint hum of discomfort had turned into a level of pain I'd never experienced.

"Mom!" No answer. "Mom!" I yelled, sitting in my underwear on my bed's edge. Irene rushed in. I cried, "It burns. It's so itchy."

"What's going on? Why are you crying?"

"It's my private," I managed to say between sobs. "It hurts." My body felt hot and cold at the same time.

Irene called out, "Melvin? Dear? Come in here." We waited. When he peeked in, she said, "Show Daddy what you're talking about."

I stood, and pain shot through me as my thighs rubbed together. I pulled down my underwear to avoid rubbing my skin, but it didn't work. The lower half of my ass was bright red with small blisters forming.

"What the fuck did you do to yourself, Joseph?" Irene shouted, confusion tightening her voice. "Is that poison ivy?"

Melvin leaned closer to examine it. "Yeah. It's either poison ivy or oak."

I stayed quiet as pain robbed my breath, words, and truth. When Melvin confirmed it, I knew I couldn't confess. I tried to sit, but the bedsheets felt like sandpaper. They stared while I stood, bowlegged, trying to avoid touching my skin.

I had to lie. "Will and I were in the woods. I had to pee. I… fell into the bushes."

Irened turned me around, inspecting the hellscape on my skin. "That's bullshit. How did you get poison ivy on your butt?"

My silence was all she needed. "It's that goddamn Will. That little fucker. I'm calling Linda." She stomped out, leaving Melvin and me alone.

Melvin glared. "Did you do this on purpose?"

I knew what he meant. "No, I fell in the bushes."

He stepped into the hallway. "I hope you're telling me the truth." Then he disappeared into the bathroom. I heard the cabinet open and close, then he returned with calamine lotion.

While Melvin dabbed calamine on me, Irene's voice echoed down the hallway from the kitchen.

She was on the phone, and I knew Linda was on the other end. Irene ranted, "I don't know what the fuck these two were up to, Linda, but Joe's got poison ivy burns all over his crotch and ass. Does Will?"

The soothing chill began to dull the burn. Melvin finished and tapped my leg. "Okay, turn around. Let me do your front."

I pulled away. "I can do my front."

He grabbed my waist and pulled me closer. "You won't do it right."

In the kitchen, Irene's voice rose. "Linda, I know Will is a fucked-up kid and all, but I can't have him messing with my son in the woods."

"You're done." Melvin set the bottle on my dresser. He leaned in and spoke softly in my ear. "Did Will do anything to you?"

"No. I tripped and fell."

Irene slammed the phone down and stormed into my bedroom, anger mixed with strange gentleness. "Did you pull your pants down in the woods?" she asked. Before I could answer, she added, "Don't lie, I know you did, and Will pushed you into the poison ivy."

I stared at the floor, knowing I could defend myself by saying Will pressured me into something I didn't understand, something not-so-innocent. But the truth lost. Sometimes telling the truth is easy; sometimes it can't be spoken.

"Not gonna answer me?" Irene turned to leave, looked at Melvin, then spoke to me. "You're grounded for two weeks. No going to Linda's house."

"But, Mommy, I didn't do anything wrong."

Will hadn't just pushed me into poison ivy; he'd twisted the blame onto me. The part I couldn't say aloud: he'd started it. I'd been burned by the leaves and by Will's deception.

Halfway down the hallway, Irene said, "And no going downstairs to see your grandparents. School. Home. Bedroom. That's it."

Irene left the room. Melvin looked down at me, then walked away.

I hadn't learned my lesson that day when Will pushed me into the itchy plants. We were back in the same situation, at least this time, I wouldn't have welts on my ass for weeks.

Will came back into the bedroom and left the door cracked behind him. He was quiet. Too quiet. A minute ago, we'd been doing something that felt fun, and now everything felt reset, as if it hadn't happened at all.

Was that part of his plan? To mess with me, send me on errands, and keep me off-balance? He could've gone downstairs and grabbed candy himself. The whole thing made my brain stutter. It didn't add up.

We heard Melvin's heavy footsteps on the stairs. Then he filled the doorway. "I'm going to bed." His speech slurred, as usual. "Go downstairs."

We grabbed blankets and pillows, shuffled downstairs, and turned on the TV to watch the preview for next week's *Knight Rider*. The episode ended, but its haunting soundtrack lingered like a strong perfume.

Will didn't mention what happened upstairs, and I stayed silent, assuming our game was over. I liked being close to him, even with layers of fabric between us. He felt grown-up, smelled grown-up, and carried himself with the casual toughness of my uncles.

We curled up under blankets, the TV's glow casting shadows across the room. I stared at the screen, but my mind kept replaying what had happened upstairs. I was so deep inside my own head that Will had to snap me out of it.

"Hey," he said. "I think Melvin's calling you."

I turned my head and heard my father's voice, low and hungry, through the dark. "Joe. Get up here."

I sat on the floor, hoping the room would swallow me whole. I'd learned a lot about the Devil, and facing him felt safer than going upstairs. Melvin was evil with a human face, convincing without horns. They both relied on manipulation and deception. If I could survive Melvin, Satan couldn't be much worse.

Sadly, I had no choice. "Alright. I'll be right back." I popped up and hauled myself upstairs, heading toward another mental execution. Downstairs, Will kept eating my Halloween candy, cradling the bowl in his lap.

Even though every instinct in me screamed what was coming, my brain still lied: *He won't do it with Will in the house. He probably wants to give you a goodnight kiss. Stay calm.*

"Hey, Dad." I hovered in the doorway, my voice casual. "We're watching TV."

"I want to do it," he said from the bed, one arm slung over his head, wearing white underwear. The room reeked of vodka, the air thick as if someone had been drinking for hours.

I whispered, "Dad. Will is here."

He pushed himself up on one elbow. "I don't give a fuck. Go downstairs and tell Will I need you here."

Fear surrounds me: Melvin touching me, Will downstairs, Will discovering, and the neighborhood knowing by tomorrow.

"Don't stand there like a fucking idiot," Melvin snarled, leaning over to take a drag from his cigarette. The dim light on his nightstand carved his face in shadow. Then he played his biggest card. "Go! Or I'll get Will to do it. He's not afraid."

Children are foolish. I thought that if Will stayed, I'd be safe. I stayed quiet to prevent Melvin from sending him home, even though I knew the real danger.

It was futile. Melvin had no qualms about another kid in the house. He only needed to keep his secrets from other adults. He believed Will was too naïve to understand.

I was the naïve one. I told myself a sleepover meant safety. In the end, I mistook company for protection. That's why it finally made sense: Melvin didn't care that Will was there. Melvin wanted what he wanted, and I had no choice but to comply.

I went downstairs, head down, battered like a soldier with no fight left in Melvin's war. Will hadn't moved.

"You *do* have a Snickers in here," he said with a mouth full of candy, not looking up from the bowl.

"I have to stay upstairs for a minute." The lie was born the moment it left my mouth. "My dad needs to talk to me."

"Hurry up," Will said, ripping open a candy bar. "I want to watch *Nightmare on Elm Street*."

Upstairs, the bedroom door clicked shut. Melvin directed me. I obeyed. I lay there, trying to leave my body, the only way I knew how, through music.

In my head, the Knight Rider theme looped as I desperately tried to escape, but Melvin's grunting pulled me back. After he finished, he sent me back downstairs. To my friend. To my innocent sleepover.

At least Melvin would be asleep by the time we started the movie. I'd be safe for the rest of the night.

THE PERFECT CRIME

Every Saturday, my goal was to spend the night at Pete's house. If Irene and Melvin managed to curb their drinking during the week, they made up for it on the weekends, with benders that ran from Friday night until Sunday evening. I'd beg to sleep over at a friend's, and Irene often said yes. She didn't see the harm. Looking back, I think she was subconsciously protecting me from the chaos that always followed when she and Melvin drank. Or, more likely, she wanted to drink all night without me giving her the stink eye. Melvin, however, always found a new reason to say no and keep me home. Even when I had been on my best behavior, as he demanded, my freedom was a carrot he dangled in front of me and yanked away whenever he felt like it. On those Saturdays when I was forced to stay home, I'd hide in my room, lost in music, listening as the shouting crept up the stairs, closer and closer.

One Saturday, I spent most of the day at Pete's. When the weather was pleasant, we stayed outside, exploring the woods. When it was cold, we stayed inside, playing Choplifter on the Atari (nobody had a Nintendo yet) while listening to Duran Duran. Pete loved Duran Duran. Hanging out with Pete felt like independence. I could be a kid without Melvin's shadow. My time at the greenhouse had just ended, so I filled my weekends with movies, mall trips, and laughter with Pete.

The sun was setting, and it was early December 1985. There was a bite in the air, but there wasn't much snow yet.

As Pete and I sat downstairs in his den, Pete's mother, Joan, called down, catching me off guard. "Do you want to stay the night, Joe?"

Joan Armstrong didn't usually offer to let me spend the night; it was always Pete who asked her, which was normal. She carried herself as if she didn't really care what Pete did. It was clear her oldest, Paul, was her favorite. I'll never know why she invited me that night. Honestly, she didn't show much kindness my way. When I'd hang out at their house, Joan wrinkled her nose and looked me over, as if I were a threat to her son. My hand-me-downs reeked of cigarettes, which probably didn't help her distaste for me. The stench of stale tobacco wasn't my fault; my parents chain-smoked in the house. I lived inside an ashtray. Joan asked Pete once if I smoked, and he told her it was my parents. I don't think she believed him.

The idea of staying up all night gossiping about girls we thought were cute made us giddy. Of course, I lied about the girls I liked. I didn't want any girls like that.

We ran over to the yellow phone by their pool table, and I dialed home.

"Hello?"

Fuck. It was Melvin. I wanted to hang up, but Melvin had trained me to believe he already knew what I was doing, who I was with, and what I was thinking. Every hour of the day, so I assumed that if I hung up, he'd still know it was me.

"Dad, Pete's mom said I can spend the night. Is that okay?" I asked cheerfully, testing his mood. As far as I knew, Irene wasn't going out, so I expected Melvin to agree.

"Your mother is going out tonight. I need you to come home."

My heart raced. Pete stared at me, chewing on a hangnail hanging from his thumb. I breathed in. I held my breath for a second, trying to steady myself, but the moment I spoke, all that control fizzled.

"Come on, please!" I raised my voice. "We're gonna order pizza, and Paul rented *Police Academy.*" Pete jabbed my arm, but I ignored him.

"What the fuck did I say?" Melvin barked. "Did you raise your voice?" His tone snapped like a belt. "Get your ass home. Now!"

I pleaded, "I'm sorry. I just want to hang out here tonight." Melvin fell silent, and the quiet pressed against my ear, forcing me to keep talking. "It's not even dark yet." I lifted my hand to Pete, palm out, shooing him back. One look at my face told him everything.

I heard Irene in the background. "What's going on?"

Melvin covered the receiver, but I still heard him. "Joe wants to spend the night at Pete's. I said no." Then he turned back to the call. "Home. Now!" The click and silence that followed hit like an exclamation point—a final, sharp punctuation mark.

I pressed the receiver into Pete's hand and started toward the stairs, tears welling. "I have to go home."

Pete followed me. "Why? Can't you at least stay for pizza?"

"No. The asshole wants me home now." I jogged up the stairs and opened the front door. "Thank you, Miss Armstrong, but I have to go home."

Before she could answer from the kitchen, I stepped outside and stomped down their driveway. Dusk had fallen, but instead of going home, I turned right and stepped off Penny Drive, slipping into the pitch-darkness of Futtner's field. I ran, tears streaming down my cheeks. My actions weren't a teenage hissy fit because I couldn't sleep over at Pete's. I ran because I knew what waited at home, with Melvin alone.

At thirteen, I constantly feared Melvin raping me when Irene was away, crushing my spirit. I spent days avoiding him, trying to defend myself, but failed. I lived a lie, pretending I controlled my feelings and body. No matter how hard I tried to stay distant, Melvin was always one step ahead, and I lost hope.

After running for a few minutes, I collapsed on a dry mound of hard, frozen soil, sitting where the onion rows had been. A place I'd despised all summer had become a place to hide, a place to wait out the inevitable. Out here in the fields, there were no surprises. I could predict what came next. And in winter, there were no bullies. Just the dark and the cold, and a sense of safety. Nothing like what awaited within our walls. Invisible blades stabbed every part of my consciousness. My chest heaved until I was exhausted. I let out a blood-curdling scream. The sound was meant for the man who hurt me, but even that felt pointless. Was there no higher authority, no force in the universe that could stop him?

Then I talked to the dark sky. "I hate you! I want you to die. You motherfucker." I could have been talking to Melvin, but I think I was talking to God, since if God were real, where was he? Wasn't it God who brought Melvin to Irene? I heard rustling in the bushes. Pete had followed me, keeping pace. I peered into the darkness and spoke to Pete.

The words came out fresh, finally true. "I hate my dad so much."

Pete half-stepped toward me, then stopped, trying to help. "Joe, you can spend the night another time. Why are you so upset?" He reassured me, but I probably scared him. Here was his friend having a full-blown breakdown as the last light drained from the sky. To Pete, I probably looked unhinged, just a brat not getting what I wanted. But if he could have peeled back the layers of my pain and the secret Melvin forced me to keep, he would have understood my anguish.

I most certainly looked like a nutjob, but confessing why I had planted myself on frozen dirt was out of the question. Don't get me wrong, the truth was hot lava on my tongue, ready to spill, but by then Melvin had groomed me to believe nothing I said or did could protect me from him. Melvin felt omnipresent, as if he could see everything. He probably saw me coming apart in the field. My pulse hammered against my wrists. My muscles turned to stone.

A thought crossed my mind: what if Pete ran to get Joan? Then I'd have to explain to Irene why I had dirt on my pants, and worse, I'd have to do it with Melvin standing behind her, staring me down, waiting. It felt like the poison-ivy shenanigans all over again, the same trap snapping shut on me.

"Dude, what the hell's going on?" Pete asked. After my breakdown, I couldn't just stand up, wipe off the dirt, and pretend I was fine.

I wiped the tears from my cheeks. It was time to put on a show. "I'm fine. My dad's just a jerk." I refused to meet his gaze. "Go home. I just want to be alone for a minute."

Pete paused. Did he believe me? God, I hoped so. "All right," he said. "Don't stay out here too long. Someone might call the cops." He walked away slowly, leaving me in the field to glue myself back together, piece by piece.

After a few minutes, when I was sure Pete had gone home, I brushed as much dirt off my pants as I could. I walked toward my condo, threading between the rows of dead green pepper plants lining the path back to Penny Drive. I rehearsed how I'd act when I got there. The worst thing I could do was let Melvin see I was upset, to give him the satisfaction of knowing he'd broken me. And that's precisely how I felt that chilly night, screaming into the darkness: broken. How was I supposed to imagine a future when this was happening in the present? I was enslaved by Melvin, with no Underground Railroad for sexually abused kids. No escape from Melvin for someone like me.

Honestly, I just wanted him dead. The thought of him gone, leaving Irene and me to start fresh, consumed me. At school, I wished he'd die in a car crash. When fishing, I hoped he'd slip and drown. Watching TV, I prayed for a heart attack, anything to stop him from breathing on me.

But Melvin dying from bad driving, overdrinking, or eating too much red meat still wouldn't be enough. I wanted the monster to suffer the most painful, dramatic death imaginable. I wanted to be smiling when it happened, repeating, *"I love you, Dad."* The exact words he'd force me to say while he violated me, again and again.

Looking back, it's strange that I believed he'd die. I wanted it so badly that I tried to will it into happening. I thought evil people suffered for their sins. There was no doubt in my mind that Melvin had escaped the notice of angels and that his judgment day was near. Near, but not near enough. When? I wanted to witness Melvin take his last breath, to see it leave him. Possibly choking on his blood, an image that soothed me in my despair.

The obsession festered, and the plan I hatched to kill him became my closest confidant. I'd figured out exactly how it should be done, at least in my mind. The violence I daydreamed about gave me a strange sense of joy. It helped me put one foot in front of the other as I walked home, where, as so often before, after Irene had left for the bar, Melvin would corner me and steal another piece of my childhood.

As an adult, it still unsettles me how dark my mind became when I imagined Melvin dying. I feel enormous sadness for that boy who had to think that way to survive. Melvin would never leave me. I understood that. Neither did my imagination of his death.

My young body stored all the emotional and physical danger, and even to this day, it still surfaces when I least expect it. I know how to manage it now. Back then, I didn't. And I couldn't stop thinking about how I should've been eating pizza at a friend's house, watching a movie on VHS, and staying up all night playing records. Instead, I lumbered toward my condo, replaying a fantasy that would shock most people who know me.

In my head, it goes like this:

Melvin's death happens over a weekend, while Irene's at one of her favorite bars. Melvin usually stays home because he prefers me. I'm outside with the neighborhood kids while he sits at the dining room table, watching reruns, drinking vodka, and pickling his liver. It's twilight. When he's buzzed enough, but still alert, he calls me in from playing outside. I usually take my time before entering his prison, but not this time. Once I'm inside, he sends me to the bed, where my small body becomes his prize. After he finishes his routine, he tells me to go back outside and play so he can sleep it off. This time, though, I'm playing a different game.

Melvin quickly falls asleep. I get dressed and slip downstairs, opening and closing the screen door once so he thinks I'm outside. Then I cut a hole in the sliding-door screen with a knife, simulating a break-in. Sneaking back upstairs is crucial, as the fifth step creaks, and if he wakes while I have a knife, he'll use it on me. Standing over him, I believe I'm doing what God won't.

I watch Melvin's chest rise and fall with each shallow breath. I picture him waking to find me standing over him. I have it now, the power. Look at me. Look into my eyes, Melvin. See what you've turned me into: a killer determined to stop you. Maybe he wakes. Maybe he doesn't. Irene won't be home for hours. I can wait.

He doesn't wake up, having blacked out from the vodka. For a second, I almost hate that. I want him to wake up for it. I want him to see me. The same way he wakes me when Irene's asleep.

I kick the bed hard, with the force of an adult.

He stirs. "What the fuck?"

"Hi, Dad. Wake up."

His eyes widen, and something in me clicks into place. He gets a brief second of understanding before my anger takes over, and the version of me I've rehearsed in my mind steps forward. The knife is in my hand, and the choice is made. I slide the blade into his bare chest, piercing his soul. The knife strikes his heart as he processes what's happening.

Our eyes lock, and I whisper, "This is for what you do to me when Mom's not around." I don't feel brave. I feel empty. My anger erupts into fury. I keep plunging the kitchen knife into his chest, even though he's already dead. When I finally stop, the room falls still.

I wash up. I scrub until my skin feels raw. I erase Melvin. Then I slip back out through the torn screen and run through the woods until my lungs burn, letting the dark swallow me. I don't stop until I'm near the pond behind Wakefield Circle. I get rid of the blade somewhere it will never find me again. The splash against the pond's surface sounds like an ending; it makes me smile. I hurry back home with the strange belief that my abuser is gone, waiting to be found by his wife in their bed. I find my friends and step back into the night as if nothing happened, as if my childhood can finally start again.

Killing my father was a doomed plan.

But it did its job. It brought me comfort on many nights.

The pain he inflicted on me and others fueled this fantasy. I wanted to save everyone: the kids he'd already victimized, those he might abuse in the future, and me. He deserved to die, didn't he? He stole my innocence, and I wanted to steal his heartbeat. Was it cowardly to think this way? To fantasize about feeling whole once Melvin's heart stopped?

I'd be caught within thirty seconds of anyone finding his body. The so-called "perfect crime" was anything but—it was messy, the product of an abused boy simply trying to survive an attack by his adoptive father.

I didn't want to be a murderer. I wanted to go to bed at night without fearing that he'd call my name.

Torn ACL

"Get off me! It hurts! It's broken! My leg is broken!" I screamed. A blinding pain erupted from my left knee as I lay on the ground, crushed beneath Brett, whose villainous laugh only made the pain worse. Tag football was a neighborhood pastime. Yet the irony was that the game, fueled by teenage testosterone, inevitably devolved into a full-contact tackle match, where the rules were always overpowered by a need to prove dominance.

"Alright, you pussy. You can't handle working on the farm, and you can't handle playing football." Brett crawled off my crumpled body, shedding his hulking frame. Sensing the heat would quickly come down on him, he grabbed his pigskin and disappeared behind one of the buildings.

My cries drew adults out. "Get my mother! Mom!" I shouted for Irene as rain threatened. Neighborhood kids dispersed, fearing rain or testifying against Brett. I begged Pete to find Irene.

I lost track of the minutes. It began to drizzle. The pain was vibrating and shooting out electric pulses. Within minutes, Irene's face came into view as I held my knee, rolling back and forth on the slightly soaked grass. The moment I saw Irene, the pain felt worse.

"Joe. What happened?" she urged. Pete and Gwen stood on the sidewalk, watching me as I gasped out my explanation.

"It snapped. My knee is broken." I was inconsolable. "It hurts so much."

Irene bent over and called Pete over to help me stand, but as soon as I put weight on my knee, a stabbing pain shot down my leg. The pain forced me back down. I collapsed again.

"I can't stand. It was Brett. He jumped me."

"Joe, for Christ's sake, stand up," Irene directed, but my leg turned into a piece of cooked spaghetti, forcing me to lean toward her and almost take her to the ground.

"If you make me fall, I'll beat your ass," she hollered.

The snap I felt when Brett landed was like a tectonic plate subducting another. My kneecap shifted like continents sliding over one another, but it took seconds, not millions of years, to change the shape of my leg. From the moment I fell until Irene arrived, my knee doubled in size, looking lumpy and deformed.

With precise care and time, Irene and Pete hoisted me while I hobbled on one leg back to our condo. After I sat on the sofa and propped up my knee, the damage became visible. The fluid in my knee had swelled to the size of a medium-sized pumpkin. This fluid made my knee stiff and difficult to move, leaving me unable to find a comfortable position.

While Irene filled a ziplock baggie with ice, her verbal rage gave me something else to focus on. "That bastard Brett," she yelled. "I'll sue him and his family. What the fuck is wrong with that kid?" She walked down the hallway toward me. "Why does he hate you? What did you do?"

"Nothing. Mom. He's a jerk."

She handed me a glass of apple juice. The cold liquid chilled me. My body felt hot; adrenaline surged through me. Carefully, she laid a towel over my knee and gently draped the bag of ice on top. She grabbed a cigarette from the pack, lit it, and continued her questioning. "Tell me what happened."

I inhaled, fighting the tightening discomfort in my ballooning knee. "Alan and Brett wanted to play football. I didn't want to, but Alan made me do it. The ball was coming toward me. I reached up to catch it, and then I was on the ground with Brett on top of me." I caught my breath. "Will I be able to walk again?"

Irene stood at the dining room table, taking a swig of her beer. "Yes. Don't be stupid, but I'll kill that asshole Brett if he comes near you again."

The next morning, Irene and Melvin sat at the dining room table, drinking coffee. With my knee feeling like a water balloon about to burst, I managed to put a little weight on it and scooted down the stairs on my behind. My goal was to reach the living room and tell them I couldn't go to school. I'd need crutches or a cane, or even better, a wheelchair. The ability to walk felt short-lived, and with each small step, my knee grew more inflamed and inflexible. I held onto the wall for support and hopped into the chair next to Melvin.

"I can't go to school today. My knee is too swollen to walk."

Melvin smiled. "You walked in here. You can go to school."

I looked toward Irene. "Mom, it hurts so bad."

She finished the last of her coffee, then turned to me. "You have to go to school. You'll be fine."

The parental agreement is one I will never understand. Two parents can hate each other, fighting day and night until exhausted, yet when it comes to their child, they present a united front. This alliance suggests that, when it comes to their kid, they agree on one thing: unless the child is hanging on by a thread in the intensive care unit, they're going to school.

I left the house early, inching my way to the bus stop. I couldn't pull my corduroy pants over my expanding knee, so I wore sweatpants. The school bus pickup was only a few blocks away, but it might as well have been five miles. My parents didn't offer to drop me off. I thought I'd miss the bus, but as I approached, a few students held it for me. I tried to wave the driver off, but she waited. I couldn't win. When I wanted to miss it, the driver waited. When I didn't, the chance of missing it tripled.

Once on the bus, the comments ranged from sympathy to blame:

You're so weak you can't even handle Brett Caren falling on you.

It's not Joe's fault; he's in pain.

If Joebosity were skinnier, he'd bounce back faster.

After I'd finished telling the kids around me about the high schooler who crushed me, the yellow bus pulled into the drop-off line at East Hartford Middle School. Backpacks came off laps. Bodies surged into the aisle. I slid to the edge of my seat, ready to make my way down the aisle, when the driver barked, "Sit down, students. Your teacher will be here in a minute."

I turned, blinking. The bell rang in five minutes. Why were we waiting? From the back of the bus, a boy called out, "It's Dr. B."

The question of why Dr. Buchanan, the Assistant Principal, was coming onto the bus hung in the air as we paused for a few moments before he boarded.

"Alright, students, listen carefully," he announced. "We're having a bus fire drill. I'll walk to the back of the bus, open the emergency exit, and jump down. Each row, starting from the back, will follow me. Grab everything you have because you'll be going directly to class. Tell your teacher you were participating in a fire drill."

After his speech, he marched down the aisle of the bus, waving off students who asked questions. The emergency siren screeched the moment he pushed against the handle and jumped to the ground with ease. I craned my head back to see him from the waist up.

"Let's go! Let's go!" His hands gestured to us to hurry. "The bus is on fire."

My row was in the middle of the bus, and when it was our turn to evacuate, I let everyone around me go first. I stayed put, waiting for Dr. B. I'd barely managed the bus steps on the way in; there was no way my knee would survive a leap to the pavement for a pretend emergency. If the bus had actually been on fire, sure, I'd have dragged my leg across burning coals to survive, but this wasn't that. So I waited until he came for me.

"Shedrick? Let's go." Dr. B. had reboarded and stood in the aisle beside me. The driver sat in her seat, watching in the rearview mirror.

"Dr. B, I hurt my knee yesterday. It's very swollen." I pointed to my injury, where the sweatpants were stretched to their limit across the swelling.

He brushed me off. "It's always something with you, Shedrick. Let's go. Every student must participate in the fire drill. It's school board policy."

Dr. B didn't understand the severity of my injury. I poked my knee. "It's swollen. I can show you." I started to pull up the left leg of my sweatpants, but I realized Dr. B wasn't concerned.

He folded his arms. This was a standoff. "No excuses. Every student."

I leaned back. "I can't do it. It hurts too much."

He moved closer, inches from my face, his hot parental breath on my forehead. "This could lead to three days of in-school suspension and a missed prom. Do you want that?"

Only three months remained in middle school, and I wasn't about to get on the administration's bad side and lose my spot at our eighth-grade junior prom. I'd been saving money from my job at the brass furniture store and had special-ordered a light blue tuxedo with a velvet collar. A bunch of us were going stag, and I didn't want to miss my chance to show off that masterpiece to the class of '86.

I reached forward and gripped the seat in front of me. Leaning hard on my good leg, I pushed myself up, flung my backpack over one shoulder, and limped toward the back of the bus. I made a show of it, fingers sliding along the seatbacks like handrails, but Dr. B thought it was overdone.

Outside, the parking lot had emptied. The late bell rang.

From the back door, I stared toward the school's front entrance. A few students streaked past the large windows along the building's facade. I'd be late to class again. I was sure my homeroom teacher expected it. I paused. Dr. B closed in behind me, close enough that I could feel his impatience. I hesitated, almost turning around, but I knew that if I resisted any more, he'd shove me. So I focused on the uninjured knee. I dropped my backpack to the ground and edged forward, trying to decide how to land.

I'm a terrible jumper. On three, I took off.

My instinct to land on my good knee betrayed me. I realized it midair, as I sailed forward and dropped like a sack of oranges. I hit the ground, most of my weight on the injured knee. The pavement's impact snapped something inside my leg, like a rubber band. A single kernel of popcorn ignited. The agony nearly knocked me out. My howling echoed across the school grounds.

I gazed up at Dr. B., still standing inside the bus, his whole body filling the narrow doorway. The rest is a blur, but

I remember thrashing as Dr. B. ran inside to call 911. The bus driver knelt beside me, trying to calm me. Useless. I didn't move again until the paramedics lifted me onto the stretcher, cinched the chest straps, and loaded me into the ambulance for the ride to the emergency room.

ACL reconstruction surgery was scheduled for later that week. Until then, I lay on the sofa, trapped, unable to escape my parents' arguing about what had happened at school and what to do next. Melvin had already contacted our family lawyer, Willie, who'd drafted a notice of intention to sue, but that didn't satisfy Irene's anger.

"We'll sue every last one of them for forcing him to jump off that bus. We're suing the bus company, the school board, and the vice principal. Every. Last. One. Of. Them."

On the morning of surgery, we arrived at the hospital at 5 a.m. Admissions. Paperwork. A quick visit from the nurse, then the doctor. Then the IV in my forearm. The nurse injected a clear liquid into the line, and the panic in my chest softened, as if someone had turned the volume down. It was my first surgery. I kept thinking I might not wake up, but the pain in my knee outweighed the fear. If I died, at least I wouldn't hurt anymore.

This ACL procedure was a same-day surgery. I woke to orange juice and a snack, all smiles because the pain medication was doing its job. The nurse checked on me every fifteen minutes, and it was the opposite of my hospital stay in New York City, where I'd crawled across the floor just to get to the restroom.

Having a stranger care for me without judgment or ridicule made me yearn to be a hospital patient—that idea lodged in my brain. A few times in my early teens, I faked stomachaches to force Irene to spend hours in the emergency room, running test after test, only to discover the truth: nothing was wrong with me except that I hated school enough to set my parents' checking account on fire.

Once the juice and snack had settled, the cast became real: an off-white fiberglass cast from my upper left thigh to my foot. I wanted to crawl out of my skin. The pressure was claustrophobic, a constant weight that stayed with me every day of my recovery. The moment I understood how constrained I was, I started counting down the days until the doctor sawed it off.

A few hours after surgery, I developed a low-grade fever. The nurse and surgeon couldn't explain it. The nurse's voice sharpened, Irene's face tightened, and my hospital room filled with a quiet urgency, but the drugs still left me in a fog. The surgeon finally came in with a saw and proved it wouldn't cut me, the kind of reassurance you don't realize you'll need until someone wheels a power tool toward your leg.

"We want to make sure the incision isn't infected," he told Irene, then carefully eased the saw into the newly set cast. I squeezed Irene's hand, certain that if the whirring blade kissed skin, I'd lose my leg. When he lifted out a section of fiberglass, my knee looked like a battlefield, purple and swollen, misshapen and angry, the skin puffed around a neat line of staples. Those tiny soldiers seemed to hold me together, fighting off infection. Thankfully, the wound was clean, with no infection. The doctor ordered more fluids and antibiotics, and within thirty minutes, my fever broke.

The nurse repositioned the fiberglass section and wrapped it tightly with a wide bandage. By late afternoon, my discharge papers were signed and handed to Irene. An orderly rolled me out in a wheelchair while the anesthesia-induced nausea kept forcing me to swallow, my mouth full of bitter, chemical spit.

I expected Melvin to show up, but when Janice pulled up with Gwen, I turned to Irene. "Mom, where's Dad?"

"He's home," she said, her tone warning me. "Don't bring it up right now."

I knew to drop it. When Gwen jumped out to greet me, I gave her my famous fake smile, the one that kept questions at bay. I didn't know what was happening at home, only that I was supposed to pretend nothing was.

"Wow. That's a huge cast. Can I sign it?"

Janice leaned across the wheel. "Get him in the car. You can sign it later."

The ride back to Wakefield Circle was quiet, heavy with the feeling that we all knew something terrible had happened or was about to. Nobody wanted to be the first to say it out loud. I drifted in and out of sleep. To this day, I don't know how Irene got Janice to drive her to pick me up at the hospital. Where was Linda? Irene and Janice weren't friends, just two mothers whose kids were friends. I think it's one of those balancing acts parents do, polite small talk and navigating relationships with people they have nothing in common with, all for their children.

I lost track of time and woke up as Irene opened her car door. She took my crutches from the trunk, and with the quick hospital discharge lesson, I levered myself out of Janice's car. The cast tugged at my leg like dead weight, and each step was a fight with gravity. Irene turned and waved to Janice at the door, she waved back. Gwen rolled down her window and promised she'd call me the next day to check on me and bring my science and math homework.

I didn't want homework.

Inside, Melvin sat at the kitchen table, a drink in front of him. "Where's the patient?" he slurred, then stood and lurched toward me. I stopped.

I hadn't expected him to be home. When we pulled in, our Chevy Blazer was gone from its parking spot. I'd assumed he was out drinking somewhere else, perhaps with one of his brothers.

Irene moved quickly, stepping between us. "He's going upstairs. He needs to elevate his leg. Did you start dinner?"

Melvin held my gaze a beat too long, shrugged, and dropped back into his chair. "No. You make dinner."

Irene led me to the stairs and stayed close as I hopped up each step, gripping the railing while she carried my crutches. Once in my room, she helped me lie down and slid a pillow under my leg. The doctor had warned us that swelling could spike quickly, so it was essential to keep my leg elevated for the first twenty-four hours.

She turned on my television. "I'll bring you some pain medicine and water in a few minutes." She rested her hand on my head. I saw sadness in her eyes, but she didn't say anything else. My mother's eyes always dripped with sadness. She stepped out of the room and left the door ajar, close enough to hear me if I called.

After I drank the pink liquid pain medication, I fell asleep. The shouting from downstairs jolted me awake. It rose through the stairwell like smoke. Irene was in the middle of a sentence when my brain cleared enough to understand.

"You have no fucking job," Irene spat. "Are we supposed to live on the money I'm making at the Grocery Barn?"

I leaned forward, remembering that I'd had surgery and that a cast was holding me down.

"We lost the truck, Melvin. We have no vehicle," she went on. "Am I supposed to ask Victor and my mother for money?"

The truth had always been within earshot. Money was a live wire in our house. Melvin rarely kept a job, and even when he did, it didn't last. Drinking always won. If I'd listened more closely to their arguments, I might have understood what was happening. Kids aren't supposed to carry adult problems, but I still wish I'd seen it coming. While I was in surgery, our vehicle had been repossessed, and the shock hit me like a second injury. Downstairs, Irene kept firing questions and accusations, faster and sharper, until something hit hard.

A loud thud.

"Get off me!" she yelled.

Then came the sound: a hard slap, unmistakable.

Her screams continued, and my rage flared. I swung my leg off the bed and nearly blacked out from pain, but I forced myself upright as the shouting persisted.

The cast immobilizing my leg slowed me for a moment, but my need to protect Irene drowned out any post-op agony. I snatched up my crutches and balanced on one foot, wobbling as I hauled myself toward the door, while my mother's pleas for help rose from downstairs.

My mind went to one place: stop him permanently, if that's what it took. The thought fueled me, and I forced myself to hobble to the top of the stairs, pain trailing behind me like a tail. I couldn't navigate the steps on crutches, but I wouldn't leave them behind. They were my only weapon.

I scooted down the stairs, using the carpet to muffle my movement, hoping to surprise Melvin, but Irene's cries grew desperate, and I began shouting as I dragged myself down one step at a time, unable to see them, only hearing her.

"Get away from my mother," I screamed. "I'll kill you!"

At the bottom of the stairs, my parents snapped into view. Irene was on the hallway floor beneath him. Melvin looked up, then shifted himself toward me, slow and deliberate, as if he had all the time in the world. My entire body tingled. Terrified. I still had the nerve to lift one crutch into the air, because it was the only strength I had. My knee throbbed, but the pressure inside me was worse.

"Look at you, you wimp. What are you going to do?" Melvin snatched the crutch from my hand and raised it like a club. "I should beat the hell out of you. Make you a man."

Irene pulled herself up off the floor. I can't remember her face. I remember her blouse crooked at the collar, the fabric stretched, her chest rising quickly, her breath uneven.

"Leave him alone," she gasped, getting to her feet. "He just had surgery."

Melvin shoved her back like she weighed nothing.

"He thinks he's a man," he sneered at me. "Come on, wimp. Get up and fight."

The bully had won. They always did. The rage that had carried me to the stairs fizzled, leaving me hollow. All my plans to protect my mother collapsed, and I stared at him, helpless, suddenly aware of how small I was. The cast, meant to help me heal, had become a weapon he wielded against me. I couldn't run. I couldn't even walk.

Irene shoved him aside. "We're leaving. I'm going to my mother's."

Melvin threw the crutch down. It hit my cast, and I grunted. "Yeah," he said to Irene. "Go to your mother's. Both of you." He curled his lip at me. "You'll always be a mommy's boy."

Irene got me back to my room and told me to pack for a few nights. Then she vanished down the stairs again, moving with sudden purpose. Everything blurred. I shoved a few shirts and pairs of underwear into my backpack. I had no idea what to take when you're leaving in a hurry. I wanted my record player. I wanted my 45s. But none of that felt like an emergency. I moved in slow motion, trying to decide what mattered while they argued below.

The storm moved upstairs. Melvin with it. I worried he'd hit her again, and then the fog in my head returned. The narcotic was still working, which was why I wanted to fall back asleep rather than flee our home as if a natural disaster were about to strike.

Irene called Mémé and Pépé and begged them to come pick us up. I stayed in my room, afraid to move. Dresser drawers flew open and slammed shut as their voices ricocheted down the hall, sharp with curses and belligerence.

Then Melvin peered into my room. "You'll be back."

Without a car, we were all prisoners. No one could escape. If this cast hadn't held me down, I might have run. Or at least I would have wanted to. But wanting and doing were two different things in that house.

Melvin sat at the dining room table, nursing his drink, while Irene smoked cigarettes on the back patio. I sat on my bed with my backpack packed, waiting for my grandparents to do what they did best: rescue me from the bed Irene had made.

A few hours later, Mémé and Pépé pulled into the spot directly in front of our condo. The horn announced our chariot's arrival. For their own safety, they stayed outside, refusing to enter the blast zone that could escalate into a confrontation with Melvin.

Irene helped lift me into their car. I kept glancing back at our front door, wondering whether Melvin was watching.

He didn't bother.

GIRLFRIENDS?

Freedom from Melvin was an illusion. Within three days, Irene and I were back on Wakefield Circle. Melvin called and lured her back with a bright new pitch: he was "this close" to being hired as a maintenance man at an apartment complex on the other side of East Hartford. The job, he said, came with a free apartment and a company truck, which would let them rent out our condo for extra income. I can only imagine what else poured through that phone line: the apologies, the promises, the revisions of history. Irene caved because the truth was simple: she didn't know how to live without Melvin, and everyone, including me, knew it.

When the leg cast finally came off, I wasn't just physically back in circulation; I was back in the neighborhood's social world. Something felt off. The boys my age seemed to have changed overnight. Suddenly, there were rules I hadn't learned yet, and one was clear: get a girlfriend.

Once the teenage boys started sprouting hair in places that had once been as smooth as a calm lake, every conversation became about one thing: girls. It didn't matter what kind of girl. No girl was off-limits. Stunning girls. Unattractive girls. Even pregnant girls. It was as if the guys had held a secret meeting behind closed doors and agreed on a new rule: from now on, we only talk about girls. And apparently, my invitation had been lost in the mail.

If a teenage boy didn't have a girlfriend or wasn't at least looking for one, something had to be wrong with him. In eighth-grade logic, not lusting after a girl meant one thing: a word thrown around the neighborhood—*fag*. There was no other explanation for why a proper Connecticut Yankee boy wasn't chasing the scent of every girl within a hundred-mile radius of his puberty-driven orbit.

As if the changes in our voices, bodies, and thoughts weren't enough, we were now expected to have one singular focus: the opposite sex. Talk about them endlessly. Inventory them. Speculate out loud about what we'd do if given the chance. Every girl and every mom, we were suddenly supposed to pretend we understood.

The illusion of chasing girls became more exhausting than working on the farm.

The pressure to show sexual interest in females weighed heavily on me. Back then, I didn't realize how many small things I did or didn't do that gave me away.

Screaming *like a girl*, as they'd say. Strutting *like a girl*. Playing Barbies while looking over my shoulder, *like a girl*. These traits came naturally to me. Drooling over girls felt performative.

The only girl I needed was Gwen. We clicked. With her, I could be loud, flamboyant, and free, and she never blinked. When I wasn't with Pete, Alan, or Will, I spent time with Gwen. We'd hang out on her bed, listen to New Kids on the Block, and stare up at her Rob Lowe poster.

But the other boys on Wakefield Circle didn't like it, especially Alan. He noticed I didn't share their interest in rehashing what girls wore during phys ed and how holding onto the image of any teenage girl in short shorts and a tank top kept them in the shower longer. And I definitely didn't have the stomach for their kind of "boy-work," either, the kind that left you knee-deep in mud, picking carrots, until you learned not to cry about it.

I cried about it. The boys hated it. To them, it was just another mark in the tally of how I wasn't like them.

At thirteen, I was trying to make sense of the rules. At fifteen, Alan was already having sex. Learning that Alan was sexually active left me flabbergasted. I didn't believe it. Maybe I didn't want to. At the time, I couldn't understand why the idea of Alan having sex upset me so much, but it felt like the next level of adolescence, too adult. Today, I realize I was jealous of the girls he paid attention to.

"Alan's at the house," Will needled. "Him and Sherry are doing it. *Right Now!*"

I had to see it. As we approached Linda's condominium, I looked up at Alan and Will's bedroom window. The blinds were wide open. The bunk bed swayed side to side, as if movers were trying to take it out of the room. When the bed frame finally settled, Alan came outside, disheveled, smiling. Sherry jumped in her car and drove off. Alan beamed with pride, wearing a hoodie and gray sweatpants. The three of us chatted, and he rattled off what Sherry had done to him. Will couldn't get enough, bouncing around as if *he* had just finished having sex. When Will disappeared into their house, Alan pulled me aside. His expression hardened. In as direct a way as Alan could, he emphasized that if I didn't find a girlfriend soon, people would become suspicious and things would get harder for me.

"Will doesn't have a girlfriend," I argued.

Alan slapped me on the back. "Will is batshit crazy," he said. "No girl in her right mind would date him. But you're not crazy." He put me in a headlock, then let go quickly. I enjoyed it when he roughed me up.

Then, in a fatherly tone, he added, "Seriously, you should find a girlfriend."

I took Alan's words as a threat, and it frightened me. Was there a teenage boy mob keeping track of who had girlfriends? Was I on the hit list? The idea of having a girlfriend felt ridiculous. I had no interest in girls, not the way they meant it. I wanted to hang out with Gwen in her room and listen to "Girls Just Wanna Have Fun." I had to approach the girlfriend challenge differently, to think like a kid trying to survive rules he didn't write. Living with Melvin and Irene, I had mastered that. I decided to do what many boys did: fake it.

Instead of dating or having a girlfriend, I created a new character: the young, desperate, horny teenager who spent every waking second searching for the right girl. I kept up the charade for a few months. At one point, I even convinced Irene that I liked girls. But the teenagers in the neighborhood had better radar than my mother and weren't invested in believing me. My time ran out, and "the mob" started sniffing around again. Alan had become their leader.

"Yes, I found a girlfriend," I said, walking with him through the woods behind Wakefield Circle.

"Cool. What's your girl's name?"

My palms went sweaty. "I don't think you know her. She's in middle school and lives far away." To add some spice, I said what all the other guys said. "She's hot."

"Yeah, sure. I'm not stupid, Joe."

"Seriously," I responded, grabbing the first name that came to mind, fresh off a Brady Bunch rerun. "Her name is Ginny. Ginny Gravel." I'd gone full Jan Brady, conjuring my own George Glass right there in the woods.

Alan didn't talk to me for a week.

Things change when we least expect them, and the teenage gods shone on me during the last week of eighth grade. There was a girl in my grade named Lisa. She was cute.

Friendly. She had short black hair, and I was taller than her, which felt like a win on the girlfriend checklist. Although her braces pushed her lips out far enough to make her look like she dipped after class, she met the only criterion that mattered. Lisa was a girl. She had a pulse. And she wasn't a bully.

"Do you want to be my girlfriend?" I whispered to her as we sat in the auditorium, waiting for the end-of-the-year movie to start. As *The Jungle Book* flickered on the massive screen, a small "Yes" slipped from her, and the tension I'd been carrying about finding a girlfriend drained away on the last day of school.

Lisa and I "dated" for the entire summer of 1986. I strutted with confidence, and I had the imaginary message—I have a girlfriend—symbolically tattooed on my forehead.

Oddly, though, we only hung out in person once, at the roller-skating rink. In the '80s, the rink was the place to be and be seen. Birthday parties. Saturday free skate. Uncomfortable first dates for thirteen-year-olds. After carefully planning our outing over the phone, our parents dropped us off, and it was one of the most awkward two hours of my life. I missed connecting with Lisa by phone. On the phone, I lived in a fantasy that we were the most incredible couple in East Hartford. But roller-skating around the rink and holding hands while listening to Berlin's "Take My Breath Away" felt like hanging out with a sister. Over the phone, Lisa and I were inseparable; in person, we were strangers.

The entire relationship was an illusion, a confusing one at that. The happiest moments were on our landline phones. We spoke every day throughout the summer. Not a single day went by without at least an hour on the phone, repeating how much we liked each other. Even though I didn't find her particularly attractive or interesting, I managed to make it work in my mind.

We watched movies "together" while hogging the phone line. We talked about music and TV shows. Our favorite was *Family Ties*. Lisa thought Alex P. Keaton was adorable. So did I.

She loved Janet Jackson. I loved Madonna and Cyndi Lauper.

We'd debate who had the better music videos on MTV until Irene picked up the phone from the kitchen and cut in: "Elvis was the best at everything. Now get off the phone before you're grounded."

Our differences distracted us from the truth.

The best part was that she lived miles away, too far for me to bike there. After our roller-skating date, neither of us brought up getting together again. We'd talk about how much fun we'd have spending every spare minute together in high school. We'd never kissed, so we giggled about how much kissing we'd have to do to catch up with our friends.

Irene offered to pick her up and let her hang out for the day, and I considered it because parading her around the neighborhood would end the whispers behind my back. But I told Irene that Lisa's mother had forbidden her from going to a boy's house. That was a lie. I made it up. I worried Irene would get intoxicated and not be able to drive Lisa home.

We kept up our phone love chats, and I told Alan, Pete, and anyone else within earshot that I had a girlfriend. Gwen found the idea of me having a girlfriend absurd. She always knew. But dating Lisa made me cocky. Being a gay boy and securing a girlfriend in 1986 felt like being a magician. I lost myself.

On my first day at East Hartford High School, Lisa and I got lost in the halls trying to find her second-period class. The bell was about to ring, so we split up, and I left her to find her own way. Dozens of students swarmed around us like bees returning to their hive. Something pulled at me. Standing in the hall was my big moment. I turned back and called out to her. Face-to-face, I leaned in for a kiss. She flinched.

"I think we should break up." Her body inched toward the classroom door. "This isn't working for me," Lisa said, with the air of someone who'd been married for over twenty years and was leaving me for the pool boy. Was he hot? If so, I understood.

I had a two-month summer fling and saw her only once. Our lips never touched. But it kept the gossip down, and that was the point. The problem was, now that I'd *had* a girlfriend, I needed another. This cycle of teenage lust never ended, a loop of angst and hormones that turned everyone around me into horny zombies.

In writing, they say you're only as good as your last piece of work. In high school dating, you're only as straight as your previous girlfriend.

When a classmate asked me if there were any girls I was hot for, I'd pull a random name from one of my classes. I didn't even have to know her. Was she breathing? If so, I'd fabricate a full-blown obsession. It worked for a few weeks.

Then, one afternoon, as I walked out of World History, I was cornered by one of the girls whose name I'd been using. Dawn, a tall, Amazon-looking girl who looked more like a forty-year-old bank teller than a high school freshman, shoved me and shouted, "Stop telling people you like me. You're gross."

And a good day to you, too, Wonder Woman.

Just days away from having my head flushed in a toilet for being the weirdo without a girlfriend, I came up with the perfect person: Gwen. Sure, she felt more like a twin sister than a girlfriend, but I was desperate. Those high school toilets were a crime scene.

I had the wrong idea, though. I thought having something in common with your high school sweetheart mattered, which only proved I'd spent too much time watching *Growing Pains*. In reality, dating was like an R-rated movie: teenagers only liked each other when they were making out or groping.

Gwen and I were different; we had everything in common, and I was surprised it took me so long to realize she was the one. We loved MTV. We loved the same movies. We laughed together. We knew every word of Bobby Brown's album *Don't Be Cruel*. We talked openly about our family dysfunction. Well, mostly. I did keep one secret close to my chest.

And if Gwen was going to be my girlfriend, I had to seal it. I had to prove I was the kind of guy she could lean on when she was mad at her mom for treating her like a free babysitter.

Desperation set in. The accusations from my peers felt like being attacked by rotten melons again. It got so bad that if your face didn't have a make-out rash, you'd better have an explanation the next time a pack of boys cornered you in the locker room, as if it were an interrogation. But these dating mercenaries were relentless. The barrage of questions about the girls in my life became more taxing than being alone with Melvin. At least with him, I knew how to play the game. High school dating rewrote the rules and blurred every line.

One day, while Gwen and I sat on the hill behind my building, I made a brave move. "Can I kiss you?"

Gwen knew I didn't like girls, and she refused to pretend she did.

After she stopped laughing, she answered with a simple "no." I didn't press her. Deep down, her honesty relieved me. I didn't want to kiss her or be her boyfriend. I wanted the pressure of dating to end so I could go back to watching *Voltron* after school and playing kickball with my friends. But the teenage boys weren't playing kickball much anymore. They were all too wrapped up in girls, leaving me bored.

A few days passed, and word still hadn't spread through Wakefield Circle about my "bravery" in asking a girl for a kiss. I don't know why the rumor hadn't caught fire. I'd told everyone I could. I guess Gwen never mentioned it. As for the kids I shared this enthusiastic news with, either no one believed me or no one cared. The point was: asking a girl for a kiss was totally middle school. This was high school. Kissing happened between class periods. It was part of the curriculum.

Pete admitted he thought it was gross that I'd asked Gwen to kiss me. He talked about her as if she were family. I played off his comparison, telling him to "gag me with a spoon." Sadly, Pete was right. Gwen *was* family, but I needed her to take the heat off me. I needed a beard.

One day after school, under pressure, I picked up the phone and dialed Gwen's house.

"Hello?"

"Hi, Janice. This is Joe. Is Gwen home?"

After a beat, Gwen came on the line. "Hey. Did you hear Samantha got suspended for throwing her gum into Michelle's hair? Sam's so grody, right?"

Gwen's gossip was gold, and I was tempted to scrap my plan and go full Sally Jessy Raphael, but I had an unbelievable reputation to uphold.

I summoned whatever version of manhood I could and declared, "I want you to be my girlfriend."

Then I hit play on my boombox. I'd queued the cassette to the perfect spot, the one where my desperation would land the hardest. On cue, Huey Lewis and the News' "If This Is It" blared in my bedroom and poured through the phone straight into her ears.

After I assumed that Huey Lewis and the News had done their job, I pressed the receiver back to my ear. "Well? What did you think?"

As politely as a friend can turn down another, she said, "Joe. You're like my brother. I can't date you." I tried to interrupt, but she barreled ahead into the one topic we always agreed on. "Meet me at the pond so I can tell you all about that bitch, Samantha."

Gwen was right that Samantha was a bitch, so I met her at the pond for the debrief. I also gave up on the idea of a future girlfriend. When the topic came up, and it still did, time after time, I either stayed silent or made a tasteless joke for an easy laugh.

My relationship with the other teenagers changed once we acclimated to high school. My new role was that of a comedian, and I played it perfectly: the funny guy, the fool, the self-deprecating husky gay boy fighting for a seat at the table. To be seen and not scorned. This moniker softened some of the bullying aimed at me, but I'd be lying if I said I avoided it altogether. Bullies don't forget you when you're sitting across from them in English class. But being funny gave me a beat to sit in my skin as a teenager. A lot happens at fourteen. Girls. High school. Dodging parents.

So, instead of chasing girls, I chased laughs.

BAD STUDENT

High school was rough, even though becoming self-deprecating eased some of the taunting, it only made me feel worse about myself. I was unpopular, the kind of kid '80s sitcoms dedicated a 'very special episode' to. Every morning, I'd throw a tantrum before being forced out the door. Avoiding school became my only goal, a ritual that caused Irene great stress every morning.

I never set an alarm. I may not have even had one in my room. Instead, I waited for Irene to wake me each morning. I'd lie in bed, wide awake, praying she'd forget to set her alarm. Then I'd hear it chiming in the distance, followed by her feet scuffling toward my room. I tried this over and over again. This routine started back in elementary school, when Irene got too drunk to help me get ready for school.

"Joseph! Get up and go to school. You're gonna be fucking late," Irene yelled from my bedroom door. I'd play opossum, hoping she'd turn around and leave me in bed. My plan never worked, though. Eventually, she pulled my bedspread off me and forced me to get dressed.

As I tossed my legs over the edge of the bed, I argued. "I'm sick. I don't feel well."

"Bullshit! You're fine. Get dressed. You have to go to school." Then she marched to the window and opened the blinds. "Every morning we go through this shit."

Since I walked to East Hartford High School, there was no bus to miss. I cursed the fact that we lived so close. The school sat about a mile from our condo, down Penny Drive, and the walk was slow and miserable, mostly because of the destination. I'd step out, turn right, follow the road until it dead-ended into the woods, then shove through the overgrown brush and slip onto the school grounds like a cat with a backpack.

Still, I was often late. Being tardy became a tactic. Stepping into the looming two-story high school didn't mean I intended to stay. My first stop was the nurse's office, where I'd report whatever ailment I'd invented that morning. The nurse disliked me, which felt fair. When I dragged myself into her office, she'd scowl, waiting for my rehearsed monologue about why I needed to go home immediately. Like clockwork, she'd lift the receiver, already bracing for the part where I demanded she call my mother.

Irene and the nurse repeated the routine a few times weekly. The nurse hung up. I sat in the stackable schoolhouse chair beside her desk, panting, catching my breath, while she delivered the verdict.

"Your mom wants you to stay in school. You don't have a fever. You haven't thrown up. Go lie down for a bit, then get back to class for third period."

Her response didn't sit well with my plan, which was less "thermometer" and more "escape."

"Can you call her back so I can talk to her?" I added a theatrical cough, angling for an Oscar for Best Dramatic Illness. "I really don't feel well."

My pleading and fake coughing fell flat. I wasn't sick. Irene knew it. The nurse knew it. I knew it, too, even though I'd spent the whole walk to school inventing symptoms as if I were studying for a test.

By the time I set up camp in the nurse's chair, several students had come and gone. If someone walked in with a real fever, I felt a stab of envy. Why couldn't I have dysentery? Not measles. Not chickenpox. Just a low-grade fever. A simple stomach bug. Enough to get sent home. That was high on my wish list.

Once in the recovery room, out of view, I'd lie on one of the two cots and peek around the corner to see if the nurse had moved on. My deceit only worked when I had the room to myself. If she was coming and going, tending to another student, I had to drag myself to class.

But if I were alone, my plan could run. Lights. Camera. Action. When the coast was clear, I leaned over the edge of the cot and did what I came to do. With careful precision, I jammed my index finger down my throat. It took about three tonsil tickles before my breakfast reappeared in the trash can. That sound, that mess, was the point. I needed evidence. My ticket out of those cinderblock walls.

From the nurse's desk, I'd hear the heavy sigh, then the dial tone. She'd call Irene, and they'd run through their little script. Within minutes, I'd be pushing open the heavy school doors, savoring the sweet freedom of skipping class as I dragged myself away from the building, still performing until I was out of sight. Then I'd sprint home and spend the rest of the day catching up on soap operas.

By February 1987, halfway through my freshman year, Irene and Melvin both had jobs, which meant the condo sat empty all day. The perfect setup for a truant kid who played hooky more than he attended class. To this day, I'm not sure what Melvin did. Whatever it was, it didn't pay well, at least not according to their arguments. After our vehicle was repossessed, they bought a used one from one of Melvin's brothers. Melvin dropped Irene off at The Grocery Barn every morning, then went to work, whatever that meant that week.

He bounced between odd jobs, and at night Irene hounded him about the maintenance-man position he'd used as bait to get us back to Wakefield Circle.

Whatever my parents fought about went over my head. I didn't care about their problems. Compared with what I wanted and needed, their troubles felt trivial. All I cared about was not being in high school. After months of exhausting the school nurse with my shenanigans, I realized it was time to cut out the middleman.

It took me a few weeks to realize that skipping school wasn't just an option; it was the answer, at least until about three o'clock. Why negotiate with the nurse when I could simply not show up?

Once I excelled at dodging my education, Irene and Melvin never noticed the shift. I stopped arguing and crying about how awful high school was and how badly I wanted to stay home. Overnight, every illness in my excuse bank retired. Instead, I was cheerful, pleasant, and easygoing. Irene loved it. The morning battles were over. She thought I'd finally adjusted. I had. Just not the way she imagined.

I'd get dressed, eat a bowl of Frosted Flakes, kiss her cheek, and slip out the door. East Hartford High and the assholes who made my life miserable were the last things on my mind. I'd close the front door and walk to the end of our brick condo building. Before I reached the sidewalk, I'd turn right and vanish into the tall bushes at the corner of our building.

Only a keen eye might have spotted me, peering through the bushes like a poorly disguised shrub. I'd sit on my bookbag, back pressed against the brick wall, counting down the minutes until my parents left for work and the day belonged to Doritos and television. I'd skipped so many days that if I didn't see what Dorian Lord was up to on *One Life to Live*, I'd probably die. Or so I thought.

If my parents were ever running late, panic would shake the branches in my hideout. I feared I'd be stuck outside, forced to dart in and out of the woods, hiding from the world until school let out at 3 p.m. That happened. On a few occasions, one of them stayed home, and it wasn't until I saw their car pull away with an empty passenger seat that I understood my fate: roaming the streets like a feral cat.

Walking to school late never crossed my mind. Not once. I'd been in high school only five months, and I was already so far behind in my schoolwork that I decided it was pointless to go back. I honestly believed I could hang around the condo undetected until graduation. The idea that I wouldn't graduate if I didn't go to class never occurred to me. It was the sunk-cost fallacy, kid edition: I'd already missed so much school that showing up felt more dangerous than skipping.

After hiding in the bushes for thirty minutes, I'd hear my parents' car start. As they drove away, the tightness in my chest eased. I knew I wouldn't be outside dodging adults. The condo was mine, and I made the most of it.

Catlike, I crept along the building, staying behind the bushes until I was near my door. I had to be extra careful. Over Christmas break, Linda and the boys moved in right next door, and if she suspected anyone was inside during the day, I'd suddenly wish I were in Algebra. Getting in undetected was crucial. I was terrified Linda would catch me on my hands and knees at the front door.

Once inside, I'd tiptoe up the stairs and change into my pajamas in the dark. I never turned the lights on. The shades stayed drawn, giving me additional cover. Honestly, this was *Mission: Impossible*-level maneuvering, and after a few weeks of successfully dodging school officials, Linda, and my parents, I'd become a pint-sized Ethan Hunt.

The only light came from the TV. Lounging on the sofa was more appealing than attending Phys. Ed., a class I was failing. I disliked all my classes except Spanish, but Phys. Ed. was my nemesis. I failed English, too, which is funny considering I eventually earned an English degree. Freshman year ended with me in summer school in 1987 because I'd failed most of my classes. Who knew missing a few weeks of school could lead to failing everything except Spanish 1 and Foods 1? It's no surprise I passed a class focused on food. I love food.

Gym class? No, thank you. The idea of taking my shirt off in front of others was unthinkable. I did it once, and that was too many times. By my second day as a freshman, I decided I'd rather get a zero for participation than remove my shirt. I ran outside often, which counted as strenuous activity. I was already bullied while wearing my clothes, so I couldn't imagine what those punks would do to me shirtless. My chest looked like a punching bag, begging to be knocked out.

Then, one afternoon, while watching *One Life to Live*, I heard the distinct rattle of keys at the front door. I thought of running, but where? My stomach dropped. I jumped up, crumbs from potato chips sprinkled on my shirt, trying to make sense of being busted. Bright sunlight poured into the living room as one of my parents walked in. Then the door closed, and the room went dim again. The only sound was the TV and the slow, unmistakable approach of an adult down the hall. I bent to turn on the lamp beside the sofa. The bulb bloomed soft and yellow, mixing with the TV's glow, and the parental ambush felt like waking inside a dream.

"Why aren't you in school?" Melvin asked curiously, his body filling the hallway. He dropped his keys onto the table. The clatter made me shiver.

So much for Ethan Hunt. After weeks of evading school officials, I was caught in my own web. I stammered, offering apologies and excuses, but had nothing to defend myself with.

Melvin realized he had caught me in a secret.

"The school called me at work and said you haven't been in class for three weeks." He stepped closer. I sank back onto the sofa.

"Is that right?" he said, smirking. "Three weeks?"

Instead of responding with anger, ordering me to get dressed so he could drive me to school, and demanding I be held accountable, he seemed… happy. Like he'd been handed a present he couldn't wait to unwrap.

"Dad. I'm sorry, I just—"

Melvin's calm made my skin crawl. He went to the hall closet, hung his jacket with deliberate care, then returned to the living room while I kept searching for something, anything, to explain why I was home instead of in my World History class.

"Don't worry," he cooed, sitting down beside me. He held something wrapped in a brown paper bag. For a second, my brain supplied the safest answer: a book.

"I'm not gonna tell your mom, but starting tomorrow, you have to go to school."

He placed his hand on my leg. I jerked away on instinct. He caught my thigh and held on tighter.

"I think you're going to get an in-school suspension."

I stopped pretending I had excuses. "I don't care. I just hate school."

"Listen," he said, almost encouragingly. "I hated school too. That shit didn't do anything for me. When you turn sixteen, you can quit. But you have to go to school because if your mom finds out, I won't be able to protect you."

Agreed. When Melvin was pleased with me, he tried to keep me away from Irene. When he wasn't, he seemed to enjoy the verbal abuse she directed at me.

"Am I in trouble?"

"No," he said, standing and then stretching out his arms wide. "I have something for you."

Melvin opened the brown paper bag. It wasn't a book. It was a brand-new VHS tape, still sealed in plastic wrap. He handed it to me.

"What's this?" I asked. Then I read the title aloud: *Sugar Pussy Jeans*.

Melvin put his hand on my shoulder. "I bought it because I think you're getting too old for magazines. You need to see the real thing."

"Is this porn?"

He noticed my hesitation and grinned. "You seem nervous. There's nothing to worry about. It's fun." Then, an afterthought seemed to occur to him. "And Peter North is in it. You'll like him. I bet he'd do it with you, too."

My breath lodged in my throat. Then the room made sense. I understood the pleasure in Melvin's smile. Nobody knew I was home except him. Melvin had me to himself for hours because there was no way Irene was walking home from the grocery store.

I knew what he wanted. I just wanted to watch TV. I'd been bracing for punishment for skipping school, but I didn't expect Melvin to impose his special punishment. He was going to reward himself. He would call it something else.

We stared at each other for a beat. "Come on. Let's go upstairs and watch it."

I set the VHS tape on the coffee table. "Do we have to?"

"Yes. Don't you want to watch it?"

"Not right now, Dad. I don't feel well."

He picked up the tape and headed for the stairs. His tone made it clear the conversation was over. "You're fine. Hurry up." Halfway up the stairs, he added casually, "I have to pick up your mother in a few hours."

Instead of running outside, I turned off the TV. I clipped the potato chip bag shut with a wooden clothespin and slid the half-eaten bag back into the cabinet. Then I followed him upstairs.

In my room, Melvin had taken off his pants. Standing in the doorway, I knew there wouldn't be an argument that mattered. I had to flip the switch in my brain to survive. I thought about anything else. Homework. How behind I was and what in-school suspension would be like.

I don't know how, but Melvin moved through what he did with the quiet ease of someone who had never been held accountable. Unstoppable. The low, drumming electronic music kicked in as the tape flickered to life. I pulled off my shirt and tossed it aside. The TV cast shadows on the wall. My pajama bottoms fell to the floor. I tried to look enthusiastic because he demanded it. Pink neon filled the small screen, the title blazing across the television he'd bought me for my fourteenth birthday, three months earlier.

THE LAST TIME

It took Melvin a full year to land the maintenance job he'd used as bait to bring Irene and me back to Wakefield Circle after we ran away to my grandparents' house following my knee surgery. While the low-income apartment management took their time hiring him, Melvin bounced from blue-collar jobs, picking up handyman work—anything for some quick cash.

At one point, he launched a painting company that quickly failed. When creditors arrived, they were directed to our family lawyer. Hiding from clients illustrated Melvin's usual pattern: he often made big promises that usually led to failure. The maintenance job also seemed like another promise he kept dangling just out of reach. Days became months, then a whole year. Still no work. I never believed this dream job existed until one afternoon when the phone rang. Melvin talked for a few minutes and then hung up. Our world had changed overnight—once again.

In the summer of '87, while juggling summer school and the usual teenage angst, we finally moved into our new apartment.

Oakridge Apartments was only an eight-minute drive from our condo, a cluster of brick buildings that resembled Wakefield Circle but not quite. The grass looked like it hadn't seen a lawn mower in years. Trash overflowed the dumpsters. Screens were ripped or missing altogether. A few cars sat abandoned, left behind by evicted tenants.

Even in the dilapidated state of this new neighborhood, my parents focused on the upsides. Melvin finally had a steady income. Irene could walk to The Grocery Barn. I didn't have to change schools. That was my upside, though it wasn't really a win. East Hartford had only one high school.

So I fixated on the downside: being torn away from Gwen, Alan, and Pete, and from the familiarity and small comforts of our place on Wakefield Circle. I felt deep fear and sadness about leaving the condo. As hard as the kids on Wakefield Circle could be, at least I knew the choreography. I knew who to avoid, when to disappear, and which corners to stay off if certain groups were roaming.

Oakridge brought a whole new kind of uncertainty, the sense that anyone or anything around the corner could be a threat. Living with my parents had already trained me for that. I lived in constant pirouettes. I learned how not to get too dizzy.

I'd be turning fifteen in a few months, and uprooting me from the handful of friends I had gave me one more reason to rebel. It wasn't just the move. It was the reason: Melvin wanted to prove he had his shit together. I understood, on some level, that he needed to make money. But as a teenager trying to find my footing, all I could think about was how this family decision affected me.

We moved our lives into the new apartment, one truckload at a time, each load making it feel like we were slamming the door on our past. Then Linda moved into our old condo with Alan and Will, paying my parents rent. That felt strange. What if our parents fought over rent? Would I still be friends with Alan? I could've done without Will after the candy bar incident, but Alan? I couldn't fathom it.

And my friends were now sleeping in my old bedroom, the purple one, the room where I kept all my secrets. If those walls could whisper… the thought of them revealing Melvin's sins sent blood rushing to my temples.

Seriously? What if the walls could talk? What if Alan and Will somehow uncovered the truth about my hidden life? They already knew I was the husky, awkward kid with a small social circle, but they didn't know the darkest part of my life, the part where Melvin exploited me. Logically, I knew they couldn't discover Melvin's crimes just by sleeping in my old room. Still, the misdeeds lingered like the TV glow, clinging to that room long after I was gone.

Like most things with Melvin and Irene, the move felt like a new skin, at least on the surface. I mourned leaving Wakefield Circle, but my parents' excitement pulled me into their conviction that this time our lives would improve. How many times had they caught a break, only to set it on fire? Too many to count.

My parents' happiness echoed through the walls and drifted up the stairs into my new room, making it hard not to feel it. I smiled frequently during the first few weeks. Irene prepared dinner every evening, filling our apartment with warm, familiar aromas and establishing a comforting routine. My top choice was pork chops with scalloped potatoes, while my least favorite was Melvin's go-to: liver and onions. He kept busy around the complex, repairing tenants' broken appliances, managing move-outs, and getting units ready for new families.

At first, I aligned with my parents because I liked how the new skin felt, but over time, it went from smooth to irritated and raw. I daydreamed about a better life, one where the drinking eventually stopped, the fighting faded into the past, and my father's nightly visits to my bedroom ended. I even told myself I could forgive Melvin for what he did to me. Or maybe it was simpler than that: I wanted to.

Life settled into something that almost felt normal. My parents even let me get a cat, a gray-and-white tabby I named Bonkers because he was exactly that, a wild little lunatic who tore through the apartment as if possessed by every cat that had ever lived. I adored him. Bonkers, however, despised Melvin, which only made me love his furry face more.

One night at dinner, Melvin told us he had quit drinking. He said the new maintenance job and our move across town had given him the fresh start he needed, a real chance to be the husband and father he could be. We'd heard the same speech from Melvin when we moved to Wakefield Circle, and it wasn't a fresh start at all—just a continuation of the same damning plot in a slightly nicer location. I was skeptical that Melvin's new job would make a difference, but I went along with it whenever Irene nodded and reassured me: *It's gonna be different this time.*

We ignored the difficulties while living in fantasies. Never mind the debt collectors and angry clients still calling, demanding payment for the jobs he'd abandoned when the painting business collapsed. The phone rang anyway, and we let it ring. We clung to the hope in Melvin's words, focusing on his promise of sobriety and Irene's renewed dream of cooking dinners and sleeping without money worries.

But happiness in our house was a perfect illusion.

After we moved to Oakridge, one of my new responsibilities was serving as Melvin's maintenance assistant. I juggled that while barely attending high school and working a new job as a shelf stocker at the large grocery store down the street.

Since East Hartford High was now across town, I had to take the bus, which conveniently gave me a perfect way to skip. I may have spent half the summer in school to recover my grades, but I hadn't learned my lesson. I was biding my time until I turned sixteen so I could drop out. I had no future plans. I never really believed I had a future. I only had now. Survival mode.

On days when school felt like a waste of time, which was most of them, I hid behind one of the buildings until the bus arrived. I watched it pick up students and pull away. Then I'd stroll back to our apartment, wearing my best innocent annoyance, as if I'd tried.

"I missed the bus."

Melvin's company truck was our only ride, and he was always off looking busy, so on mornings when I came strolling back inside from the bus stop, Irene rolled her eyes and told me to stay in my bedroom until the end of the school day. Score. I settled into my twin bed, curled up with Bonkers under my *Return of the Jedi* bedsheets, which carried the unmistakable scent of teenage boy, no matter how often Irene washed them.

A sudden knock rattled my bedroom door. Before I could react, Melvin barged in, yanking my attention from the episode of my favorite cartoon on TV.

"Get up and get dressed. You're helping me paint Unit K today."

I curled my lip. "Can I finish this episode?"

He didn't look back. "No school. Then you gotta work."

Tenants left their apartments in disarray when they moved out, even those who weren't evicted. Nobody seemed to care about getting a deposit back. They rarely cleaned, patched holes, or even took everything with them. Piles of trash. Abandoned furniture. Stained carpets.

When Melvin put me to work, I often wished for a giant dumpster right outside the door. But I never wished to be in class. The idea that high school was "safe," with assholes calling me derogatory names, never felt true. If I had a choice back then, I'd rather have sat with the Devil than studied the Civil War.

"When you're done clearing out the trash in the living room, come help me paint the bedroom," Melvin ordered, unfolding plastic sheets to cover the grimy, stained carpet. The management company rarely approved carpet replacements, so it reeked of old pet urine, sour milk, and whatever else had seeped in over the years.

I dragged my feet. Slow on purpose. Distracted by birds outside, the wind, anything that wasn't this. When I finally finished clearing the trash, I shuffled into the bedroom.

I knew what awaited me. The story had been written before I ever stepped into Unit K. It was inevitable. Melvin didn't need my help. The "maintenance assistant" title was a cover, something for Irene to believe. Melvin knew why I was there. I did, too. And it had nothing to do with painting.

"What do you want me to do?" I asked, hovering in the doorway, trying to keep my distance for as long as I could. It was pointless. I already knew how this was going to go.

"Come here. Stand in front of me," Melvin directed. He knelt on a folded painting tarp and unzipped his pants. I moved toward him, positioning myself as he stared up at me. Melvin's focus was singular: the task.

"When we're done, you can go back home. Tell your mother I'm done with you."

Used and discarded.

A few weeks after we moved in, I began to notice a change in how I approached my relationship with Melvin. A shift.

Puberty? I can't be certain. But a strong urge to protect myself consumed me as I never had before. I'd rarely argued with Melvin about what he did. For years, I'd been groomed to go along with it. When I didn't, he made my life harder: an unnecessary grounding, an unnecessary spanking, a slap across the face.

But standing in Unit K, looking down at this pathetic motherfucker, I felt something I didn't recognize at first. Not courage, exactly. More like resistance, a thought that didn't belong to him. Something that went against Melvin's idea of "love." He didn't love me. He didn't love Irene. He loved himself. That truth landed in Unit K and overpowered everything, even the rot leaking from one of the garbage bags in the living room.

Heat prickled my skin. My neck turned crimson. My breathing labored, but I controlled it. I hated how he said, "When we're done," as if this were a collaboration, as if we were two people huddled over the same problem, trying to find the best way for him to consume parts of me illegally.

Part of what he did was sexual, but the engine beneath it was power. Melvin was a man married to a woman who abused young boys, and he used that abuse to maintain control and keep his secret intact. If his gaze ever broke, if his control slipped, he'd lose me. That was inconceivable to him. And suddenly, it wasn't to me.

"I don't want to do this anymore. I'm almost fifteen."

Silly me, thinking age mattered.

Melvin shook his head and grabbed my leg. I pulled away. He tried to justify himself, but I didn't let him.

"We need to stop," my voice was strong, sounding as adult as possible.

Melvin rose to his feet, his zipper still unzipped. "You don't love me anymore?" he whispered. Then came the insults. "You're just a selfish coward. That's all you are."

The verbal assaults were not new and had become a regular part of our daily interactions, but they didn't land as they once had. I heard his words differently. I didn't wince when he offended me. Over the previous weeks, his disparagement began to bounce off me. I heard it for what it was: noise.

As a child, I blamed myself for my parents' cold words, thinking it was love and their cruelty was my fault. By fifteen, I knew better; their anger wasn't about me. Melvin, a man-child, couldn't handle his teenage son's independence. He knew he couldn't buy me with VHS sex tapes or a crumpled twenty when I whined about our sessions. No more "candy" from his unmarked van. That era was over. I had a job, made my own money, and for the first time, had a little freedom and leverage, even if I didn't know how to use it.

I had found a power source deep within. Power, the thing Melvin loved more than kneeling before me. For a split second, standing there, I almost didn't mind that we were here, in this moment, because the darkness had been shattered by a newly found light that had been switched on. Everything changed in a single breath, the one I took right after I told him we had to stop, and he called me a coward. One thing became crystal clear: if I could survive my parents until I turned eighteen, I might make it out without having to listen to the part of my brain that whispered, *Kill him.*

"You're not a fucking man!" He dropped to his knees again. "Now unzip your pants."

I did what he demanded, but something in my chest detonated. A bomb that had been dormant for years finally went off, an ugly, righteous force that made me feel, for the first time, as if the ground under us shifted. I stared out the window at the building across the parking lot and made myself a promise. I had skipped school that day. I needed to make it count. My body. My rules. Not his. He had claimed it long enough.

Melvin's mouth would never touch me again.

FINDING MY TEENAGE VOICE

My part-time job after school and on weekends was at Finest Grocery, a mile away on School Street. I'd turned fifteen a few weeks earlier, still too young to run the cash register but old enough to spend four-hour shifts in the aisles, making sure every label faced forward for the "optimal shopping experience."

Boring doesn't even begin to describe the job. Whenever the shift manager's voice echoed throughout the store, "All stock and floor employees to the checkout," I lit up. It meant escaping Campbell's soup towers and stepping into the action, bagging groceries, and chatting with customers.

In late 1987, Finest Grocery paid me $3.37 an hour, but the real bonus was that it kept me out of the apartment. On the mornings when I managed to catch the school bus and survive a full day of 10th grade, I'd come home, change, and head back out the door for my 4 p.m. shift.

The payoff wasn't the paycheck. It was adulthood, and more importantly, distance. If I worked every available shift, I didn't have to be around Melvin, and that alone made the hours spent staring at spaghetti sauce worth the ache in my legs.

The four of us, Bonkers included, had been living at Oakridge Apartments for almost five months, still believing Melvin was on the wagon. Thanksgiving was behind us, and Christmas was already in view. The quiet in the apartment felt like proof he was sober. Irene and I really thought a full-blown alcoholic could quit cold turkey. That he could give up the fuel that kept him functioning.

Irene and I believed it because we had to. We craved regularity, even as Irene kept crushing Budweiser cans to dull the ache beneath it all. I didn't even know what "regular" looked like after years of living in my parents' emotional wreckage, but deep down, I think we both knew the truth: it was temporary. The farce would fracture. Melvin held on to plenty of ugly habits, and we should've known drinking was one of them.

Our apartment had a basement, a third space I instantly claimed. Until then, my only experience with cellars was Pépé's workshop, a dark, eerie underworld I avoided at all costs. But the basement at Oakridge on Henderson Street became my sanctuary. Surprisingly, Melvin and Irene let me take it over, and what had been a den for the last maintenance man's family became *Joe's MTV Zone*, with the TV tuned to MTV whenever I needed refuge from adults.

The decor in the basement was dreary: dark paneling, tiny windows that peeked up at the sky, and shag carpet with a faint, musky odor. Crunchy under my socks. I loved it. It might've creeped out other kids, but to me it felt like the last day of school. Magnificent.

The number of friends I had at Oakridge teetered near zero, so I spent hours underground, dancing and lip-syncing my little gay heart out to Whitney Houston's "Greatest Love of All," Janet Jackson's "Control," and Madonna's "Open Your Heart." Madonna had become my entire world. I breathed, dreamed, and lived on her music. Don't believe me? I played *True Blue* on repeat until the batteries in my Walkman died in the middle of "Papa Don't Preach."

One later afternoon, downstairs in my teenager lair, a commercial break hit. Downtown Julie Brown told us to "stay tuned… Wubba Wubba Wubba" on *Club MTV*. I drifted, got restless, and found myself snooping around Melvin's workshop. It was a compact space behind a door separating our basement from a long, prison-like hallway that stretched the length of the building.

What started as typical teenage nosiness turned into something else. Paint cans lined the wall. Hammers hung from pegs. Unopened boxes made the space feel like an obstacle course. I opened the ones not sealed with masking tape, rifling through them without really looking.

Until something stopped me.

An empty gallon bottle of Popov Vodka.

The bottle was hidden inside a box labeled TOOLS. I yanked it out by its handle and looked it over. My smirk felt earned. The thrill of stumbling onto one of Melvin's secrets felt like leverage, another coin I'd pocketed since the last time he'd touched me.

I had kept that promise. Months had passed since Melvin even looked at me sideways. I don't know what made him back off, but he showed little interest in me. Maybe it was because I was fifteen. Maybe I was too old for him.

The thought made me shudder, because it fit together perfectly.

Melvin's fading desires became a reward.

I carefully placed the evidence back in its hiding place. The whole sobriety act was a ruse. Melvin was *still* Melvin. He hadn't quit drinking. He'd just gone underground with it. And now his secret was mine to reveal.

"Mom, I found Dad's bottle of vodka downstairs."

Irene had been preparing dinner, her long brown curls clipped up with a barrette. "What? Dad doesn't drink anymore. He hasn't been drinking since we moved here." She kept chopping whatever was in front of her. "Please don't start any of your shit right now."

But I was in the early stages of perfecting the art of stirring shit up, and my giddiness got the best of me. I turned toward the basement stairs and walked away. "Follow me."

When I handed Irene the empty bottle, her tears came first, then outrage. In that moment, Melvin's sobriety act collapsed, and the apartment filled with the old dread. I felt a strange pride in it, in being the one who proved he hadn't changed. I'd become my own kind of private investigator, dragging the truth back into the light.

Most of the time, life feels like it's spinning out of our control. We tell ourselves we're steering, then the universe yanks the wheel. We fixate on what we want to happen and are surprised when chaos shows up anyway. So we cling to the few things we can control. I didn't control much in our apartment, but that afternoon I controlled the truth.

I hadn't found the bravery to shout from the rooftops about the abuse Melvin forced me to endure, but I could rip off the bandage on his drinking. Naming that truth, out loud, was how I began to find my voice. I wasn't the frightened kid anymore, swallowing everything whole. Like everyone else my age, I'd mashed together the terrible twos, the fuck-you fours, and the sassy six-year-olds into something I found delightful: my defiant teens.

Calling out another one of Melvin's lies granted me a new type of strength: insubordination. They say the truth will set you free, but it also prompts reactions from everyone it reaches.

After dinner, Melvin's truck pulled into our space out back. Irene sat at the kitchen table, working through the last of a six-pack she'd opened after finding his vodka bottle. It wasn't lost on me that she was inebriated and furious that Melvin was still lifting a bottle to his mouth. In her mind, I suppose, his devotion to hard liquor was worse than her love for amber ale.

That was another lie she told herself. They were both drunks.

I heard three thuds as Melvin kicked slush off his boots on the stairs outside. Irene barely gave him time to step inside before unleashing her frustration. "You asshole. You liar. You're drinking again."

Act or not, Melvin seemed genuinely shocked. "What are you talking about? I've been working," he stammered, shutting the door and heading for the kitchen table. Then he saw it: the empty gallon bottle Irene had hauled up from the basement, sitting beside her like a witness. She had the proof and her own liquid courage, and she planted him firmly on the spot.

"Where did you find that?"

Irene pulled herself up and swayed toward the refrigerator. "You think you're so smart, don't you? I'm not fucking stupid, Melvin! You know where it was."

The hiss-pop of her beer can rang out in the pause. It sounded deadly. Then the room filled with shouting again.

"Joe found it downstairs, in your little workshop," she confessed, grabbing her Winston 100 from the ashtray and sitting back down, in control, or so she thought. After a long drag on her cigarette, she leaned on her elbow, cigarette raised, like a movie star from the 1940s.

I wanted to disappear into the sofa. We hadn't heard Melvin's truck pull up. If we had, I would've already been hiding in my room. Exposing the truth while he was gone had given me a fleeting sense of courage. But now he was home, with the flames of anger flickering off his aura, the trepidation surged. Dread bubbled in my throat. The urge to flee poked at my ribs, a reminder to always be on alert.

Melvin aimed his gaze at me. I held Bonkers tight. Too tight. The cat had become my hostage, a shield against whatever might come flying my way. He squirmed, claws out, annoyed by the vise grip I had him in. We were all bracing for impact. Bonkers understood it first. Even at fifteen, I knew that once I'd shown Irene what he hid in his workshop, she'd present the bottle to him, Melvin's trophy for best deceiver. The confrontation would be nasty. The only question was how bad.

As Melvin stared at me from the kitchen, his expression shifted from confusion to anger to something resembling pain.

I wasn't safe for him anymore.

He looked bewildered, like his son had betrayed him. Like I'd broken the father-son bond he'd been carefully constructing ever since he met Irene at The Silver Dollar and learned she had a boy at home.

For Melvin, the real betrayal wasn't the exposure of his drinking. He had to know we'd find out eventually. No, it was my change in behavior. By uncovering his deceit, I'd shifted my allegiance, and he could feel it. A crack had opened in the story he kept us trapped in, the one held together by wishes and disappointments. It toppled easily with the truth. If I could "switch sides" and run to Irene to lay bare his lies, what else might I tell her? Would my mother believe me this time if I told her that Uncle Johnny had been right?

I didn't fully trust Irene, but I loved her deeply. She needed to face the fact that we lived in chaos, not comfort. I wanted to take Melvin down without revealing our secret. He'd spent years shaping me into his toy. Honestly, at that age, I still couldn't find the words to describe what he'd been doing to me.

But I had words for his drinking. When I found the bottle downstairs, I told Irene. It wasn't for her. It wasn't for him. It was for me.

Ever since the last time I stood in front of him in Unit K, my pants down around my ankles in that dirty apartment, I'd carried one clear thought: *if I didn't drag some of this bullshit into the light, no one else would.*

At fifteen, I was the adult in the room.

Melvin shifted into the living room. I focused on Bonkers' straw-like hair. I knew Melvin's intimidation was trained on me. Irene fell silent. I tracked my father's movement. We made eye contact. My courage evaporated.

"Did you tell your mother this was mine?"

I refused to engage. Bonkers had my tongue. Maybe the cat was more intelligent than all of us. He sensed something boiling in the room and squirmed free, sprinting to my bedroom.

"Answer me!" Melvin demanded. "Did you tell her?"

Irene jumped from her chair and stubbed her cigarette out in the ashtray. "You leave him alone. I'm tired of you giving my son a hard time."

He pivoted to face her. "Your son? Sit down, you drunk bitch. He's my son."

A burst of movement caught my peripheral vision. Melvin loomed over her, then shoved her into the nearest chair. The legs of the chair screeched across the floor as Irene crashed against the table. Her breath punched out in a wet gasp. She fought to stand, but his strength was no match for her stupor. He shoved her down again.

Melvin's hand gripped her throat. "Don't make me hurt you."

The raw fear in her yelps triggered my fight-or-flight response. When it came to Melvin, I'd spent years frozen, trying to stay invisible even when his light shone brightest on me. Don't move. Let him say and do what he wants, and maybe it'll end quickly. I fled when I could, especially once I had a job and an excuse to be away.

Even though I had daydreamed about his demise, fighting Melvin like an adult had never crossed my mind. But as Irene gasped under his grip, the idea no longer felt ridiculous.

I had to be the man he thought I wasn't.

"Get off my mother, asshole." The words escaped before I even realized I'd said them. Adrenaline lit me up. I was off the sofa and standing in the threshold between the living room and the kitchen.

Melvin released Irene's neck. "What did you say?"

Reality hit. I realized I might get hurt. Refusing to acknowledge Melvin's question, I instinctively raced for the stairs, following the cat's escape, though I'll never understand why I ran toward a dead end. Melvin was faster and blocked my path. Panic and confusion flooded my mind. *Where do I go? What's my next move?* His rage locked onto me like a torpedo, and I had no defense.

Who was I kidding? There was no defense. I was guessing in the dark. The questions cascaded over me, but no answers came. In the brief moment I managed to shake myself clear, there he was, a towering inferno.

Melvin crept toward me. I had nowhere else to turn. He'd backed me into the corner, wedged between the wall and the blinking lights of our Christmas tree. I cowered, lifting my right hand to shield my face.

"Put your hand down. I'm not going to hit you."

My hand dropped. I straightened.

THWACK.

The right side of my face burned after Melvin backhanded me.

By this point in my life, I was accustomed to being hit. I'd been spanked. I'd been slapped across the face. Hell, on

Wakefield Circle, Irene once knocked out my bedroom window screen, pulled me to the window, hung me halfway through it, then tossed me onto my bed and beat me like a punching bag.

Melvin's smack felt personal. Not routine, not punishment, but something else. I'd unleashed a new level of his anger by exposing him. Our struggle was now man-to-man. But he sucker-slapped me right after promising not to hit me.

Who was the wimp now?

"You bastard!" Irene yelled from the kitchen. "He's bleeding."

I touched my lip with my finger and stared down at the bright red blood. Melvin's pinky ring (yeah, a pinky ring, like he thought he was some kind of mobster) had split the corner of my mouth, tearing skin from my lower lip. The sting of the air on the wound was nothing compared to the shock of being backhanded.

"Go to your fucking room. Don't come down." His voice snapped.

Melvin didn't move aside. I shrank back and worked my way around his larger frame. His rigidity, a statue of violence, came with a sly smirk hidden just out of Irene's view.

I took the stairs two at a time. I found my teenage voice.

"Fuck you, Melvin. You aren't my father."

The seven words echoed off the walls. Clean. Genuine. A truth that cracked the story open and exposed what had become my new reality, one that finally catered to my needs.

Once in my room, I slammed the door and locked it. Whoever had lived there before me had wanted privacy. I fell onto my bed, and tears came fast and hot against my flushed cheeks. Not sad tears. Angry tears. Bonkers positioned himself beside me and nuzzled his head against my arm, offering the connection I desperately needed.

I'd broken the father-son bond, the only thing, in some strange and twisted way, that had kept me safer from him. Funny to think I'd ever been safe with Melvin, but in retrospect, playing along with his wishes had been its own kind of protection.

LET ME KILL HIM

The mayhem at home finally cost me my job at Finest Grocery Store. My supervisor knew my life was a rolling disaster, but sympathy doesn't rewrite policy. I was late too often and called in sick too many times. At fifteen, I was trying to juggle school while surviving two selfish adults. Something had to give. In the end, it was stocking shelves.

But I still needed money, and I needed to be anywhere beyond Melvin's reach.

Before Irene quit her cashier job at The Grocery Barn, she called her boss and got me hired at the small corner store. For a few months, she worked the day shift, and I came in at four to relieve her. We'd pass each other at the register as coworkers, not mother and son, and I'll admit, I liked it. It was another level of adulthood I welcomed. She'd drop the keys into my palm, smile, and for a second, we were equals.

Then one day, she quit. Amicably, everyone said.

I missed those handoffs more than I expected. In the store, Irene looked like a version of herself free of Melvin's influence. She told me she was happy to quit, but I didn't buy it.

Melvin treated Irene's employment like a switch he flipped to suit his own benefit. When he didn't have a steady paycheck, he pushed Irene to work. When he did, he talked her into staying home. He liked her at the kitchen table, beer in hand, soap operas flickering on the little TV, spending more time under his eye and less time around anyone he hadn't personally approved.

Circumstances in our apartment had intensified since Christmas. My lip had healed. I'd acted as if I'd forgotten, but I hadn't.

At home, smiles only appeared on Friday-night sitcoms. At Oakridge, there was nothing to perform. Behind the front door, there was nothing to fake. Irene was caught between Melvin and me, caught in our crossfire. The war between us had moved past any semblance of agreement or a cease-fire. We could barely stand to be in the same room longer than necessary.

If I were home, there was often trouble, and it was usually my fault. Or I'd "instigate" Melvin. (I was a teenager. Instigating was part of my résumé.) There were rarely quiet moments. Even in my basement hideout, I was still within earshot of the verbal altercations.

The arguments that erupted in our house often started small. Spontaneous. Each one was as devastating as the last or the next. Something as simple as forgetting to shut the front door could trigger a systemic quake that shook the walls. It was as if Melvin waited for a reason to throw a glass across the living room. There was no difference between taking too long a shower and telling Melvin to fuck off, which became a pastime of mine once I turned fifteen. A fog of disagreements. Raised voices. This became our routine.

Then one day, for reasons forgotten, Melvin stopped buying groceries. Was there a point? Not really. He was just an asshole. He convinced Irene to quit at The Grocery Barn, erasing any chance she had to earn money. If she didn't have her own money, she couldn't buy anything without his approval. I had some money in my savings account, but it was mine. They didn't know how much I had, and I wasn't sharing it. Truthfully, it wasn't any of their business, and I wasn't spending my money to feed that house.

In reality, his behavior had nothing to do with food. In Melvin's mind, he was punishing me for exposing his hidden vodka and for taking my body off the market. Melvin had lost control over me. The fact that I was rarely home incensed him. He may even have drunk more when I wasn't there. When we had to be together, he ignored me unless we were cursing at each other. But when I was away, his anger festered and waited for me.

One night, I came home from work hungry, tired, and in no mood for any bullshit. That last part was my mistake. Irene hadn't prepared dinner. Not a total shock. I often found myself eating a bowl of Raisin Bran. Melvin had fallen asleep in his living room chair. Irene sat at the table, focused on a crossword puzzle. I started foraging through the kitchen, searching the cabinets and the refrigerator for dinner. I noticed, as cliché as it sounds, that the shelves were bare.

"Where's all the food?"

Melvin's response surprised me. "I threw it out. I make the money in this fucking house," he mumbled from his chair, a glass in his hand. Trust me, the liquid was vodka. He tilted his head, finding volume in his garbled speech. "I decide when and if there's food in this house. Do you hear me?"

We heard him. Bonkers heard him. I'm sure the new neighbors did, too.

I'm going to break the fourth wall here. I'm talking to you, reader. As you've seen, I'd been under Melvin's thumb for years. I thought I knew him well, better than Irene did. I'd learned how to keep him happy, piss him off, and, once I became a teenager, how to avoid him. But I never thought the asshole would go so low as to stop buying food.

Never underestimate the level of assholery an asshole can reach.

That night, I had a few Little Debbies stashed in my closet for dinner. I had won. His immaturity wouldn't leave me hungry.

Melvin's grocery boycott went on for weeks. I have no idea what my mother was eating. He consumed vodka as if it were Gatorade. I managed with school lunch and by stealing Doritos and Coke cans from The Grocery Barn to snack on during my walk home. That's why, even now, when I can't decide what I want to eat, my first thought is always a bag of chips and a soda.

Mr. Gay, the manager at The Grocery Barn, spent most of his day in a small office overlooking the cash registers. One afternoon, he was passed out there while I hid out of sight, stuffing soda cans into my pants and trying to stroll out casually.

Sometimes I'd buy cereal and other goodies to hide in my room. I had to sneak them into the house. Melvin threatened to throw away the food I brought in. Villainous behavior. I believed him, but now I realize he would've had to wrestle the food from my hand. After backhanding me, I didn't think he had the nerve to face me in another physical confrontation.

Most nights, the squabbles turned into barroom brawls. Even when I tried to stay out of everyone's way, I'd still get caught up in my parents' upheaval. One night, I locked myself in my bedroom, eating junk food and watching *Full House*, with Bonkers at my side, when I heard Irene's nightmarish scream slip under my door.

"Joe! Help! Call 911. He's trying to kill me!"

I took the stairs in three leaps. Protecting Irene had become part of my daily routine: wake, eat, go to school, work, and keep an eye on my mother to make sure she was still alive in the morning.

Irene sat in the chair closest to the kitchen sink, pinned there by Melvin's hands on her shoulders, unable to escape his grip. The side of her face reddened. His anger was tangible, sharp enough to smell. Have you ever smelled anger? It's hard to describe, but it clung to him like a dark atmosphere, a vibration of uncontrolled hatred and fear. The veins in his arm stood out beneath his T-shirt. All he had left was brute force. And damn any teenager or wife who challenged his position.

I stopped at the kitchen threshold. I stretched. My eyebrows furrowed. My nose flared. My ears rang with my heartbeat. I clenched my fists, ready for the showdown.

"Get away from her, Melvin!"

That always set his fuse. He despised it when I called him Melvin.

A sudden chill ran down my spine, like a divine shock. I wasn't sure what it was, but as I prepared for whatever was ahead, I crossed my arms firmly over my chest. My parents stared at me—Irene looking desperate, Melvin unsteady and struggling to keep his balance.

Then a surprising thought flashed through my mind: *Melvin is weak. Not strong. You, Joe. You're strong. You're fifteen. You could beat the shit out of him with one hand tied behind your back.*

My anxiety about Melvin evaporated. It became the sweat on my brow. I wasn't afraid anymore. I was ready to fight. He looked pathetic. Nothing to fear. Not his bloodshot eyes. Not his stinking vodka breath. I stepped forward and told him to let go of my mother.

I could imagine myself killing him with my bare hands.

I leaped toward him, but he pulled away. Irene fell back as the chair gave way beneath her. Melvin stumbled, and I came at him again, snagging his T-shirt at the shoulder and spinning him around to face me. Abusive father. Teenage son with zero fucks to give. I shook him hard. He tried to stay focused, his arms thrashing. I tore into him with words I can't remember. Vulgar. Heinous. My mind went hazy. Autopilot. The same autopilot I used when he lusted after me. Only this time, I had the controller. I was player one in Melvin's sadistic game.

"Get off me!" Melvin lunged for my waist, but I twisted out of his reach. He crashed into me anyway. I let him; it was easier to overpower him that way.

I used my weight against him. I'd never thrown a punch before; I didn't know how. So I leaned in and clawed at his face and scalp, wild and clumsy. I yanked his hair until he bent over in front of me. The three of us shouting into the air. I dragged him deeper into the kitchen until we were by the cabinets near the back door. I could hear Irene screaming, but she felt miles away—a distant emergency, with a more urgent one in my hands. I threw my body into his, and we crashed onto the linoleum. My leg clipped another chair, spinning it into the living room.

"Don't hurt my son!" Irene cried as we twisted on the floor like two hateful pretzels.

A surge of adrenaline washed over me, and I finally felt like He-Man, my muscles suddenly stronger and more powerful. In what felt like slow motion, I flipped Melvin onto his stomach. The slap of his body hitting the floor filled me with conviction. He fought hard, but I had the leverage. My plan was simple: sit on him until he calmed down or passed out. I straddled his back as he squirmed beneath me, spitting curses and promising I was "fucking dead" the second he got free.

Then the realization hit: one of us might die tonight. It wouldn't be Irene or me.

I was younger. Huskier. Sober. For the first time, I realized I might win. I could walk away from this family nightmare alive while his lifeless body took up space on the kitchen floor. He'd held me in his grip for over ten years, under his body, under his rules. I'd been forced into his cult. Now the tables had turned. Rage rose in me, an ugly mix of hatred, vengeance, and the need to make Melvin suffer.

Not just suffer. But die. Killing Melvin felt justified. Overdue.

"Leave my mother alone!" I grabbed his hair in my fists and yanked hard. Then, with every memory of him sneaking me off to some secluded place, I lifted his head and slammed it into the floor.

Thwack.

"You're not my father. I have a father out there."

Thwack.

"It's not you."

Melvin threw his head back, dazed but still fighting. I wanted to break his neck again, to finish what the tractor-trailer accident had started. He tried to push himself up, threatening to send me tumbling. I let go of his hair and started punching between his shoulder blades, hard. His breath came in gasps. I could feel him weakening beneath me. I forced his head back down, grinding the side of his face into the cold linoleum like a bad dog. His left eye caught mine.

All the abuse had to end.

I looked up at my mother. She shivered, pressed against the wall like a tarnished statue, watching her teenage son try to save her.

My energy began to wane. My breathing crackled. My chest tightened. I could feel the heat in my ears. If Melvin broke free, it would be over for Irene and me. I didn't believe there was another way out except to end his life.

Then I saw it. A weapon. The chef's knife rested on the edge of the counter.

A sharp kitchen knife, like something out of a horror movie. But it was real and within reach.

With my right hand, I grabbed it off the counter. It was heavy. Irene must have left it out while she was cleaning her smelly weed. When I leaned forward to grab the handle, Melvin twisted onto his back. His arms kept slapping and pulling at me. I fell on top of him, the shiny blade waving in my hand. I pulled myself up to a sitting position and drove my weight into him. He panted for air. Our eyes locked, with pure hatred between us. It felt ancient and raw.

That rage had been buried in my heart since I was five, but only now was I ready to act on it.

I raised the knife above my head, both hands gripping it. Ready to bring it down. Prepared to end him. He struck my stomach. I tightened. Screaming became the chorus of my actions. Finally, the perfect crime. I'd get caught and spend the rest of my life in prison. But it felt monumental. Necessary. I made peace with that and stopped worrying about my future.

I sensed Irene move closer. She inched in front of us, half-hidden behind one of the fallen chairs. "Joseph. Don't do it. Please." I glanced up as she lifted a chair and set it upright, grounding herself in the small, ordinary motion. "He's not worth it."

No, Mom. I have to do it. I want to.

And then my arm began lowering the weapon.

Why? Why couldn't I do it? I stared down at him, his chest straining to rise. I pushed the blade back onto the countertop and jammed it into the sink. My brain snapped a picture of the scene, the image imprinting itself on me even now. We stayed motionless for a beat, as if we all had to catch our breath before the next move.

I lifted myself off Melvin, pushing up with my legs and pressing my hands against his chest to keep him pinned. On the floor, he looked elderly. Harmless. I knew he was anything but harmless. With my strength now matching his, maybe even surpassing it, I saw I didn't need to beat him, kill him, or run from him. I could defend myself. That was the win I'd been chasing.

Irene babbled over me. I ignored her, kicked the other fallen chair aside, and sauntered, not ran, through the living room toward the stairs. I expected Melvin to attack me from behind, but I didn't let that possibility change how I left the room. Freedom from your abuser will do that. By strutting up the stairs, I was practically daring him to try me.

Melvin did not chase after me, and I never turned back to look at him and Irene in the kitchen. I moved forward, one step at a time, until I locked my bedroom door behind me. I sat on the floor against the door, grabbed my trusted friend Bonkers, and finally let myself breathe.

No Longer Compliant

Irene struggled to manage a drunk husband and an increasingly defiant teenager. She barely left the kitchen, as if standing too long would make the apartment try to escape. Her constantly swollen ankle held her back, and even the chair she sat in for hours felt ready to bolt.

She worked hard, downing her Budweiser, chasing the bitter relief it offered. Funny how she could sit inside a burning building and still imagine herself safe. That's what drinkers do, self-medicating to escape reality. Irene had a refilled prescription.

Maybe she believed she was outpacing the danger, but the illusion of safety had vanished long ago. I knew we weren't safe. Even Bonkers knew it; he spent most of his time outside. I envied that cat. I wanted him to take me with him into the dark alleys he disappeared into. The darkness of an alley felt better than the brightness of our living room. Melvin's drinking had escalated and never let up. There was no more hiding vodka bottles in the basement, no need for excuses to pretend he was working. He drank until he blacked out.

Irene drank herself gray.

Living with my parents felt like riding a rickety wooden roller coaster in an abandoned amusement park, all creaks and rot, with the car threatening to fly off the track at every turn. It never gave you a moment to catch your breath. One minute it crept along, and the next you were jerked side to side, tossed by unforgiving turns. You were either going to make it to the end or smash on impact.

Living with my parents felt relentless, with no way to get off and no idea what wild turn would come next. A few weeks after I fought off the urge to bury a knife in Melvin's skull, we went back to pretending—all under one roof, each of us surviving in our own way. Irene believed we were a family; Melvin believed he was in charge; and I believed there might still be a speck of good left in them. We kept our distance and reached an agreement: you do you.

Or it seemed.

Irene and I were suckers for thinking a quiet month would last.

My parents loved to fish for trout. Being out in the woods, fishing pole in one hand, beer in the other, rearranged their DNA. Something about the canopy of red maples and the crisp air made them act like loving spouses. Fishing was the one hobby that cooled the friction in our apartment. They actually laughed, embraced, and nobody took any verbal swings. It was as if the woods called a truce. Even in winter, if the day felt spring-like, Melvin and Irene met Linda and her boyfriend for the afternoon to cast. Some parents drown their sorrows in a bottle. Mine went fishing on the river.

Actually, they did both.

I didn't like freezing my ass off beside a fast-moving river, with ice forming on the banks and my hands numb with cold. But being around my parents when they were civil gave me hope. Sure, the affection was an act. I knew it. They did, too. I just didn't want to accept it. I clung to the scene anyway, greedy for the peace, for the idea that we'd be okay.

How long do we cling to these healing fantasies that our circumstances will improve before we embarrass ourselves?

Too long.

One mild Saturday in early March 1988, Irene made sandwiches and loaded the cooler while I complained that I didn't want to go fishing. She had an answer for every excuse I offered. I would've lied about picking up an extra shift at The Grocery Barn, but she had Mr. Gay's number and could check my schedule whenever she wanted. What I didn't want to tell her was that I had grown content with keeping space between Melvin and me. When we ignored each other, I slept better at night.

Then came the surprise I didn't see coming: Alan was tagging along.

Alan was a senior at East Hartford High. I was a sophomore. We rarely talked anymore. We never even shared a class. He felt unreachable, as if graduation were closing the door between us. I missed roaming Wakefield Circle with him. He played my therapist and charged me for bad teenage advice. Alan outgrew wandering the neighborhood. He had a driver's license, a car, and independence. After my parents moved to Oakridge Apartments, I rarely saw Alan, except when we passed each other in the hallway between classes. Spending the day in the woods with him while our parents caught fish, just the two of us, felt like the end of a chapter.

A new story was about to begin for both of us.

We always returned to Melvin's favorite fishing hole along the Blackledge River, a shallow waterway that meandered through central Connecticut. The highways were lined with gravel pull-offs, each supposedly leading to the best rainbow trout in Connecticut, a claim repeated every time we turned off the pavement and parked to unload our gear.

On that perfect day, while our parents set up camp, their voices drifting in from the distance, Alan and I hiked along a muddy trail, wet grass slapping our ankles. Birds were returning from winter. He tried to splash mud at me. I cursed. Now I think back to him, seventeen, still holding onto his playful side before he aged out of it. As usual, Alan peppered me with rules and predictions about life as an upperclassman. I didn't have the heart to tell him that when I turned sixteen, I planned to close the book on high school.

We hiked toward the adults. I kept rambling. Alan stopped and raised his hand. "Shut up." Raised voices carried over from the campsite.

"Come on."

I fell a few paces behind him.

"Hurry up, Joe. Someone's fighting."

Let it be Linda and her boyfriend. Please.

I jogged to catch up. "I hope it's your mom and her boyfriend."

Alan shook his head, disappointed. I thought I was just telling the truth. We continued toward the parking lot, a familiar dread creeping up the back of my neck.

We broke through a curtain of branches, and the brightness hit me first. Then I saw the scene a few feet away: Linda helping Irene into one of the collapsible vinyl chairs lined up near the water's edge. An engine revved, and the ass end of Melvin's truck disappeared onto the highway, dust rolling back toward us.

The sight hit me hard. It was a lead sinker, cold and final, dragging my hope under. I bolted to my mother and knelt beside her. She doubled over, gasping, clutching her ankle.

"What happened?"

"They fought," Linda said. "He pushed her down."

The truce was over.

Anger, hate, sadness, fear, revenge, every teenage emotion I had, fused into a single, cold absence: indifference. Linda ran to the cooler to grab ice for my mother's ankle, already turning blue. I watched Irene rock back and forth in the chair, cursing the day she stayed with Melvin. I felt the distance click in. I didn't have the energy to care.

Irene's pain was her fault. I didn't blame Melvin. He showed her, over and over, what kind of man he was. She kept telling herself he'd change. Every bad hit we endured while living with Melvin came back to Irene. I wanted to feel sorry for her, but I didn't see her as a victim.

I grabbed Alan's arm and dragged him back into the woods. I was desperate to delude myself. I wanted a normal Saturday—a simple fishing trip. I didn't want a mother thrown to the ground. We later learned her ankle was fractured.

Alan and I hadn't gone far down the trail when Linda's voice called us back to her car. Irene climbed into the front seat. Alan and I squeezed into the back with Linda's boyfriend. I remember Linda telling Irene to get an X-ray at the ER. Irene stared out the window, reshaping the story in her head. A sliver of a lie, just enough to help her forgive Melvin, who'd broken her this time.

Linda pulled up in front of the apartment and kept the car running, likely expecting Melvin to rush out. I nearly fell as I opened the door and eased Irene out of the front seat, even as she yelped with each movement. I watched Linda drive away. I'd wished she'd taken me with them.

Irene carefully hopped down the sidewalk on one leg, moving slowly. As she climbed the few stairs to our door, she leaned on me for support.

"Just get me inside the house. I don't need anyone to know about this shit."

Assisting her up the stairs reminded me of my knee surgery, when she helped me out of Janice's car. Whether Irene knew it or not, we had only each other.

My mother turned. "Don't say anything to Melvin. Go right to your room."

I nodded and grabbed the rusty handle of the screen door.

She stopped. "Don't tell your grandparents, either. I know you tell them everything."

Unbelievable. Irene would rather protect Melvin from my grandparents' I-told-you-sos than protect her own body.

Keep the family's secrets close. Keep the family's pain private.

It's hard to imagine, but Melvin's drinking worsened. He started slacking off as the apartment's maintenance man. It was only a matter of time. He'd once taken the job seriously. Now he barely bothered. Melvin walked around like he didn't have a job. Tenants asked for help. He acted as if they'd bothered him: fuck them and their broken faucet.

First, he stopped buying groceries. Then he stopped pretending to be the family's provider.

Most days, Melvin slept in late. Or he left late and came back late. Same day. Same loop. Irene waited until dark, then called their favorite dive bars, frantic, asking for him.

To no one's surprise, Melvin hadn't been seen all day.

At least, according to the bartender.

Those guys loved Irene when she planted herself at their counter all afternoon, slapping down dollars for another beer. But when she called them scared, afraid her husband might be dead on the side of the road, they closed ranks.

They always did.

To keep a roof over our heads, Irene and I picked up Melvin's slack at the complex. Melvin getting fired was out of the question. Nobody could know the scheme Irene had pulled me into. Another secret, born to hold our life together with scotch tape and scrap paper. Melvin knew we were doing his work. He didn't care. But Irene loaded me up with more worries. Some I understood. Some I didn't. Some I held tight to my chest. She warned me that if we failed to cover for Melvin, we'd have to crawl back to Wakefield Circle. Linda would be evicted. Irene would lose her best friend. Alan might hate me forever.

Will might tell everybody that he let me rub his dick for candy.

Melvin preached that our move to Oakridge was a new beginning. To me, it felt like an epilogue. While I was at school, Irene hobbled on a tightly wrapped ankle, giving tours of empty apartments. When I was home, not at The Grocery Barn, I cleaned those apartments and coordinated move-in days.

Apartment management never realized Irene and I were doing the work, not Melvin. The checks kept coming. Irene kept depositing them. Melvin kept drinking and disappearing, grateful to have two servants cleaning up his mess.

Irene and I seldom discussed our situation openly; our behavior revealed everything. When I complained about having to go to school while working two jobs, Irene turned on me, insisting that covering for Melvin was for our own good. She'd remind me of what we'd lose if we had to move back to Wakefield Circle.

I didn't want to lose Alan. I didn't want any secrets to get out, so I kept my head down and tried to contain my anger. I was helping Irene, not him. I did it for her.

Then, late one afternoon, I came home from my shift at The Grocery Barn and walked into a doozy of an argument.

"You've fucked up this time, haven't you?" Irene snapped.

I darted for the stairs. Steer clear of Melvin. That was the rule. But Irene's words snagged my attention. I lingered on the bottom step, out of their line of sight, listening as the noise grew louder.

Ever since I'd pinned Melvin to the kitchen floor, we'd do our best to keep our distance. We still interacted, but only in short, tense exchanges, like unfriendly coworkers passing in a hallway, each determined not to engage. Honestly, I think he was slightly nervous around me after that. He'd never admit it, but it hung in the air between us, my private victory. Melvin had never tried so hard to avoid me. It became a game to stay out of each other's sight. He'd get bolder as he drank, but deep inside, he couldn't stand to look at me, the boy who'd betrayed him.

"Why the hell were you drinking and driving the company truck?" she demanded. "We're going to lose everything."

We didn't have much left to lose, but I understood her panic.

Melvin braced himself against the back of a chair, swaying. "It wasn't my fault," he murmured in defense. "The car came out from a side road. I swerved."

Taking responsibility wasn't exactly one of Melvin's strengths.

Irene pushed herself up. "You wrecked the side of the goddamn truck. What are you gonna tell your boss?"

I leaned over the railing to watch. I noticed my mother was sober. No familiar red-and-white Budweiser can in her hand, no can perched on a coaster. She tried to limp past Melvin, but he caught her by the arm.

"I'll have it fixed before anyone notices," he said, gripping her.

Irene yanked herself free. "With what money, asshole? The whole side of the truck is damaged."

The shouting grew louder as they moved into the living room, hurling insults at each other like playing softball with no gloves on.

I headed up the stairs. I wondered what life would be like if they clawed each other apart, tore themselves in half. I let the thought go. I couldn't worry about them. I had to protect myself now. I closed my bedroom door, pulled the receiver off my Garfield-shaped phone, and dialed my grandparents.

"Hello. This is Lorette," Mémé answered, always announcing herself like a switchboard operator.

"Hi, Mémé. It's me. Can you guys come get me?"

I hadn't spoken to my grandparents in a couple of weeks. They'd been in Florida with Pépé's brother, Emile, and his wife, Carmen. I'd planned to spend the weekend with them when they returned, so why not this weekend, at 4 p.m., while my parents were acting dysfunctional? Their behavior would only get worse as the night progressed.

I'd kept my promise to Irene. I hadn't told Mémé and Pépé about her fractured ankle.

That promise would be broken by morning.

Protecting Irene's secret no longer mattered. What mattered was that I needed my grandparents to rescue me.

Again.

"What's going on? Are you okay?" I heard Mémé's breathing quicken. "Is your mom alright?"

"We're okay," I said. "Dad wrecked his work truck. They're fighting." My voice cracked. "Please come get me."

Mémé called out to Pépé. "Vic? Victor? Wake up."

He was passed out in his recliner.

"Melvin's acting up again. Joe wants us to come pick him up."

A pause. Mémé covered the receiver with her hand. When she returned to the line, her voice was brisk: "We're on our way. Give us thirty minutes."

I grabbed my school backpack and stuffed it with a few days' worth of clothes. I'd packed like this before—too many times. I sat on my bed, watching my new digital clock on the nightstand. Bonkers was out prowling. I wished he were here. When twenty-eight minutes had passed since my phone call, I picked up my bag, closed my bedroom door, and headed downstairs. The shouting had died down. Irene sat quietly in the kitchen. Melvin slumped in his scratched-up *I-only-sit-here* recliner.

"Where do you think you're going?" he challenged.

I rushed past him into the kitchen and kissed Irene goodbye. I didn't answer. I let his question fade. I locked eyes with my mother, silently counting the seconds until I was out the door. Irene sat there, clutching her beer, her eyes full of resignation. Her bandaged ankle was propped on a chair. My heart ached for her, but enough was enough. If they wanted to destroy each other, I wasn't staying to witness it. I was escaping to my grandmother's for a weekend of peaceful dinners, 8-Track tapes, and a house free of surprise blowups.

Melvin hauled himself up. I zipped past him toward the front door.

"Hey, you little shit," he yelled. "Answer me! Who said you could leave?"

He had no idea I had backup on the way. My parents should never have allowed me a phone line in my bedroom. Not in that house. Just then, my grandparents pulled up in front of our building. Their Dodge Caravan's horn cut through Melvin's questions. My ride had arrived.

"I'm going to Mémé and Pépé's house for the weekend," I called out to the room, not to him. I opened the front door. The early-evening air smelled of wet pavement and gasoline.

Melvin lurched toward me, as fast as his drunken body would let him. "The hell you are," he growled. "Get your ass upstairs and don't come back down until I tell you."

I stopped on the small front porch, holding the screen door open. I chuckled as if Melvin had told the funniest joke. I turned to face him. My sharp, bitter laugh mocked the man who once had me tangled in his web.

"I'm fifteen," I said, steady and defiant. "You can't tell me what to do anymore." I released the screen. It slammed into the frame. I jumped down the steps and glanced back, forcing warmth into my voice. "Bye, Mom. I love you."

I threw open Pépé's car door and quickly slid into the backseat, breathing heavily, feeling relief and a hint of surprise at my own courage.

So bold.

Holy shit.

Did I just walk out of the house? Did I just laugh in his face?

I tried to act tough, but my body trembled as if I had a fever. Without a word between us, Pépé pulled away. I glanced through the back window just in time to see Melvin on the sidewalk, his figure outlined in the fading light. I don't know if he saw me, but I saw him.

I kept my gaze fixed on him until Pépé turned right onto School Street, then headed back toward Prospect Avenue.

THE BIG NEWS

It took me the whole ride to unload the secrets I'd kept bottled up: Melvin had been drinking again, he'd broken Irene's ankle, and he'd ripped my lip with his pinky ring.

No lies. My life had become messier than a soap opera; there was no need to embellish. As I recounted it all, Mémé didn't respond; she just shook her head, disappointed. What else could she do? She'd already done what she could: she'd picked me up. Pépé stared straight ahead. He didn't say a word.

As we climbed the back stairs, I shuffled behind Mémé. Pépé went straight to the cellar. My stomach growled. I looked forward to spending the weekend without a grocery-shopping ban.

"What's for dinner?"

She unlocked the door, stepped inside, and set her purse on the kitchen table. I followed her in, and she shut the door behind us. "Your Aunt Jean is coming downstairs tonight. I'm making goulash."

Mémé wasn't Hungarian and never pretended to be, yet she made goulash at least once a month. I've always assumed Pépé picked up a taste for it while stationed in Europe during the Second World War. Goulash was comfort food. Maybe Mémé knew that's exactly what I needed.

Of course, her version was Americanized, like most recipes that crossed the Atlantic. Her goulash was made with elbow macaroni, ground beef, potatoes, green beans, and peas. Looking back, it was more of a beef stew with pasta than traditional goulash. But it was hearty, comforting, and delicious, better than a bag of Doritos.

"Aunt Jean's coming?" I asked, walking toward Mémé's bedroom, where I stayed whenever I visited. She hated sleeping with Pépé but put up with it during my visits. Secretly, she hoped he'd doze off in his recliner. Years of truck driving followed him into bed. He shifted gears in his sleep, kicking at her legs. They'd had separate bedrooms my entire life.

"Yes, she should be home from work soon. She likes living upstairs." Mémé bent, pulled a large pot from the cabinet, and set it on the counter. "When you're done, fill it with water and put it on the front burner."

My grandmother returned to Jean. "She's on the right track. No men right now. I remember when she lived here with your mother—"

I turned on the faucet and filled the pot.

"That was a lot for everyone," she finished. "I hope she'll be all right when she has to move."

"Why is she moving?" I asked, turning off the water and carrying the heavy pot to the stove.

Mémé lowered her voice. "She'll have to move one day. We can't stay in the same place forever."

After dinner, Jean went back upstairs to my childhood home, and my grandparents and I retired to the living room. I figured we'd settle in and watch whatever game Pépé had on TV, as we always did. I caught a spark in Mémé's eyes—anticipation laced with tension.

Pépé sat in his recliner, usually a silent sentinel who barely looked away from the screen during a game. Tonight, the TV didn't matter. His attention was fixed on me. In that stillness, my heart fluttered. Big news was about to break.

"What's going on?" I asked, looking from one to the other. I had a feeling something bad was about to happen. I thought about it before either of them spoke. Gravity cemented me to the sofa cushion.

Mémé exhaled. "Well…" She glanced at Pépé, then back at me.

"When we were in Florida last week," she stood and walked toward the dining room table, then came back and handed me a folder. "We bought a house."

Joy radiated from her. Heat from happiness. A dream coming true. For years, they'd driven back and forth between Connecticut and Florida, imagining the day they'd trade Hartford's snow for months of sunshine.

I felt cold and dreary. All my blood seemed to drain to my feet.

The folder sat in my lap, untouched. "A house? What about this house?"

Pépé said it flatly. "We're selling this house."

I couldn't believe it. "What?" I asked. Were my grandparents going senile?

"You can't sell this house," I continued. "This is *your* house." I glared at him, waiting for him to snap out of it.

Mémé plucked the folder from my lap. "You'll love it, Joe. It's just outside Orlando, in Buenaventura Lakes." She opened the brochure and ran her finger along the floor plans. "It's beautiful. You're welcome to visit anytime. The locals call the neighborhood BVL. Right, Victor?"

My grandparents were thrilled. I felt the roof begin to cave in.

Pépé nodded. "Things are going to move quickly. We're putting the house on the market in a few weeks. We hope to be in Florida by the end of May."

Yes. My grandparents were going senile.

"But Pépé. It's March." They could tell their message wasn't landing well with me. I tried to be brave, but my voice rose higher than I expected. "What do you mean you'll be gone by the end of May?"

The news suffocated me, as if I were being held underwater without a breath first. I had come to their house seeking a break from misery, not to face a death sentence. That's what it felt like: Dr. Tyrell, my childhood doctor, telling me I had two months to live.

I appreciated that my grandparents treated me like an adult. They'd taken the time to sit me down and explain it all, not over the phone. This is how you tell someone their lifeline is moving a thousand miles away: in person. They even told me before Irene. None of it softened the blow.

I knew they wanted me to be happy for them and to celebrate the new chapter they'd planned for decades. But moving to Florida?

How could they do this to me?

Then a little clarity. It made sense. Mémé and Pépé raised their children. They'd practically raised me. I wanted to be happy for them, to celebrate their joy and their upcoming retirement to Florida, the classic New England dream of soaking up the sun and warmth for the rest of their lives. But I couldn't match their enthusiasm. It reminded me of the excitement Melvin and Irene had poured into me when we moved to Oakridge Apartments. That move ignited a firestorm. Significant changes led to trouble.

I avoided eye contact while Mémé rattled off the details: three bedrooms, two bathrooms, a retention pond in the backyard—whatever that was. I heard the brochure crackle as she continued. My mind blocked out what I didn't want to accept, which was 99% of it.

They were abandoning me, a nightmare worse than the vampire in my dreams.

I knew one thing for sure. I couldn't stay in Connecticut without my grandparents, trapped under Melvin's control and drowning in Irene's tears, until I turned eighteen. Another three years with Melvin and Irene felt impossible.

I paced as the conversation continued. Mémé kept throwing information at me, and I dodged it like homework, my eyes on the wallpaper, my brain elsewhere.

An idea formed. One of those solutions so obvious I couldn't believe no one had said it out loud. We were looking at their move all wrong: me, negative; them, positive. But moving to Florida could suit all three of us. Hell, even Irene needed a break from me. Maybe not Melvin.

They had answers to everything, but I hadn't asked the one question that mattered. I sat back down. I interrupted whoever was speaking.

"Can I move with you?"

I couldn't read them, and there was no thunderous applause, so I knew my question wasn't the genius move I'd imagined. In fact, it sounded like the last thing they wanted to hear. This was their time to enjoy their lives, not to become my parents. My question came out pitiful. A teenager with only one path forward: his grandparents. I wanted it to land as desperation. I wanted them to cave.

Pépé answered first. "The house won't be built until later this year. We'll be staying in a motel in Kissimmee until then."

He didn't stop there, attempting to pull me back from my foolish idea of becoming their Florida roommate. "And you need to stay here and finish school."

"I can finish school in Florida."

Mémé jumped in, trying to change the subject and avoid the spotlight of my question. "The motel is excellent. Same one we stayed at last week."

My eyes never left my grandfather. Since I could walk, I went to Mémé with everything, not out of fear of him but because I'd always been Mémé's boy. I figured that if I spoke to him like an adult, he'd understand. "Pépé, I can go to school in Florida."

Desperation flooded me. "I have to go with you guys. I can't stay here."

Then my eyes began to water, and I realized I was not an adult. "Please. I can help around the house."

Mémé put her hand on my knee. "Honey, you can't move to Florida. Your parents would never allow it." She leaned closer and handed me the brochure.

"This is our new house. It has a nook in the kitchen and a sunroom." The brochure went limp in her hand. "They're called lanais in Florida."

She was talking about Melvin. He'd never go along with it. She was right.

Melvin avoided me when he was sober, but he still wanted me under his influence. If I lived with him, I belonged to him. Fucked up, right? Our father-son relationship had disintegrated, and he knew it. I couldn't stand being in the same room with him. But for Melvin, a son who despised him was better than no son at all. As long as I was there, he didn't care that I cursed him out without fear, pushed back, and retreated to my room, drowning out everyone with Taylor Dayne music videos.

I was free of his sexual advances, but now we argued like men. Melvin had found a new way to keep his hold on me: I had nowhere to go. I could yell at him all I wanted, but I wasn't escaping his roof until I turned eighteen. Trapped like my mother, exactly as he liked it.

My mind was made up. I knew what I had to do next. My grandparents didn't realize it yet, but I was going with them to Buenaventura Lakes. I'd leave behind East Hartford High, Alan, Gwen, and—the hardest of all—Bonkers. It hurt enough to make me wonder, once or twice, whether I was making the right choice. Whenever doubt showed up, I went back to the only thing that mattered: getting far away from Melvin and Irene, away from that apartment.

The details of my escape to Florida hadn't formed yet. I nodded as Mémé continued, listing the perks of her new ranch-style home nestled in the peaceful landscape of Central Florida: no more stairs to climb, no snow to shovel, and no roaring cars speeding up and down their street.

Time suddenly mattered. Mémé and Pépé planned to leave at the end of May. That left me only a few months to build a plan the adults could swallow—even Melvin. I decided nothing was off-limits. I'd beg. I'd lie. I'd manipulate. I'd lie some more. What's the phrase? The ends justify the means. Yeah, that.

Mémé waited for a response, so I smiled. "Is it near Disney World?" A flicker of hope gleamed in her eyes.

When I first sat down with them in the living room, their announcement hit like a thunderstorm with all the windows open. The idea of them leaving me never crossed my mind— a problem I never expected to solve. My grandparents had lived fifteen minutes away from me my entire life. When the shit hit the fan at my house, they were always there, pulling the plug before the unnecessary splatter.

Mémé beamed. "Yes, it's very close. We'll take you there when you visit. Maybe next summer." She waved the brochure at me. "Would you like that?"

Next summer? Mémé, you have no clue.

I took the brochure and skimmed it. "Yeah, that would be fun." I pointed to one of the spare rooms on the floor plan, circled in red. "I guess this will be my room."

She tilted her head and smiled tenderly. "You'll always have a room in our house."

Pépé pushed himself out of his recliner. "You should look into colleges in Florida," he said gently. "You might find one you like."

As he walked past, he reached down and patted my head, a tremendous kindness. My grandfather wasn't a hugger. A pat on the head was his way of telling me that the ground eventually steadies, even when it's crumbling under me.

I set the brochure on the coffee table. "We'll see about college." The truth settled in my throat, suddenly sweet now that I was going with them. "This is wild. I wonder what Mom is gonna think."

A question in search of two answers. What she'd think of their moving. And what she'd feel about me leaving with them. I faced countless obstacles before summer.

"There's nothing for her to think about," Pépé called from the dining room. "She chose to stay with that asshole. She made her bed. Now she sleeps in it."

He forgot his innocent grandson had to sleep in the bed she'd made, too. I kept that to myself. Once the TV landed on whatever game was on that night, Mémé focused on the blanket she was crocheting. Pépé fell asleep before the first commercial. I excused myself to my room and started plotting how to leave Connecticut. Happy. Exhilarated. My life wasn't a dead end with Melvin and Irene at the wheel. I had a new path. The goal was to leave Melvin's authoritarian world behind for good. My road to happiness included sunshine, BVL, and Disney World.

Oh my god! I was moving to Florida. No one knew about it but me.

Nonrefundable

By the end of April, I sat across from Irene at the kitchen table and unveiled what I thought was a brilliant, foolproof plan to get the hell out of Connecticut. She looked nervous. I usually avoided talking to Irene about anything real, but this mattered. Melvin wasn't home, so I took advantage of the silence and the few beers she'd had. She'd even smiled earlier—I took that as permission to shake up her world.

"Mom, I want to visit Mémé and Pépé in July for two weeks. We can tell Melvin I'm going down there to help them get settled. It's not even a lie. They'll need me. But here's the part you're not going to like: I don't want to come back. I'm serious. I've got to get out of here for real. I'm failing tenth grade; I know I am. I keep telling myself I don't care, but I do. I don't even think I hate school. I think it's this. The drinking. The fighting. The way you two are either screaming or silent.

"If I go to Florida, it'll be calm. That's the whole point. I'll actually have a chance if I'm not living in this mess every day. And if I come back here, Melvin will trap me until I'm eighteen. I can't do three more years of this. I've got my own money. I'll pay my way there. He ripped my lip, Mom. Please. Just help me get there."

I was gazing at a statue. Irene never blinked and seemed to hold her breath to avoid breaking apart.

I tried one last time. "Can I go?"

Still, not a thing.

I'd practiced the speech alone in my room until it sounded convincing. Now I wasn't so sure. Did it come across? Had I made it clear how much this mattered? What if she said no? What if she sentenced me to life in Melvin's world—forever stuck beneath the weight of their decay? I needed a pardon, and this was my last appeal.

A small gasp escaped her. She fell quiet, doing math in her head. I watched the gears turn as she processed the idea, already subtly reshaping her reality to fit around my departure.

"Have you talked to your grandparents?" she asked, her expression neutral, though I knew the calculation had already begun.

I'd spoken to Mémé the previous weekend. The house on Prospect Avenue had sold faster than any of us expected. With only weeks left before they headed south, my weekend visits had grown more frequent. I rarely asked my parents for permission. My grandparents would pick me up on Friday night, and I'd return home on Sunday after Mass.

When I visited them, I had to go to church. It wasn't optional.

Pépé put me to work clearing out twenty-plus years' worth of tools, dust, and junk he had collected in the cellar. I hauled boxes and packed dishes in the kitchen with Mémé. The constant replay of the conversation with her—on the school bus, at the cash register, and in my bedroom—culminated in a moment of clarity: it was now or never.

My plan had to work.

"I have an idea," I said, helping her wrap the antique glassware. The etched-golden goblets felt like a handful of gems. She had to be on board before we approached Pépé. He'd be the hardest sell. Melvin wasn't the problem yet. I planned to lie to him until I was safely in Florida.

"What if I come to visit you this summer and never leave?" I said it nonchalantly, as if I were asking her to pass the salt. I set the wrapped glass in a box, and she handed me another.

We went back and forth for what felt like hours. I'd done my homework and had an answer to every concern. Just when I thought I'd gotten through to my grandmother, when the urgency finally seemed to sink in, she'd pause, considering it.

She was so close to agreeing that I could almost smell the swampy Florida air.

Then her hands went to her hips. "I'm sorry, Joseph. We can't. You can come visit during a school break, once Pépé and I are moved in."

It was a script she'd been practicing, just like mine—clearly, the apple hadn't fallen far from the tree. I could tell she was fighting the urge to say yes; I told myself she wanted me with her in Florida just as much as I needed to be there.

I finished wrapping the last goblet. Mémé hadn't budged. I had to bring out the big guns. I'd already promised myself I'd lie, beg, and manipulate if I had to. I was at the end of my rope.

"Mémé. I can't stay here. He's going to kill me. Or Mom. Maybe both. His drinking is out of control, and you know it. He broke Mom's fucking ankle and wouldn't let her see a doctor. It's too much. I just want to be with you."

She placed her hand over mine. "Watch your mouth."

"If you say no, I'll just run away. I'm coming to Florida either way." I squeezed her hand. It was small in mine. Silence stretched between us, uncomfortable and heavy. I let it hang for a beat, then dropped my last line.

"I just hope I don't get killed while hitchhiking."

Mémé took a deep breath and looked up at the ceiling, as if praying she wasn't agreeing to a mistake.

"You can come live with us, but your mother must agree."

Step Two: Irene.

Mémé let go of my hand and reached for her iced tea. As she took a sip, I realized I hadn't swallowed in minutes.

"I hope Melvin doesn't cause any trouble," she continued. "You know Pépé won't tolerate any nonsense."

I bounced on my toes and threw myself at her small frame. She tried to set her glass down, but iced tea splattered onto the floor. I refused to let go.

"Thank you, Mémé. I won't be a problem. I'll go to school and do chores. You won't even know I'm there."

I was already lying.

I kept embracing her, and she held on, too. When I finally let go, I grabbed a sheet of newspaper and reached for the stack of dishes on the counter. "What about Pépé? Is he going to say yes?"

"You let me handle him."

That's all she said. And she did. Pépé was on board before dinner hit the table.

Irene studied me, waiting for my response. She expected me to say I hadn't asked them yet; she wanted to be the gatekeeper. As usual, my mother was wrong.

I folded my hands on the table and tried to look older than fifteen.

"I spoke to them last weekend. They said yes. I'll go for the summer, but I won't come back. They're saving space on their moving truck for my stuff. I just have to get it to the storage facility before it leaves, sometime in July."

Silence.

"You can call her if you want," I added. "You probably should."

A slow drag on her cigarette. The last gulp of her beer. The stillness felt like the long pause before a judge delivers a sentence.

"Fine," she sighed. "You can go. We have to be careful about what we tell your father." Her hand wrapped around the empty Budweiser can, trembling.

"He won't be happy," she concluded.

After that first curious look, Irene showed no concern about my leaving. No tears. No fight. No begging me to stay. I was her son, but at that moment I wondered if she hadn't been lying all those years ago when she'd claimed I was really her cousin Lana's kid. The lack of concern was so complete it felt like proof.

I didn't want much pushback, but when she barely flinched, it stung. I hovered in confusion, wanting my mother to fight for me even though I didn't want an argument. Would I have changed my mind if she begged me to stay? Absolutely not. But the truth was unavoidable: she didn't fight because she didn't want me there.

Her relief gave her away.

In her eyes, I was the problem. She'd later confess that if I were gone—thousands of miles away—her marriage could reset. No more bickering. No more violence. She was trading her son for a delusion of happiness that Melvin would never provide.

I spent far more time protecting her than she'd ever spent protecting me. For months, Irene hobbled on a fractured ankle that refused to heal—untreated because she was too terrified to seek medical attention. The problem wasn't me; it was Melvin. We both held unrealistic expectations of him—mine had long since been broken, which was precisely why I was leaving.

Her blind faith in him saddened me, but I couldn't afford to carry her grief alongside my own. I sat with the sharp sting of my mother letting me slip away so easily, then pushed it down. I had to move on.

Time sped up. By the end of May, Mémé and Pépé had left the house they'd bought in 1971, the same one where I'd spent my first eleven years. Their belongings sat in a Hartford storage unit, waiting to be loaded onto a semi and hauled to Florida once their new place was ready.

I cried during my last visit. The house was bare. Just a bed and the sofa remained; the last pieces were going to Jean. Saying goodbye felt final, and I kept reminding myself I'd be with them in a few months. Worry and thrill wrestled in my chest.

To stay cheerful, I typed up a countdown and taped it to the inside of my closet, turning the dark space behind my clothes into a private war room. Each morning before school, I slashed through another day. Turning it into a game made survival feel like a winning streak. I'd planned to leave in early August, closer to when the Florida house would be ready, but Melvin's drunken aggression escalated. I couldn't wait. I moved the date up to mid-July.

The sooner, the fucking better.

My sophomore year at East Hartford High finally sputtered to a stop. On the last day of school, I boarded the bus, knowing it would be my final ride down those same predictable streets. That made everything real. I blurted to random classmates that I was moving to Florida over the summer. They shrugged. They'd seen this movie before—the dramatic exits followed by quiet, defeated returns. They'd heard versions of this every time we'd tried to leave Melvin.

I was the broken kid who was always leaving, but I'd be back in class on Monday morning, sliding into my desk as if nothing had happened.

This time, I wasn't coming back. As expected, my final report card was a total wreck: seven Fs and two Cs. I even managed to fail Photography 1, which took a specific kind of effort to blow—it was honestly shameful. I'd be repeating the tenth grade, but not here. Not in East Hartford.

One night in late June, I sat with Irene, eating dinner. Melvin was within earshot. Irene lit the fuse with the casual indifference of someone who didn't realize they were holding a match. I didn't have time to duck for cover.

"When your grandparents register you for school," she said, "make sure they—."

She didn't finish.

Fuckity fuck!

"Why would he need to be enrolled in school in Florida?" Melvin asked, leaning against the counter. The air in the kitchen turned cold. I kept my head down and mechanically shoveled cereal into my mouth. For the moment, I wasn't the target.

His eyes remained on her.

"What the fuck are you talking about?"

This wasn't Irene's first slip. She had a long history with them. Sometimes it was the alcohol; sometimes it was just Irene being Irene. We'd agreed on the exact moment she'd tell him I wanted to visit my grandparents over the summer, but she jumped the gun and fired the shot straight into the wall.

At first, I was pissed. I'd picked the date. I'd replayed the conversation so many times in my head that it became a prayer that kept me up at night. I was superstitious about it: I figured any change to the script would jinx the whole thing. I'd failed enough this year; I couldn't afford to fail at leaving.

Her first mishap happened a few weeks earlier. I was at The Grocery Barn one afternoon. Gwen had been hired, so I hung around even on my days off. We laughed. We screamed. I loitered until Mr. Gay told me to get my ass home. While I goofed off with Gwen, being a normal teenager, Irene was at home dismantling my safety net. How? She told Melvin she wanted to send me to Florida as an end-of-school-year gift.

Wrong, Irene. Stick to the script.

The plan was to say I was going to help them move in—a job, not a reward. A gift for finishing the tenth grade? What was she thinking? Again, she wasn't. The irony was thick enough to choke on. She spent more time with him than I did; she might not have let on that I'd flunked, but rewarding a wrecked school year was a neon sign that something was up. I knew Melvin would eventually hear about the two-week trip, and I'd rehearsed every detail, but the tension settled in like a squatter in my chest, gut, and lower back. Even thinking about Florida gave me heart palpitations. Deep down, I still believed Melvin could read the betrayal in my eyes and see exactly what I'd orchestrated.

The secrecy was so intense that even a "Visit Florida" commercial during the nightly news made my armpits sweat; I was sure the upbeat music and bright sand were sounding an alarm in the middle of our living room. The plan was never to keep Melvin in the dark forever. I couldn't just vanish into thin air—never to return from my vacation. My original plan had been for him to find out the truth after I arrived in Florida, leaving Irene to answer his questions about how my two-week vacation had turned into a permanent exit. She said she'd handle it. Eventually, I stopped worrying that she might end up with another broken bone as payment for my trickery.

As expected, Melvin grumbled about my "vacation." Two weeks? That was too long for him to go without his favorite target. One night, on my way to bed, he stopped me on the stairs. He tried to cut it down to one week. I leaned on the railing while he lay on the sofa, a king on a throne of ripped pleather. I swallowed the dry rock in my throat. With fake politeness, I told him my grandparents had already bought the plane ticket.

Nonrefundable. The word landed like a deadbolt sliding into place. Lie, beg, and manipulate. The rules had not changed.

A few days passed. Whenever we were together, Melvin talked as if the whole trip depended on his permission. I kept a stone face, glancing only at Irene when he turned away. Sober, he was "thinking about it." Drunk, he said there was "no fucking way."

He eventually invaded my sanctuary and cornered me in my bedroom. "Who do you think you are? You don't tell us what you're doing."

I'd bitten my lip long enough. What did I care? The haggling felt ridiculous. I'd leave in the middle of the night if push came to shove. To me, Melvin was just a problem with a visible expiration date.

I kept my voice even, using the flat, compliant tone he demanded. "Dad, I thought you were letting me go as a gift."

The room fell quiet. Melvin realized he was losing. I had used Irene's words against him, making him look weak. After that, he dropped it.

Back in the kitchen, Irene's words hung in the air like smoke. *Grandparents. Register. School.* That was it—no more games. We'd have to come clean. I wanted to crawl into my bowl of Cheerios. He cursed before Irene had a chance to recover. I had always known she'd somehow screw this up.

Fucking Irene.

Melvin went still, his eyes widening as the last few weeks snapped into focus. He was sober, which was good. Like he was checking off a list, he started calling out the things that had been disappearing from my bedroom. I kept my door closed, but he had been peeking in whenever he could.

First, my most prized possession was missing from my dresser. An eight-inch ceramic bear, Mémé had painted brown, with her name carved on the bottom, a gift from when I was four. I'd displayed that bear in every bedroom I'd ever lived in, front and center. He knew how much I worshipped it.

Now the bear was gone.

My posters had vanished as well, leaving only tiny thumbtack holes in the drywall. Nothing in my room suggested it was occupied, except for the furniture and a single set of sheets.

Melvin's anger had two targets: us and himself. You could see it in his face as it all clicked—how foolish he'd been. While he was sinking into a vodka stupor on the sofa, I'd been pulling the rug out from under him, planning my escape. I'm still proud of myself.

His questions, laced with threats, pelted us like hail. Irene stuttered until she froze, nothing coherent coming out. Panic carved itself into the lines of her forehead. With nothing to lose, I let my spoon clatter against the bowl. I met Melvin's gaze and delivered the truth.

"It's not Mom's fault. This was my idea. I'm leaving, Dad." My legs tensed, the last part of me that still feared him. Thank God I was sitting. "All my stuff is already in storage. It'll ship down with Mémé and Pépé's things when their house is ready."

He listened, his eyes narrowed in a way I'd never seen before. I sat straight. Tall. No fear in my voice. No hesitation.

No need to pad the story. Each word was another foot of distance between us. Every exhale felt like getting myself back.

I'd spent months moving behind his back, whispering to Irene when he passed out, and packing my closet in silence. Sue, our neighbor across the street, had driven me back and forth to the storage unit. She kept my secret because I kept hers—an affair.

"Sue helped. She drove me to the storage unit with my stuff while you weren't home."

Melvin stepped toward the table. "You've got a lot of nerve, wimp. You're nothing without me." His right fist worked at his side, coiling and uncoiling, searching for a target. He kept slashing threats at me like swords, but my emotional chainmail held.

He paused to catch his breath. That was my opening. I stood, grabbed my bowl, and carried it to the sink. I brushed Irene's back as I passed—a quiet message: *I'm here. He won't hurt us.*

She was too paralyzed to react.

"I'm going, Dad. It's over. I'm moving out." I stepped past him, drawing a line in the sand that he was no longer allowed to cross. No flinching. No distress. No hand covering my face to anticipate a blow. He had spent a lifetime training me to fear him, but the lesson had finally worn off. Now I was unmoved, and he couldn't stand it. My confidence stripped him of his power, and it pissed him off more than my words.

Melvin's mind raced in loops. He kept muttering that I was his "former" son. I'd backstabbed him with a serrated knife, twisted it, and left it in. My actions, this months-long game I'd played against him, hurt more than the day I exposed the vodka—even more than when I nearly stabbed him on the kitchen floor. I wasn't just untrustworthy; I was a snake. Unforgivable. In his version of the story, he'd saved us and asked for nothing in return.

That almost drew a reaction, but I let him run his mouth. I've probably never been that calm since. My confession was over; now it was his turn to rant.

Melvin bombarded me with insults. He should never have adopted me. I didn't deserve his last name. *I agreed. I despised carrying his surname.* He wished he'd never met us. We were pieces of shit.

Ditto, Melvin. Ditto. He said life was better before we "ruined" him, before he had to become an instant father to a bastard. Back when he was content being a bachelor behind The Silver Dollar.

I coughed to hide my laugh.

Then came his closer: "You're just like your mother."

He delivered it like a knockout punch, but it landed like lines I'd already memorized. Melvin's voice exhausted me. Same words. Same threats. The same old, predictable Melvin bullshit that no longer made my heart race.

Hearing him say that about her, Irene turned her silence into hysterics. Slobber bubbled at the corner of her mouth. Melvin and I watched her performance—an audience of two watching a play we'd both grown tired of. Irene wasn't crying for the loss of her son; she cried because the toxic rhythm of her life was finally breaking. She'd have been happy with the status quo: me failing high school, Melvin breaking her into splinters, the grocery-shopping bans. Irene rocked the boat only enough to keep Melvin "behaving" when he drank.

When I rocked the boat, I tipped the fucker straight into the icy Blackledge River.

See, I was nothing like my mother.

Irene's tears hadn't affected Melvin in years; he enjoyed the spectacle. Her tears were just gasoline for the family's fireworks. I'd lost interest in the performance, too. Yes, Irene put on a great show, but Melvin and I both saw the hollow routine beneath the hysteria.

My father and I did have something in common after all: a cold, identical annoyance at her theatrical pain. Then came his final swing, a twist nobody saw but him.

"If Joe moves to Florida, you might as well leave, too."

The declaration tugged at my collar like a hand. I didn't think Melvin had that in him. Irene could've had X-ray vision and still missed it. The tears stopped instantly, like a faucet being shut off. Her glassy eyes caught the fluorescent light. I planted myself by the staircase, a ghost already halfway out the door. She focused entirely on Melvin. I was no longer her concern. I was Mémé's problem now.

"What do you mean? He's going. I'm staying here with you." The groveling was unbecoming, even for Irene. "I didn't do anything wrong. I want to make our marriage work."

My Cheerios crawled up my throat. I almost threw up right there on the living room carpet; my body was physically rejecting her voice. Irene's genuflection to her abuser made me sick. Truly. It was a gnawing, acidic disgust in my gut.

Tonight, the truth burned hot: I hated Melvin. Melvin hated Irene. Irene hated losing Melvin.

My mother had never been on my side. She was never the protector she claimed to be. I should've accepted it that afternoon on Wakefield Circle, when she walked in on Melvin and me in the storage unit, with that porn magazine lying on the floor. But I was a kid. If I'd admitted my mother was willfully ignorant back then, I might not have come back from it.

My mother wasn't a victim; she was an accomplice to what Melvin put me through. For years, it was hard to blame her because I'd always believed we were in the mud together, trying to haul each other out. But in the kitchen that night, the truth cut through the delusion: I was the only one pulling. She was just holding on to me so she wouldn't sink.

How could I ever love this woman again?

Irene was team Melvin through and through. I had told myself she wore blinders about what Melvin was capable of—not just to me, but to herself. There was no excusing her now; the betrayal was seared in. She bargained until she ran out of air, begging him for another chance. I watched it unfold from the shadows, a spectator to my own abandonment.

She threw herself at him, teetering on one leg to keep weight off the injured ankle. If it weren't so sad, it would've been hilarious. Grabbing. Pulling. Their face-off had nothing to do with me anymore; Melvin had moved on to a new target. I wanted to run to my room, but if he got violent, I'd have to intervene, even though the sight of Irene made my skin itch.

Melvin didn't touch her. He leaned back, avoiding her embrace as if she were contagious.

"Without Joe, there's no family," he said. "You might as well leave with him. I'm done with you both."

I remember feeling relieved he didn't hit her. Actually, he did nothing. No violence. No more shouting. These were the new rules of engagement: a surgical, freezing silence. Melvin left Irene perched at the kitchen table, her hands dropped to her sides, shocked by the rejection she hadn't rehearsed.

He hurried past me, and I stepped aside. As he climbed the stairs, he glanced back over his shoulder and dropped one last piece of shrapnel. "Your cat hasn't been home in a few days. He's probably dead."

Melvin's sword finally shattered my armor. Bonkers never came home.

As much as my heart felt crushed by sadness, I couldn't afford to sit in grief. I had to keep moving. Bonkers was my only friend at Oakridge Apartments—the buddy whose quiet presence kept a scared kid from running away every other week. He made biscuits on my stomach before I had to get up for school. He smelled like grass after being outside, and he'd stare at me until I gave him a chip. Bonkers snuggled with me in my *Star Wars* sheets and gave me the only unconditional love in that apartment. Leaving him behind hurt all over. Irene said she'd take care of him. I counted on that.

He deserved better than to die alone outside.

I waited for Melvin to close his bedroom door, then ran to my room. I didn't even check on Irene. She'd become a burden. I had to think. Recalculate. I started to panic, then reminded myself: tonight still worked in my favor. Well, kinda. Melvin had excommunicated me from his world. That was a win. Nobody got hurt. Double win. If he'd been drunk, someone would've bled.

It was too late to call Mémé, so I'd do it first thing in the morning. I grabbed a bag of Cheetos from my closet and sat on the bed. Then the heat hit me: my neck flushed, sweat beading on my back. I turned on the A/C.

Frustration surged. Melvin had flipped my plan on its head. Yes, I'd manipulated everyone to get to Florida, and he hadn't derailed that. My bright future was still intact. But in the last ten minutes, the stakes had shifted. I was still getting out, but now I had to drag along the one person I despised as much as I despised him.

My mother.

ONE WAY. NO RETURN.

The final few weeks with Melvin were surprisingly quiet, mostly because we stopped engaging. I can't speak to his motivation, but I made avoiding him my full-time job. Just the sight of him sent a surge of bile and raw anger up my throat. Whenever I was forced to talk to him, I'd let a sharp comment slip. He'd bark a threat, and I'd back off before the explosion. Then I'd remind myself, like a mantra: in less than a week, I'd be a Floridian. The strategy was simple—total avoidance.

I spent that final summer in Connecticut, balancing shifts at The Grocery Barn while aimlessly cruising East Hartford with Alan. He'd graduated in June, and the whole world was wide open to him. I'll never forget how handsome he was in the hazy light of 1988. Every girl adored him. And so did his closeted gay best friend.

One afternoon, he picked me up after work, with Gwen already waiting in the back seat. The three of us raced toward Misquamicut Beach in Rhode Island. Other days, we spent killing time at the East Hartford High pool before retreating to Gwen's house, where we'd sip her mother's boxed wine and snack on cheese and crackers. It was my first taste of "adult grape juice." Living through those last weeks, I finally felt the pull of transition—the electric lure of burning the map and starting over. The very thought of leaving became intoxicating.

Or maybe that was just Gwen's mom's wine.

The three of us sat on Rhode Island sand as a salt-heavy breeze blew in from the Sound. Alan was on a mission to scare me about Florida. "You know they have huge-ass bugs down there? Flying cockroaches. They'll get tangled in your hair." He shook his head, barely holding back his laughter. "They hiss, too."

"You're full of shit. There's no such thing as a flying cockroach."

"There are," Gwen chimed in. "My cousin went to Disney once. She said they're everywhere." She scowled at the very thought. "I'm never coming to visit."

"You guys are nuts," I laughed, sifting sand through my fingers. "But even if there are monster bugs, at least my asshole father won't be there. I'll take my chances with the roaches."

Alan kicked up a spray of sand at me, and I threw a handful back at Gwen. In a moment that felt straight out of a John Hughes movie, the three of us tumbled in the surf, our limbs entangled, laughing like the foolish teenagers we were.

The only real sting of saying goodbye to this chapter wasn't the bugs or the unknown—it was leaving these two behind. They had always been my lifeline to normalcy.

With only two days left before our departure, I ran down the stairs, the adrenaline of my last shift at the Grocery Barn already kicking in. The plan was simple: clock out, grab my final paycheck—the payday I'd been living for since April—and deposit it at the bank across the street. I watched the teller stamp the book; that final entry was more than a deposit—it was my official discharge papers. The bank book felt heavier in my hand, weighed down by the promise of freedom. The total balance: $400 plus change. My ticket to a new life. Now, only two obstacles stood in my way: finding a ride to the Greyhound terminal downtown and surviving the next forty-eight hours trapped in that apartment.

Irene looked up from her coffee at the kitchen table as I walked into view. Her voice was flat, agonizingly matter-of-fact. "Your father's driving us to the bus station Saturday morning."

She looked hollowed out, withdrawn. The weight of her grief was etched in the dark, bruised circles beneath her eyes. A heavy void had taken up residence in our kitchen. I didn't think it was possible, but the moment Melvin decided he no longer wanted her, her addictions, the constant drinking and smoking, consumed her. I clung to a desperate confidence that her crutches would disappear once we arrived in Florida, as if sunshine could bleach the trauma away.

Irene acted as if she'd finally accepted the reality of being discarded. Any flicker of joy she'd nurtured about a fresh start with Melvin had been extinguished. She finally saw the truth: without me to manipulate, Melvin had no use for her. She was merely an appendage, easily amputated.

I grabbed a can of Coke and cracked it open, the sharp pop echoing in the quiet kitchen. "Two days left," I said, a lightness spreading through my chest. "Do you need me to bring anything home from the store?"

The heavy silence swallowed my question.

Then came her response, a whisper so fragile it barely reached me. "I'm giving up everything. My life is over."

How could the very thing that felt like my salvation be the very thing that signaled her ruin?

Irene had indeed given up a lot. She still had me, but our relationship had grown brittle, a cautious dance around what went unsaid. She had to distill more than forty years of her life into two meager boxes. One held pictures, mementos, and a few essentials. The other cradled her prized possession: a golden ceramic cat the size of a Maine Coon. That green-eyed, soul-sucking creature followed us like a curse from Hartford to Florida. I reviled it, but Irene loved it enough to have it shipped south. Everything else—the bulk of her clothes, her furniture, her kitchen utensils—was left behind with Melvin. He had already evicted Linda from our Wakefield Circle condominium and would end up living there until my parents finalized the sale in the wake of their looming divorce.

Thankfully, Alan didn't blame me for the sudden exit. Will had returned to his birth mother, and just like that, he began to fade into the blurred edges of my memory.

Back in Connecticut, the financial arrangements were as clear as paper: my parents agreed that Melvin would pay Irene rent while he stayed at the Wakefield Circle condo and provide child support until I turned eighteen. In reality, the checks were a fantasy. He never sent a dime, effectively ghosting us.

When the condo was finally sold—sometime in late 1989—Melvin grudgingly handed over a lump sum to cover the back rent and the child support he'd conveniently ignored. He had his lawyer, Willie, handle the entire divorce agreement. Irene, defeated and drowning in grief, never hired a lawyer of her own. She simply accepted whatever they deemed she was worth. There was no alimony, despite the years he'd spent stifling her independence and dictating whether and when she could work. She left Hartford with nothing but pocket change and a hollowed-out spirit. As for me, the state appraised my existence at twenty-five dollars a week until my eighteenth birthday. You can't put a price tag on a stolen childhood, but that weekly pittance was a final mockery—it felt like the court was legally codifying Melvin's abuse.

In the end, Melvin's worst fear finally came true. The carefully curated excitement of moving to the Oakridge

Apartments—with his self-proclaimed "incredible" maintenance job and the promise of a second chance—had run its course. To those watching from the outside, the outcome wasn't surprising. Our little family didn't just go bust; it imploded. He retreated to Wakefield Circle alone, soaked in vodka and self-pity, with no wife to browbeat and no "precious son" left to groom.

But Melvin was a con man; he was never truly down and out. He was a scavenger of circumstances, with an uncanny knack for slipping under the radar. Within a month of Irene and me leaving, we learned from Linda that he had already moved a new girlfriend into the condo. They became an instant family, a carbon copy of the life he'd just destroyed. When my parents' divorce was finalized, he married this woman within days.

The cruelest part of Melvin's "fresh start" was that his new wife came equipped with three children: two daughters and an eight-year-old son. Those poor lambs. Especially the boy. I didn't need a witness to know exactly what he endured. I saw it with terrifying clarity. I watched the phantom replay in my mind—the way the thrill of having a father figure curdled into a nightmare, and how an innocent trust was shattered in the most violating sequence imaginable. I saw him with his pants around his ankles, wondering if being a "better" little boy could have prevented the impossible. I knew how quickly safe moments could warp into scenes that would scar him for life. My own scars are like that, slightly healed by time and therapy, yet still visible to anyone who dares to look closely.

Trauma-induced lifetime tattoos.

I know what it's like to have that kind of trauma pumped into your veins, a toxic circulation you never asked for, and to carry it forward while fighting off demons that never truly go away.

I sometimes wonder about that boy now, as a grown man. Has he found peace? Has he learned to live with the shadow, or does it still dictate the architecture of his life? For us—the survivors—the rest of life becomes a slow, painstaking effort to rebuild on the ruins our parents left behind. We never ask to be born. We never ask for parents who prey on our innocence. But the universe deals its cards without clemency, and we're left to survive the hand we're given.

On Saturday morning, July 16, 1988, I didn't so much wake up as stop pretending to sleep. I'd spent the night paralyzed on my sheets, staring at the ceiling as the minutes ticked away. I ached for my cat, missing the familiar weight of his warm body against my leg. This was the last time I'd ever rest in this apartment. The last time I'd reach out to shut off my window-unit air conditioner. After I stripped the bed in a final act of "I'm outta here" defiance, my once-expressive bedroom looked like a blank canvas. I found myself hoping the next person trapped in this room had a better story to tell than mine. I left the linens in a heap; Melvin's brothers were coming to help him move out all the furniture. I didn't know then that my "replacement" was already waiting in the wings, that another boy would soon be forced to sleep in my bed, probably on my *Star Wars* sheet, enduring the same torture I had.

Because I'd woken before the sun, I descended the stairs with precision, sidestepping the creaks and groans that might alert my parents. Before heading to the kitchen, I detoured one last time to my basement lair. Once, it had been a musty sanctuary—the stage for a thousand solo danceathons where I'd crank the music to drown out the poison drifting down from upstairs. Now it was just a cold, excavated concrete box. I stood in the dark, giving the haven one last moment of silence. I'd spent the last few days performing these tiny rituals, saying a private goodbye to every corner of my life that had offered me a shred of safety.

Eventually, I went back upstairs and poured a bowl of cereal. I sat at the table, slurping milk, waiting for the house to wake up and for the end to officially begin.

Upstairs, the reality was far more twisted. Irene was still sleeping in the same bed with Melvin, even after he made it clear he was done with her. The thought confused me then and haunts me now—the image of her choosing to spend her final night huddled beside the very man she was supposedly escaping. It's a riddle I've stopped trying to solve.

Until the very last moment, Irene extinguished any possibility of her son seeing her with anything but contempt. Disgraceful. What hurt most was that she couldn't even summon the strength to cross the threshold of that bedroom. Like so many women entangled in the gears of abuse, she couldn't cut the cord. She could have slept in the basement. On the sofa. Hell, I would have shared my twin bed with her if she'd asked. But she never asked. Instead, she clung to the desperate fantasy that her life wasn't fracturing—maintaining a charade that this wasn't an ending and that somehow she and Melvin would still be together.

Melvin never had to force her into that bed; he knew true control didn't require a struggle. He had already tossed her out like roadside trash, yet he relished that she still crawled back to him at night, unable to face the darkness alone. Maybe behind closed eyelids, she could still summon the image of the husband she'd once hoped for, the savior she'd invented when they first met. But this morning, the nightmare didn't fade; it opened its eyes and demanded she face the end.

We all moved in a heavy, mechanical silence that morning. In the kitchen, Irene and Melvin shared a hug that felt entirely performative. In the car, they held hands. She sniffled as we rode down the highway. It was the final, sickening act of her charade.

Our luggage was tossed into the trunk of Melvin's gray-and-black Buick Skylark, a used car he'd scrounged through a connection. It felt like a step down, a physical manifestation of his fading status. The apartment management had already reclaimed the keys to his work truck; he'd finally been terminated, and they'd given him only a few weeks to vacate. I thought that was generous. The truck sat lifeless in the parking space out back, a stationary reminder of how quickly Melvin's "incredible" second chance had crashed into a guardrail. Fitting.

Melvin pulled into a parking space at the bus terminal. The Greyhound bus bound for Orlando was scheduled to depart around eleven. As soon as the engine stopped, I leaped out of the backseat, eager to grab the bags from the trunk. Irene had her suitcase; I carried a smaller bag and a box clutched to my chest.

Inside the cardboard box was my full-sized Garfield comforter. It sounds absurd now that I'd carry that oversized comforter with me, but it was more than fabric. Imprinted with Garfield in a multitude of mischievous escapades, it was my safety blanket. Mémé had bought it for me. It was only fitting that I bring it to Florida. The soft plushness reminded me of countless nights spent cozy with Bonkers. I used it to wrap myself up into a tight burrito, anything to hide my body from Melvin.

"I'll go buy the tickets," I announced, leaving our belongings next to Melvin's car. He didn't offer us a cent, but I didn't expect him to. We were leaving him behind, after all.

Irene didn't have a single nickel to her name; she hadn't worked in over a year. I, on the other hand, had more cash than she'd seen in a long time. I was the one providing our way out.

I walked up to the ticket window, the weight of the bills in my pocket feeling like adulthood. "Two one-way tickets to Orlando."

The clerk didn't even make eye contact. In a raspy voice, he said, "That'll be three hundred fifty-five dollars."

My heart sank. I had planned that after buying my own ticket, the rest of my $400 fortune would carry me through the rest of the summer in Florida until I could find a job. But having to pay for Irene's ticket left me with only forty-five dollars. She promised to pay me back once her divorce settlement came through.

And eventually, she did.

The ticketer handed me the two tickets and my meager change. I thanked the man, probably looking far too excited about a twenty-four-hour bus ride crowded with people who couldn't afford to fly. Us included. But the shock and wonder of it all washed over me.

I made all this happen.

As I walked back to the car, tickets in hand and wearing a smile that felt illegal, I came to an abrupt stop. Irene had her arms wrapped around Melvin. His back was to me, and her face was buried in his shoulder. She yelped and cried out in raw, sharp pain—like a tooth extraction without novocaine. Howls of sorrow poured from her as she said goodbye to the love of her life.

We were boarding a bus to the Sunshine State; to me, her reaction was completely misplaced.

"I'll always love you. Please don't make me leave," Irene pleaded as I stepped closer to the dysfunction. Those words burned into me. *Jesus Christ, Mom. Have some dignity.* Melvin kept holding her until I walked up and bent to pick up my box. Only then did he release his grip.

"This is the way it has to be," he said. He leaned in and kissed her, and she began wiping away her tears with fierce determination. I couldn't bring myself to look at her.

I handed her a ticket. "Here, Mom. We've got to go. The bus leaves in about twenty minutes." She was still limping on her slowly healing, fractured ankle—a parting gift from the "love of her life."

Without looking at Melvin, I asked, "Could you help carry her bag?"

"Are you going to give your father a goodbye hug?" he asked, the word "father" hanging in the air like smog.

Without hesitation, I set the box down and walked toward him. I had won. The wall had come down; our Cold War was over. Irene stared at us. I leaned in, and Melvin hugged me with the quiet understanding that he'd never see me again.

All the history we shared and all the secrets we kept pressed into that moment. The pain he had inflicted from age four until I began fighting back—the pure loathing I carried for him—was still there, simmering beneath the surface. I squeezed tighter, letting the full weight of my fury and survival press against him.

I had planned countless ways to destroy him—while he slept and while he was awake. And yet the hand that now rested against my back in a gesture of affection, the same hand that once ripped my lip in a fit of demonic rage, felt powerless. Melvin had groomed me to be his sex toy. He never gave up, even after I told Irene what he had done all those years ago. Melvin knew Irene was weak and that she would never truly defend herself—or her son's innocence. I had always known it was wrong, but I didn't have a voice that reached beyond those walls. Muted, shut away in a world where a predator meticulously dictated every corner of our lives.

The hair on my arms stood on end as he held on. Sweat trickled down my temples, mingling with the heavy humidity and the crushing weight of my emotions. I wanted him to feel the loss, to see what happens when you abuse the son who once worshipped you.

This outcome was the pangs of karma in action.

I wanted him to understand that, no matter how desperately we had clung to the dream of a normal family, it would never be realized. I learned this hard life lesson at fifteen: never get swept up in the illusions of what you wish would happen while ignoring the reality of what is. Meeting a drunk predator living in a run-down duplex behind a bar could never provide the stability or safety a single mother and her child deserved. Instead, he brought exactly what Irene had once believed he could cure: our pain.

Melvin released me. "Take care of your mother. I'll send you some money soon."

I nodded, noting a slight softening in his voice, but I met it with total indifference. My primary concern was no longer his empty promises; it was getting two suitcases, a box, and my mother onto that bus.

Melvin didn't help us walk to the boarding platform because he said it was "too painful to watch us leave." It was one last act of cowardice, leaving me to haul our luggage while Irene struggled on her healing ankle. But the "pain" didn't keep him from watching. As the bus backed out of the terminal, we both spotted him standing and waving beside the car. He was still playing the part of the loving family man for anyone who might be watching.

Away from Melvin, Irene moved like a zombie, one foot dragging after the other. I lugged our two bags and the box, urging her along as the bus driver helped stow our luggage in the compartment below. Because of Irene's shuffling, we were the last passengers to board the half-full Greyhound. I guided her toward the back. She now reminded me of a lost child, needing all her decisions made for her.

I didn't want her there. This wasn't part of my adventure. Now I had a pathetic person I was forced to care for. I had no hope for her yet, but that didn't matter right now. What mattered was getting away from Melvin. The prime objective: save yourself. Save your mother.

I found seats in the back of the bus. Irene took the window seat so she could prop her swollen, still-painful ankle on my leg, and I took the aisle seat. There was a restroom right there in the back—first class. I quickly used it before we departed.

Back in my seat, Irene continued to whimper, wiping away crocodile tears. Was she really sad, or was this just a performance? I didn't dwell on it. I was too excited as the bus lurched backward, signaling we were finally on our way.

We caught a final glimpse of Melvin waving. That final act unleashed uncontrollable sobs from Irene, a full-blown emotional storm. "I love you," she sobbed, repeating it on a loop. It was painfully clear she had spent too many years immersed in ABC soap operas. The passengers around us watched with pity.

I just sighed. I really wished I were alone.

EPILOGUE

The Sunshine State

I remember snapping photographs of Irene with my Kodak 110 camera, trying to catch her in the act—walking down the stairs, washing dishes, or cradling her chihuahua with a tenderness that might have done me some good if it had been directed my way. Whenever she spotted me squinting through that plastic viewfinder, angling for the best shot, she'd force a smile. For years, I accepted that her smiles were just a curtain to hide behind. But in the shutter-click between the flash and the reality, those seconds didn't feel fake. They were a real shared moment between mother and son, existing in the rare quiet space where Melvin wasn't allowed to follow.

When I look at those pictures now—her long, brunette hair pulled back in a barrette, that same flannel shirt layered over a rotation of T-shirts—I see I wasn't just capturing her in a moment. I was curating a version of her that no longer existed. I was hunting for the mother I wanted her to be: the one with the laissez-faire smile I'd only seen in faded Polaroids from the 1960s. After years of Melvin's "programming," her lightness had vanished. His presence had so thoroughly jilted her spirit that by the time I was behind the lens, every grin was an act of labor.

In those brief flashes, she looks ordinary. Jovial. Content. She isn't the woman crying at the kitchen table or stumbling through a drunken haze to fetch another beer. Through that lens, I captured her stripped of Melvin's weight. I edited out the pain that had carved deep lines from the sides of her nose to the corners of her mouth, the trenches where her sorrow gathered, front and center for the world to see.

***

The Greyhound pulled into the Washington, D.C., terminal for a transfer, and—holy shit. It was pure, unadulterated chaos. More people than I'd ever seen were packed into one space, all vibrating with the same frantic energy: catch the bus before it disappears. I looked at the sea of faces and wondered how many other women and children were doing exactly what we were, quietly dismantling their old lives and slipping away in the middle of the night. I guarantee we weren't the only ones, all survivors hoping the next bus we took would erase our pasts.

The pressure built until it felt like a physical weight; I panicked we'd miss the next bus. Irene had checked out mentally, leaving me feeling entirely alone in that crowd. I wasn't technically solitary, but she had become a heavy, stagnant anchor, determined to make us miss the connection. I lugged our bags across the terminal, constantly prodding her to hurry, dragging her toward a future she didn't even want. I asked if she was hungry, but she just shrugged—a gesture of unresponsive vacancy. Was she mourning Melvin? It was absurd. She stared at me with cold contempt, her anger redirected at her lifelong scapegoat. She should have been furious with the man who broke her, but her body language and curt, biting responses told me I was the true villain in her story.

During our bouncy, jarring ride down I-95 South, she repeatedly threw it in my face: I was the one who had forced Melvin to make her leave.

"I wanted to stay," she hissed, her voice cutting through the bus engine's hum. "You ruined it."

At the time, I believed these were the words of a woman ripped from her routine, a life rearranged without her consent. By making the bold decision to move to Florida, I had ignited a warhead that destroyed her happy life. She believed she was being forced to give it all up, when in reality she was being offered a chance at rebirth. I thought it was a gift. A guarantee that Melvin would never hit her again.

As she blamed me throughout that grueling ride, I ignored her, brushing off her accusations like annoying flies. She hadn't had a drink in over twenty-four hours, and her behavior resembled a spiraling detox. I took the brunt of it. I told myself a change in environment would snap Melvin's hold over her—that the Florida sun would act as a catalyst, allowing her to finally realize that leaving her abuser was the best thing that ever happened to us.

I held out hope for Irene, not yet understanding that our path together was a dead end. I was gripped by a healing fantasy, wanting her to be someone she wasn't, someone she simply couldn't be. She'd been broken by men long before I was even a thought. Robert. Frank. Larry. Melvin. A lineage of ghosts that had reduced her to dust.

Irene's behavior taught me a cold, vital lesson: never expect anything from people. Never believe they will act according to your logic or hopes, because you will only end up disappointed. You have to accept each individual exactly as they are, damaged and all, and then make the conscious choice to stay or leave. I know it's easier to put in print than to put into action, but Irene taught me that expectations are future resentments. Letting go of them is the only way to stop the suffering, a path to forgiveness for yourself, not for them.

I kept expecting her to snap out of her obsession with loving a child rapist. As usual, Irene disappointed me.

One afternoon in 1991, I asked Irene if I could borrow twenty dollars. A normal, mundane request. She was in her bedroom and told me to grab her wallet from the kitchen counter. I riffled through her saved receipts, looking for my payday, but when the leather folds fell open, an internal shockwave hit me.

There, tucked into the clear plastic window—front and center—was a picture of Melvin, staring back at me. Four years later, after all the miles we'd put between us and that life, he was still the first thing she saw every time she opened her wallet. It was proof that her heart still lingered in sin.

I pocketed the money, grabbed her wallet, and stormed into her bedroom. She stood in front of the bathroom mirror, probably fixing her hair. I didn't say anything at first; I just held the wallet up so she couldn't deny the evidence. I wanted her to look at the man. The one I spent my entire childhood fending off. The one she carried with her all day long.

"What the hell is this doing in your wallet?"

She was unfazed. Almost relieved. "He was my husband, Joe. I love him."

Before I could even find the words to respond, she drove the final nail into her own coffin. "I still do."

The heat spread across my neck, that familiar warning that my body wanted to react. I forced down the urge to lash out. Part of me wanted to hit her. I felt the hate bubbling under my skin, hot poison.

"Melvin was our abuser, Mom. He molested me as a kid. You know this!"

She walked past me, heading into the kitchen of the house I'd helped her rent in BVL. "I don't know what to tell you. I'm sorry about that. I really am, but he was my husband. I'd have stayed."

"He's the one who didn't want me." She pulled a beer from the refrigerator and looked at me with vacant eyes.

"He only wanted you."

I moved this woman to a new state. I gave her a *real* second chance. It wasn't one of Melvin's failed plots. Only for her to stand in that kitchen and confess that she'd have rather preferred abuse over rejection.

For decades, I tried to piece together the abstract jigsaw puzzle of my relationship with Irene. No matter how hard I tried, the pieces never fit—not because they weren't available, but because I'd been looking at the image upside down. I couldn't understand how she could see Melvin, know exactly what he was, and still remain loyal to him over her son. It tormented me through my twenties. thirties, and forties—a constant, throbbing ache of confusion and betrayal.

The answer didn't arrive until 2020, while the pandemic raged outside and most of us were stuck inside. It came during a therapy session: sudden, undeniable, and life-altering.

Halfway through a session, I stared into my computer's camera. On the other side of the Zoom call, my therapist watched me from behind his desk.

"It's so weird," I said, the words coming together as if a ghostwriter had written them for me. "The only answer that makes any sense of the fuckery from my childhood is that Irene didn't love me."

The Fourth of July had nothing on the fireworks exploding in my mind as this truth finally crystallized. The answer had always been there, buried beneath years of denial and pain, simply too raw to confront. I finally understood why she allowed all of it to happen, why she spent years cowering in the corners and trembling in Melvin's shadow. My safety never mattered to her. I was never her concern.

At forty-eight, after a lifetime of soul-searching and thousands of dollars in therapy, I accepted the unthinkable: Irene couldn't love me the way a mother should love her child. Her heart was already occupied. She loved her sadness. She loved *and* hated herself. She loved the drink, the smoke, and the jagged illusion that Melvin was a good man.

Love for me? There was simply no room left for that.

On the bus, I pressed my headphones to my ears to drown her out. Somewhere over the South Carolina state line, I realized she was still hoping the driver would turn the bus around. I daydreamed that we'd spend the night at a Disney World hotel, finally reclaiming that flicker of happiness from the Sheraton Hartford.

Irene wanted to go back.

As the Greyhound rolled into the Orlando terminal, I leaned toward my mother. "There's Mémé and Pépé."

I waved, though I doubted they could see me through the tinted windows. Irene's sniffles faded, her tears drying up as quickly as they had started. Crying on command was her superpower; the tears flowed as easily as breath. She began to compose herself for the performance ahead, wiping her face with a moistened Burger King napkin. She had cried for hundreds of miles, I wondered how there was anything left in her.

When the bus finally pulled in, I urged Irene forward, practically pulling her toward the exit. Down the narrow steps we went to where Mémé and Pépé stood waiting. Mémé's eyes lit up at the sight of me, but Pépé's grin carried a different relief; his daughter had finally left her husband. He was pleased, despite the updates I'd given them on the drama that had played out ever since Melvin moved on from her.

Staring at my grandparents, standing there in the Florida sun, I felt something I hadn't in years: Hope.

I'd made it. My plan had actually worked. Some days, even now, I find it hard to believe. I had survived Melvin, mapped out an escape down to the smallest detail, and pulled it off with only one slight, emotionally fragile hiccup tagging along in the seat next to me.

I rushed into Mémé's arms. I thought back to that afternoon in her kitchen, surrounded by newspapers and boxes, the day I had finally broken her down and convinced her to take me with her. Now I was hugging her again, but in the blinding white heat of a Florida summer.

"We're here, Mémé. We made it," I said, my voice cracking under the weight of the last fifteen years. Then I leaned into her ear, slipping instinctively back into my role of family informant.

"Mom is upset."

She shushed me, a soft dismissal of the warning I'd just whispered, and handed me a semi-wrapped gift. "Here," she said, her voice bright with cheer, "We bought this for you. I know how much you love Garfield."

I tore open the package, my fingers sinking into the soft, furry plushness of a Garfield stuffed animal. In my hands was more than a toy; it was the first tangible proof of my new life. It was a gift from the only two people who had actually built a safety net for me, wrapping me in a kind of love that didn't require me to be a buffer or a hero.

Irene greeted them with a quick hello and embraced her mother, a brief flash of the daughter she was supposed to be.

As the driver unloaded the bags, Pépé took Irene's without a second thought. I tucked my new Garfield securely under one arm and gathered the rest of my belongings. I was fifteen, and I'd mastered how to carry my own weight.

"When can we go to Disney World?" I asked as the four of us walked toward the Dodge Caravan.

"In time," Mémé said, keeping pace with me. "We're going to dinner tonight. Remember, it's Pépé's birthday."

I did the math: July 17. We had arrived on his birthday. I opened the sliding door of the van. "Happy Birthday, Pépé. I wish I had something for you."

I climbed into the back seat, settling in right next to Irene. Pépé caught my eye in the rearview mirror as he turned the key. The engine hummed to life, and the air conditioning, the cure for the Florida humidity, began to blast.

"Don't worry about it," he said, shifting into reverse. "You guys are my present this year."

The End

FINAL THOUGHTS

I'll keep this brief; you've read enough of my words already.

Let me be direct: writing this memoir has been, without exaggeration, the most challenging undertaking of my life. The process wasn't uniform. There were easy days, and there were difficult ones. Days when I simply refused to write. Days I spent crying, sometimes for Irene, and other times for myself. There were moments I longed to write inappropriate jokes about airline pilots, and days when I spent more time lip-syncing to '80s music. I used those tunes to break up the emotional sludge. And, finally, there were the days when I couldn't wait to type the very last word.

Even though forcing myself to relive the worst memories was incredibly difficult, I always knew I had to write about this experience. I promised myself I would write it, even before I ever dreamed of becoming an author and without knowing how it would happen. In 2009, I started to jot down ideas and moments from my childhood. I managed to write out a few chapters, specifically those titled "The First Attack" and "Gaslighting," but then I couldn't go any further. I froze. Fear took over, mimicking blindness. Despite over twenty years having passed since 1988, the old wounds were immediately torn open. The only relief was to avoid the task entirely.

As I grew stronger and felt ready to confront Melvin and Irene, my memory returned, leading me back through specific rooms and moments in time with those who had hurt me most. *Thank goodness for cannabis.* Yet, not everyone in my past was a villain; many shielded me, like holding an umbrella against the storm.

I'll tell you this: walking side by side with the ghosts of Melvin and Irene for the past two years while writing this memoir has given me strength. They no longer hold power over the boy I was and the man I've become. And perhaps, reader, you wouldn't be reading this without some very important people in my life.

To my husband, Matt. You've heard these stories to the point where you might be able to tell them yourself. You know my history. My pain. When I referred to myself as a victim in my story, you reminded me that I was the hero. You love me unconditionally. I just realized something—you are Mémé's successor. I know she'd think you were doing an incredible job of loving her grandson. I love you, Schmoopie. I'm so happy that you are my person.

To Mémé. I miss you terribly. I had to dedicate this book to you because, without you, I honestly don't know how my life would have turned out. Thank you for taking me along with you to Kuh·si·mee. (I remember how long it took us to learn how to say Kissimmee.) I never doubted you'd say yes. I was your favorite; everyone knew it. I hope Heaven is everything you wanted it to be.

To Pépé: Thank you. I'm so sorry that Irene treated you terribly later in life. It fills me with regret that I wasn't always there for you, especially since you had always been there for me. You did so much for us. For her. And she never appreciated you the way she should have. When this memoir got difficult to write, when words escaped me, and I'd start to panic, I'd remember advice you gave me when I was sixteen. "Joe, if you don't relax, you'll give yourself a heart attack." I'm still working on not having that heart attack.

To Irene: Mom. I haven't called you that in decades. I forgive you. I understand. It wasn't easy. I will always daydream about who you were before I was born, the lady dressed up in hats and beehives. Real smiles. I wish you had found someone like my husband, Matt, to love you. To show you there was a different way. To mend the broken pieces. No matter how much you blamed me for disturbing your routine, I wouldn't have changed a thing. You're welcome.

To W.T.: My childhood friend. I changed your name for your privacy, but I couldn't go without thanking you for being such a huge part of my early teen life on Wakefield Circle. When we were living it, time felt still. Now, as I think back to those afternoons sitting under the weeping willow—M.D. with his nunchucks—it freaks me out how much time has passed. I remember once at East Hartford High, I knocked on your classroom door and told the teacher, "I need to speak to her," and he just let you leave. We went to the beach. The '80s. What a time to be a teenager.

To M.D.: There was so much pain in my childhood, but you brought me normalcy. All the advice you gave me about dating girls, it never stuck. Sorry. I remember the time we sat on your bed, planning to run away to California. We'd worked out every detail, but you got pissed off and refused to go with me because I wanted to bring too many things. HA! I'm smiling as I type that out. You've been gone since 1997; it's hard to believe. Your kids are incredible. You'd be proud of them. I'm living it up, just like you always told me to do.

To Dr. Ann Amicucci: What can I say? This book might still be sitting in a folder on my hard drive, slipping further out of reach of being told, if it weren't for you. It was in your Advanced Rhetoric and Writing class, while I was earning my undergraduate degree, that I decided to write about Irene for your online journal assignment. You responded by letting me know that when I was ready to write this history, it would be a gripping story. Your words and confidence opened those forgotten folders for me, and I went to work. It's important for me to let you know that you are the kind of college professor your students remember forever. I'm serious, Ann. Forever!

To Angelica Guevara: My editor, former classmate, and friend. I remember when you pulled me aside in class one day and asked me if vulgar language offended me. It was sweet, the idea that you didn't know me yet. As you edited this book, you learned a lot about me. I wanted to work with someone I trusted, and ever since we sat together in class, you've shown nothing but warmth, thoughtfulness, and compassion. You are one of the great ones. Thank you for editing this memoir. I knew that I could trust you with the most important story I'd ever tell. You get me, and that's hard to find.

Finally, to the countless people who did their damnedest to protect me from the two people who were actually supposed to protect me. From teachers to friends to farm owners and grocery store supervisors—thank you. You'll always be part of this story.

Until next time.

ABOUT THE AUTHOR

Joe Thomas is the author of *Fasten Your Seat Belts and Eat Your Fucking Nuts*, *Flight Attendant Joe*, *I'm Just Here for the Layovers*, and *First Class Cocktails with Flight Attendant Joe*. He was the co-host of the podcast *Confessions On the Fly* and the host of *Grounded with Joe Thomas*. He lives in Colorado with his husband, Matt, and their three cats: Harvey, Fred, and Nash. ***Bad Catholic*** **is his first memoir.**

Instagram: authorjoethomas